Borderwork
in
multicultural Australia

Borderwork in multicultural Australia

Bob Hodge and John O'Carroll

ALLEN&UNWIN

First published in 2006

Copyright © Bob Hodge and John O'Carroll 2006

Allen & Unwin
83 Alexander Street
Crows Nest NSW 2065
Australia
Phone: (61 2) 8425 0100
Fax: (61 2) 9906 2218
Email: info@allenandunwin.com
Web: www.allenandunwin.com

National Library of Australia
Cataloguing-in-Publication entry:

Hodge, Bob (Robert Ian Vere).
Borderwork in multicultural Australia.

Includes index.
ISBN 1 74114 680 1.

1. Multiculturalism – Australia. I. O'Carroll, John. II. Title

305.800994

Set 10/12 pt Minion by Midland Typesetters, Australia
Printed by CMO Image Printing Enterprises, Singapore

10 9 8 7 6 5 4 3 2 1

Contents

Acknowledgments

The authors wish to thank many people who have helped us in this project. Foremost among these have been the students of our unit *Multicultural Australia*, whose enthusiasm, honesty and willingness to engage with the themes at the deepest level have inspired both the book's existence and, to no small degree, its content. Colleagues in the School of Humanities at the University of Western Sydney contributed a congenial intellectual environment, and we especially thank Chris Fleming for his timely and supportive comments on two early chapters. We are grateful to the estate of the late David Mowaljarlai for permission to use the map reproduced in chapter 10. Given the nature of this book, the families of the two authors have made far more substantive contributions than can be covered with a formal acknowledgment. Gabriela Coronado had a deep knowledge of multiculturalism which she contributed in many readings and commentaries on the emerging text, and she produced the idea of multiculture, which was a key concept for the work. Nathalie O'Carroll was one of a number of people writing about detention centres before they became a big political issue. John also thanks his wider family, especially his father for the trip to Victoria described herein, and Helen in Behernagh for thinking that one day he might have his name written on the cover of a book. Finally a special word of thanks to Elizabeth Weiss, our publisher at Allen & Unwin, who encouraged and supported the project beyond all expectations, many times providing acute if severe comments which we didn't always want to hear at the time, but are now so glad that we listened to.

Discussion questions and tips for further reading can be downloaded from http://www.allenandunwin.com/Shopping/ProductDetails.aspx? ISBN=1741146801

1. Trials and triumphs of multicultural Australia

Introduction

This is a book for the current stage in Australia's ongoing search for its place and role in a multicultural global world. Not so long ago, most Australians took pride in their multicultural identity, but more recently this faith in multiculturalism has been badly damaged, by ferocious attacks from its enemies and a sense of crisis amongst its friends. A shadow has fallen across the land, an image of 'Fortress Australia', displacing the old talk of multiculturalism as if it were the mere construction of the 'chattering classes', cut off from the reality that has always been there. Discussions take place as though idealism and hope are now taboo. Yet without such aspirations, there could be no Australia as we know it. Without the commitment to tolerance and diversity that characterises the daily reality of multicultural Australia, it would be a very different place.

This book is intended for students fascinated by Australia's unique way of being multicultural, drawing on an undergraduate course we have taught for some years. It is also for anyone who wants to be inspired anew by the promise of multicultural Australia, without evading any of its difficulties—past and present. These aims explain the form and style of our book, why it is as it is, and what we do not try to do. Our aim as teachers is to stimulate good discussions (lively, diverse, well-informed, passionate, critical, open-minded, transformative) as the best foundation for good citizens.

Good discussions are not fact-free zones, however. There are many things we believe informed citizens of Australia ought to know about their history and society. We indicate some of these, pointing out where to go for those who wish to know more. We also have our own perspective, which comes across clearly enough, so that readers know where we stand. More important for us is that our readers also come to know better where *they* stand. For this reason, we do not gloss over the difficulties and contradictions in our own position as in others—a necessary approach to a topic that is so complex, so open to change.

The book proceeds by dealing with current 'hot topics', situating these against the social frameworks that give rise to them. These hot spots typically cluster around **borders**, boundaries that mark territories, identities, and values to be defended or proclaimed. Some of these borders are massive and concrete, seeming like facts of nature into which multicultural processes will have to fit, whether they like it or not. The border around Australia as a nation state sometimes seems like this, creating the self-evident identity of those it defines. Yet borders are not simple or self-evident—even the border that defines Australia. Borders are constructed at many levels, right down to the smallest and most private. They can be solid walls, fences, doors, clothes, or less material signposts or internalised rules. These countless borders cover social space like an infinitely complex network. Borders exist to be crossed, as well as to exclude. **Borderwork** is what we will call the many processes by which humans construct, maintain, police and negotiate a variety of relationships, whether based on similarities or difference, love or fear. Borders are often seen as the enemy of multiculturalism, as though multiculturalism is really only about harmony and ease of relationships. But multiculturalism is about managing differences and similarities alike, in ways that may be positive or negative in different circumstances, according to different perspectives. Borderwork is not opposed to multiculturalism: it is basic to it.

Our students have found it helpful to ground these debates in their own multicultural experiences, and that is what we will do in the book that follows. These experiences are mainly positive. Our own experience as teachers in this area is similar to the results of one study that found only about 10 per cent of Australians had a negative view about multiculturalism and cultural diversity, and these figures are not very different in rural Australia (Ang et al. 2002, p. 4). In spite of all the bad press, the vast majority of Australians know they live in a multicultural society, and they are delighted with the fact.

Unshrinking 'multiculturalism'

Part of the problem for **multiculturalism** is the word itself. The term has suffered drastic shrinkage over the years as it is used in public debates. It has become a code word for government policies towards minority immigrant 'ethnic' groups, and their quaint and colourful customs ('cultures'). There are many (*multi*) of these groups, but not many people all up compared with the majority group, 'Anglo-Celts'—who in this view have no ethnicity, no need for 'culture' themselves, and hence no vital stake in multiculturalism.

We want to unshrink this limited sense of what it means to call Australia a multicultural society. We draw attention to something remarkable that has happened in Australia's history. The British penal colony out of which the nation grew was as harsh, unjust and intolerant a society as you could care to name. But sometime between then and now a kind of miracle took place. A *multicultural* Australia emerged in which diversities are tolerated and valued, to a significant degree. How did it happen? What exactly is it that happened? What does it tell us about *where* it happened, about *Australia*? That is what the rest of the book tries to find out. We need this specific concept of **multicultural Australia**, to see it as something unique, formed by the play of many forces, inextricably connected with the core issues affecting all Australians.

Confusions in words may seem a minor matter, but such confusions can trap us as we use these words to think with. For instance, we find it useful to mark a clear difference between 'multicultural' and 'multiculturalism'. English -isms usually have negative connotations, and 'multiculturalism' is no exception. 'Multicultural', in contrast, has the potential to hold more diverse associations, describing everything about a society that is 'multicultural', not just a policy or problem (Hall 1990). Yet in popular discourse the -ism noun has taken over the adjective, sucking 'multicultural' into its orbit as though the adjective only describes whatever 'multiculturalism' is.

In presenting a new view of multicultural Australia, we have tried to go back to the very basics, to think anew about what multicultural Australia really is, and what it really does. We have used the new word **multiculture** to describe what *happens* in a multicultural society. For us, this noun refers to a shifting, dynamic interweaving of cultures and diversities such as that which exists in Australian society today, as well as to political policies and aspirations.

How does multiculture relate to official versions of multiculturalism? To start with, multiculture in Australian life has been protected by government policies, so we do not want to set up a false opposition between social life and policies. For all their faults, policies have played a vital role, and if they were weakened Australia would be the worse for it. But to understand the possibilities of multiculture, we need to look at more than policies. As one clear instance of how misleading definitions built around policy can be, Indigenous Australians are often left out of discussions of 'multiculturalism' because the policies were mostly not designed with them in mind—they fall under a different government department. This is also a symptom of the discrimination they have suffered in multicultural Australia. Their role in Australian multiculture is complex but essential—the idea that multicultural Australia could *not* include Indigenous cultures is nonsense.

At the heart of 'multiculture' is the important, difficult term **culture**. Culture can have a narrow sense, referring mainly to artistic culture; however, it can also have a broader sense, covering a whole way of life. For anthropologists who have used the term, it has typically referred to the coherent way of life of pre-industrial societies, but Raymond Williams, one of the founders of British cultural studies, applied it to class cultures in complex modern societies (1976, pp. 90–91). Within this broader sense of the term, it becomes impossible to see an Australian multiculture that does not also include the Anglo-Celtic majority.

With this greater scope comes greater complexity. When Australian social scientists Cunneen and Stubbs (1997) studied violence against Filipino women in Australia, they found they needed to use what they called 'intersectional analysis' to study how basic social categories of class, gender and ethnicity intersect and interact in real-life problems. Culture and identity are shaped by class and gender as well as ethnicity. As Jeannie Martin (1996) puts it in her analysis of representations in the media, the problem is that women of non-English speaking backgrounds are 'either subsumed to the general category "women" in contrast to the general category "male" or subsumed to the general category "ethnic minority" in contrast to the general category "dominant culture"' (1996, p. 147). These categories are not *lived* separately, and our analysis must reflect their interaction in real life.

Since multiculture is formed out of the interplay of class, gender and ethnicity, it makes no sense to ask whether gender issues are relevant to its study. These factors are *all* intrinsic. All cultures have ways of constructing gender, class, age and occupation (as well as geography, education and a host of other variables). None of them is an optional extra in a culture, and hence not in a multiculture either.

Borders and borderwork play a crucial role in mapping the complexities of multiculture. Categories that are too rigid and simplistic—expressed through high borders—inhibit complex exchanges of people, ideas, meanings and even goods, and borderwork will consist mainly of setting up or breaking down obstructions. If there is a multiplicity of movements across a multiplicity of borders, then the task of borderwork is to do justice to this complexity, balancing the continual needs for difference and connection.

Stories

In discussing issues of Australian multiculture with our students, we have found it best to use stories. Stories go beyond the points we are making, connecting to other situations that raise other issues. We draw on many examples from everyday life—some from our own lives as citizens or teachers who have learned from our students over the years.

Others come from the media. Unlike many books on multiculturalism, which treat mainstream media with suspicion, we view the media as a representative weave of viewpoints. They are not a window to truth, but they are what people see each day when they buy the paper, connect to the internet, or turn on the radio or television. In our teaching, we make a practice of highlighting stories that strike us as instructive in one way or another. In each chapter, we make use of text boxes to provide readers with striking examples of multiculture, aiming to provoke questions that go beyond our own analyses.

We found that stories helped the many different kinds of students in our classes to get a handle on issues of Australian multi-culture. A narrative approach restores human faces to the irreducibly complex experiences of multiculture. Take this mostly negative example. In 2001, in the weeks after the September 11 attacks on the World Trade Center in New York, fear and vengefulness hung in the air. A few days after the attack, one journalist reported:

> Islamic communities around the country have been abused, attacked and had their mosques fire-bombed and smeared with faeces in a frightening backlash over the US terrorist attacks. School children have been stoned, women harassed, and hate-mail sent via fax and email as Muslims become a target for public anger over the carnage in the US. (O'Brien et al., 2001, p. 9)

This report carries a fine, ethical plea for calm. It gives a general picture, and readers need that. But the pluralised 'communities', 'women' and 'children' form a blur; however many stories are compressed into this one, it sounds like a string of clichés. Readers cannot connect directly with faces or stories of the day. In this form, much of the complexity and multiplicity has been ironed out, and so has the scope for action—for not only seeing what happened, but going on to do something.

Stories can come from anywhere. Australians cannot understand their own multiculture unless they know much more about the global world that is its context. New York and Australia are closely bound together today. Other stories have other lessons. Our next one comes from long ago (Bhabha 1994, p. 76). Frantz Fanon, a young Algerian student in France in the 1930s, is in a public space. A child stares at him aghast: 'Mama, look at the Negro! I'm frightened.' The event was burnt into Fanon's consciousness, the border created by the child's prejudice becoming for him a wall he had to shatter at any cost. He became an advocate of violent revolution, for a war in which Algerians expelled the French colonisers, but which left the country still rent by civil war 40 years later.

His anguish led him to see no option other than violent rejection of colonial power, a view shared by many Algerians. Australians today, in their relatively safe part of the interconnected globe, need histori-cal understanding of anger of this kind, which today drives the madness of Al Qaeda. That anger is part of multiculture. Those who feel it need to find another way forward. That too is multiculture.

Indeed, in France and Australia today, the stark racism confronting Fanon is no longer commonplace. *Something* has changed. But what? The human race has not suddenly become better. But the way we see and are seen has changed. The way people feel and are felt has changed. The change is unsung, but it is important. We call it multiculture.

Coping with complexity

We all know we live in a turbulent, unpredictable world. Many see multiculture as another complication coming from the outside world, the cure being to keep things simple as they once were. But that 'simple' world was never so simple. Wars, disasters, genocidal episodes and financial catastrophes litter the history of the 'good old days' of the twentieth century.

How do we analyse all this? How do we make sense of Australia and its complex histories, and cope with all the challenges which face us today? First we must be interdisciplinary, drawing on ideas and approaches from social sciences and humanities. Interdisciplinarity is in fact an example of multiculture at work. Different disciplines have their own cultures. Bringing differences together in effective, respectful collaboration is the mark of multiculture. The many cases where disciplines clash show how much the principles of multiculture are needed in academia, as in other spheres of life.

An even broader form of interdisciplinarity can help us cope better with the extreme complexity inherent in a multicultural global world. In this spirit, this book will take some ideas from **chaos theory**, an area which emerged first in science. We offer this theory not to 'prove' anything by it, but as a rich source of metaphors, models and orientations that can open our eyes to the strangeness of so many things associated with multiculture, and make sense of many things we already know but find it hard to recognise or represent.

Academics and others find it hard to accept and think about extreme complexity because of the authority of linear thinking in the way we are trained to think. We are told from an early age that crisp, linear thinking, modelled on classical science, is the only real way to think about everything: analysing problems into distinct parts, with simple causes linked to simple effects, keeping concepts and descriptions as precise as possible.

Chaos theory comes from good scientists who present a richer set of options. Take **far from equilibrium dynamics**, an idea which came from Ilya Prigogine and which we use throughout this book (Prigogine & Stengers 1984). Prigogine argued that the linear laws of cause and effect only work well in conditions that are close to equilibrium, where things are balanced and stable, where A always causes B and processes are always regular. In far from equilibrium conditions, processes can accelerate rapidly or change direction abruptly, producing contradictions and unexpected outcomes. Small causes can have remarkably large effects.

Yet Prigogine insists that chaos is not something just to fear. Order grows surprisingly out of chaos. In fact, the edge of chaos is the site for all new, unexpected kinds of order, richer and more complex than could come by design imposed from above. The history of multicultural Australia in the twentieth century shows all these qualities in abundance. Out of the turbulent years of the 1970s, Australian multiculturalism was dramatically born as a policy, precipitated by one man, Al Grassby, whose taste in ties would be as amazing now as it was then, briefly minister in a government which didn't last long, bequeathing a consensus policy that endured more or less unchanged for the next 30 years. An achievement so sudden, so surprising and so lasting needs a special kind of theory to understand it.

For the kind of concepts and descriptions required for such situations, we draw on another branch of chaos theory, **fuzzy logic** (Kosko 1994). Its inventor, the engineer Lotfi Zadeh (1986), was interested in improving control systems, not in complexity for its own sake. But he recognised that extreme complexity does not go away just because it is hard to think about it. He distinguished 'crisp' (precise, definite) categories from the 'fuzzy' (imprecise) categories he felt were usually better for dealing with complexity. He proposed a general principle: the more complex and dynamic a system or condition, the less relevant or meaningful are precise ('crisp') categories. In other words, if things are very complicated, you will struggle to understand them if you fall back on rigid, precise categories. Indeed, such rigid thinking can cause new unforeseen problems, making a difficult situation worse. Simple, crisp thinking in these circumstances is not only useless, it is dangerous. Australian culture and society have always been too complex and dynamic to be understood through crisp categories and definitions, and this applies even more to Australian multiculture in a global world.

One kind of simplistic thinking has proved especially dangerous in thinking about the issues of multiculture: **binary** (either-or, black-and-white) **thinking**. The problem with this habit, more deeply ingrained in most of us than we are aware, is that it reduces the complex set of players and the many possible options down to just two parties locked in struggle, which only one can win: Anglo-Celts versus 'the ethnics'; Us versus Them; Coalition versus Labor; Australia versus globalisation; and many others. **Three-body analysis** is a powerful aid to seeing the actual plurality of situations that are commonly reduced to just two terms (Hodge 2005). The idea comes from the nineteenth century French mathematician Henri Poincaré, analysing the 'three-body problem' posed by Isaac Newton: how to predict the trajectories of three interdependent bodies, the sun, earth and moon. Poincaré showed that the dynamics of three bodies are much more complex than those of two. For instance, the sun affects the earth, and vice versa. But the earth also affects and is affected by the moon, which puts the earth in a different relation to the sun, which from this different position acts differently on the earth, and so on. The moon, seeming too small to matter much, in fact affects the whole system.

Used as a model for social analysis, this reminds us never to be content with just two objects, two sides. Many writers in social theory have also become aware of the need not just to question the apparent self-evidence of binary oppositions, but also of the need to displace this way of seeing (Derrida 1981). Three-body analysis is a powerful visual aid in the work of social analysis because it literally allows us to 'see' bodies in space. By looking for a third body, we restore the inherent complexity of what is almost always in fact a many-body system (like the full solar system). Even three bodies is a simplification, and our choice of a third is likely to be arbitrary. But looking for the third is *always* productive, taking us outside the predictable moves open to two contenders to explore the always multiple structures that frame apparent oppositions. In practice, three is enough to capture dynamic, open-ended complexity.

Rethinking racism

Sometimes the opposite of multiculture is called **racism**. We feel this term is too narrow and misleading about what is going on across many cases, where 'race' is not directly at stake yet the processes seem similar. 'Racism' is a powerful word, yet it distorts and limits debate and understanding. Many critics of multiculturalism set up racism in a way that makes almost any vision of multiculture seem impossibly idealistic or utopian. For such critics, racism carries with it the idea that difference (especially of race) always has the same basis, the same terrible effects. In this view, the human species is genetically programmed to reject difference. If this were really so, then multicultures could never happen, not in any deep sense. Multiculturalism could only be a policy of minimising the natural hatred between different ethnic groups.

We draw on the work of anthropologist Gregory Bateson (1972) to present these issues differently. Bateson coined the word **schismogenesis** (from Greek *schismos,* a split) to refer to the main ways that splits develop in groups, cultures or social systems. He did not call the divisions he witnessed 'racism' because he saw them as part of a more general and complex pattern. We present this argument at greater length in Chapter 5. Bateson's account allows us to see that tendencies to split and to come together coexist in all kinds of groups, and that splitting happens in many different ways under different conditions.

Bateson made a useful distinction that goes to the heart of the enigma of racism. Most people suppose that racism is a response to difference, and that difference is always a problem. But some of the bloodiest, most intractable conflicts have been between peoples who are very similar. Irish Protestants kill and are killed by Irish Catholics who look indistinguishable from them. Of course, in keeping with our observations on three-body analysis, we need also to recall that there was indeed a third force present in many of these struggles—the British—and that this was no neutral framework, but one that actually motivated or affected the schismogenesis within.

Bateson points out that difference can as easily come *after* schismogenesis—an effect not a cause. He calls schismogenesis that is truly based on difference *complementary schismogenesis.* Classic racism is usually of this kind, as in the treatment of Australian Aborigines. But where problems arise because of the near similarity of the different groups, he refers to it as *symmetrical schismogenesis*. Working-class fear of immigrants who 'come to take our jobs' is a good example. The problem is similarity, not difference.

Schismogenesis is a social process, not one built into our genes (as people think is the case with racism) and it must have a counter-tendency. Otherwise the human race would be unable to climb out of episodes of schismogenesis, as it clearly does, as Australia has done. We call this capacity **cosmogenesis**, the creation of order (Greek *cosmos*, order, harmony), the mirror image of Bateson's schismogenesis.

We do not offer this new framework to minimise the terrible things perpetrated in the name of racism. Our aim is to better explain its complex twists and turns. For instance, Nazi Germany is the most notorious example of racism in modern history, but Germany now is (mostly) a multiculture. The speed with which genocidal tendencies sprang up and then were reversed after the war warns us not to assume that multiculture or its opposite are stable conditions— permanent qualities, say, of all Germans. In the case of modern Australia, multiculture has been a positive force in recent times, reversing earlier schismogenesis. But these achievements are fragile, not to be taken for granted.

Multiculturalism and the left

Parties who oppose multiculturalism are usually seen as being on the right of politics. Yet the intellectual left in Australia *also* presents a negative analysis of Australian multiculturalism. This view did not arise in a vacuum, and we feel it is important to sketch some recent history to make this point clearer.

Outside Australia, in Britain and the United States, many people on the left had become disillusioned with the failures of multiculturalism. They wondered whether there was anything more to multiculturalism than official policy, cliché and manipulation. A few questioned the whole idea (see Gunew n.d.). Many more expressed qualified support. Under the banner of critical multiculturalism, they proposed an even more sustained critique, especially as part of a concerted anti-racist strategy. **Critical multiculturalism** is a left critique that looks at the failures of multiculturalism, pointing out imbalances of power and patterns of racism (May 1999, pp. 11–34). While we agree with the need for critique, our approach sees the constructive aspect of multiculturalism as central, and this includes—though it isn't confined to—official policy. To indicate the way we see things, we would like to examine two relatively recent Australian books that typify important traditions within the Australian left. One, a work edited by Vasta and Castles (1996), has much in common with the then emerging international idea of a critical multiculturalism (cf. Vasta & Castles 1996, pp. 43–44); the other, by Ghassan Hage (1998), presents an even bleaker outlook. Despite the fact that we see things differently, we set both as class texts at different times, so important did we view them as being.

In 1996, Stephen Castles was director of Wollongong University's Centre for Multicultural Studies. The subtitle of the landmark book he edited with Ellie Vasta explains its focus very clearly: *The Persistence of Racism in Multicultural Australia*. The work, in other words, was an attack on continuing racism because multiculturalism:

> is incomplete and unstable so long as it co-exists with various kinds of racism. Discourses of tolerance and diversity are not unimportant— indeed they are a great step forward compared with our racist past—but they can only be seen as genuine anti-racism if they are matched by a fundamental change in institutions, attitudes and practices. (1996, p. 5)

In many ways, the approach the framing theoretical authors (Castles, Vasta and Collins) took was consistent with tendencies in multicultural studies around the world.

But there is always also a local story. The facts presented in Vasta and Castles' analyses are solid, and they are part of an internationally significant critical social science idiom. Yet with hindsight we can see some problems with the strategy they took. In some moments it is balanced and judicious, acknowledging the changes that have happened, yet it is also a polemic, a battle cry against the racism that still dares to persist in multicultural Australia. It tells a broad story in which there is still one last 'Great Battle', the final defeat of racism— its complete elimination. Before this has happened, before the change is 'fundamental', everything else falls short of being 'genuine'.

But, however persuasive this call to action, its terms are dangerously binary: either multiculturalism or racism. Even a small amount of one makes the other unstable (though Castles doesn't note the

Borderwork and multicultural Australia

converse, that even small amounts of multiculture should destabilise racism). There is a longing for a harmonious, balanced, stable world without traces of racism, and nothing less will do. But, in a far from equilibrium world, contradictions are the norm and cannot be eliminated. Government efforts over two decades to control and eliminate racism were likely, if Zadeh is right, to lead to more chaos, less order if applied too crisply, in too linear an exercise of power.

Perhaps the biggest problem with binary thinking is that if the enemy becomes the focus of attention, then the richness of the positive—in this case multiculture—is lost. In this case, multiculture is far broader and more diverse a value than anti-racism on its own, though it should indeed include values and ways of being that work against racism.

In venturing these criticisms, we do acknowledge the value of their approach. Precisely because of their interest in international patterns, Vasta and Castles' book makes good sense of the process of globalisation. Globalisation is the process of internationalisation of economies, populations, political and cultural ideas, and products. It is a process that dates from the Industrial Revolution, but which has had pressing relevance in the last half-century. The finest aspects of the framework chapters of Vasta and Castles' book emerge when the various authors in their different ways specifically emphasise the increasing complexity of racism under globalisation (1996, p. 19). We can learn from this, but must also always pay attention to local circumstances and not treat these as mere examples. In addition, we must look at the positive contribution of multiculturalism, not just its faults. In retrospect, now, we can see that the story they were telling was too crisp, too linear for the time, and too negative for the place at that time.

It is true that in the same year as this book was published, the focus on racism seemed vindicated when Pauline Hanson, then Liberal candidate for the Labor seat of Oxley, on the outskirts of Brisbane, made a speech that was immediately denounced as racist by both major parties. Despite being disendorsed by the Liberals, Hanson won the seat as an independent, and was briefly seen as the new voice for racist Australia. Yet, in these far from equilibrium times, Hansonism as it was called—which seemed to fulfil the authors' worst fears—also made their project, a final push against racism, seem utopian and irrelevant. The strategy of stressing the 'persistence of racism in multicultural Australia' left Australia in urgent need of a companion work, on the 'persistence of multiculture in a racist Australia'.

Let us take another example. Only two years after Vasta and Castles' book, anthropologist Ghassan Hage published *White Nation* (1998), which captured the anger of the left against multiculturalism in the wake of Hansonism. Later, we deal with other aspects of his brilliant, provocative book, but here we will use it to point out the dangers and inadequacies of his kind of left approach. Hage refers to an anti-racist video made by some film studies students, in which a Muslim girl is shown being harassed by some boys, who tear off her scarf. But a white girl steps forward, picks up the scarf, and puts her arm around the girl. Hage comments:

> I could not help focusing on the movement of the White girl's arm. Protective though it was, it kept reminding me of the hand it was supposedly negating—the hand that pulled down the scarf. Like it, it was a hand that had a sense of its spatial power. (1998, p. 96)

This film, which we have not seen, was maybe simplistic, as student productions can be. It was made by students who no doubt empathised strongly with the plight of the Muslim girl. That was not enough to soften Hage's critique.

It is not only sympathy for the student filmmakers that is missing. His basic geometry of the situation is defective. He is aware of power, but networks of solidarity—between student filmmakers and their subject, between the two girls in the video—seem invisible to him. His geometry contains only two kinds of player—white and Muslim—but this situation is clearly a three-term situation, in which the white boys are separate from both the Muslim girl and the white girl. Hage is so intent on only one dimension, ethnicity ('white' versus everything else), that he does not seem to notice that gender is clearly also involved. It is one motive for the boys' aggression, and a bond between two girls against the boys. Gender is part of the situation itself. The white girl defies gender conventions that the boys might be relying on (boys are allowed to be violent), perhaps also mobilising other gender conventions to protect her (nice boys can't be violent to nice girls).

Hage notes the resemblance between the two arms, both white, and because they are similar he treats them as almost the same. But for the white girl this is a split around sameness (ethnicity) at the same time as it reflects gender difference. Hage interprets the white girl's protective arm purely in terms of power, not solidarity across the boundary of ethnic difference, which it surely also is. The idea that the arm that tears is more or less the same as the arm that enfolds and protects is problematic. It ignores the huge differences between oppressors (thugs or even the Nazis) and those who may put their lives in danger for someone they do not know. We will deal with the complexities of tolerance in detail in Chapter 3, but surely positive contacts and acts of goodwill across differences are valuable for any society.

This is an analysis of a mere moment in Hage's text, but it illustrates wider issues addressed by our own book. The Australian left has mostly been sceptical of multiculturalism, too aware of persistent racism and governmental hypocrisy (both of which undoubtedly exist) to be able to *make sense* of innumerable positive connections made by ordinary people. Hage's is an intelligent, updated version of this tradition. Yet it also contains in stark form the rigidity and blindness that the theme and the times do not need.

Revisiting consensus histories

In this book, we also seek to understand aspects of the present by rereading some partially forgotten histories. We are not talking about inventing histories here. Our counter-histories rest on facts which also have a place in mainstream histories, though usually with details so reduced that other, more creative, readings are hard to see. We do not present our versions as 'complete' in a way that historians might aim to do. We do it only to shed new light on current debates, in which versions of the past are always at stake.

One history we will return to at different points in this book concerns what most people think is the history of Australian multiculturalism. This history implies assumptions that we believe are dangerous for the present, and misleading about the past. In the **consensus history**, policy occupies centre stage, and the often different story of Australia's multiculture is ignored as though it were the same, as though Australia is more or less the same as its governments. Australian multiculturalism is usually described as a policy progression that conveniently begins in 1901. It goes like this: 1901–45 (bad white

Australia policy); 1945–65 (not-quite-as-bad assimilationist policy); 1965–72 (even-less-bad-integrationist policy); 1972–96 (trying-to-be-good multiculturalism policy); 1997–present (bad new regressive policy).

We challenge this story on many grounds. It ignores the complex connections people have always made in Australia, even before Federation. It does not try to understand policy achievements prior to official multiculturalism, and it is not helpful today. It makes limited sense of the present, and offers little hope for the future.

The consensus history treats multiculturalism as a monopoly of the left (mainly the Australian Labor Party, or ALP) when the political reality has always been a profound bipartisanship. Let us say this very plainly: from the point of view of multiculture, there is little historical basis for preferring one political party over the other. And lest this be thought a merely historical point, let us say equally sharply: there is still little difference between the two main parties on multiculturalism.

So let us tell part of this story in another way to show what we mean. In January 1951, Harold Holt, Immigration Minister in the conservative government of Robert Menzies, rose to speak at a conference he had convened to mark 50 years of Australian nationhood. The 'Commonwealth Jubilee Citizenship Convention' was part of a long liberalising chain of events that saw policy-makers, intellectuals and much of the postwar Australian community committing itself to a new, pluralised world, one conceived not just in fear, but also in a positive spirit around a project of transformation. Five years later, a report on the cultural integration of migrants in Australia by the Department of Immigration remarked that ethnically based clubs were not a problem because government policy did not 'entail conformity to Australian patterns of life in all, or even in the majority, of the immigrants' social and cultural activities' (cited by APIC and AEAC 1979, p. 12). Two years after that, the *Migration Act* 1958 swept away the previous Acts, many of which had overturned aspects of the *Immigration Restriction Acts* of 1901, 1908 and 1910 that legislated for the infamous 'White Australia' policy. In the watershed conference of 1951 itself:

> delegates saw some of the arts and crafts and were entertained by the musical talent that has been brought to Australia by new settlers from so many countries. Great value was set by delegates on the need for new

Borderwork and multicultural Australia

Australians to be encouraged to maintain their talents and culture and in presenting them to the Australian people. Opportunity was advocated for new Australians to teach their handicrafts to Australians. Equality of opportunity was also urged for the children. (Commonwealth Jubilee Citizenship Convention 1951, p. 3)

This massive program aimed to absorb people from refugee camps in Europe, and from war-ravaged Britain, which Holt as minister hoped would supply over 80 000 of a proposed 200 000 intake, stating this as 'our preference . . . and to say understandably that this country wants all the British migrants it can get . . . [there is] a maximum number of aliens that any community can be expected to absorb and assimilate' (1951, p. 18).

The preference for British over 'aliens' is indeed there, but these constitute less than half the intake. We should not miss the scale and vision for the time. Nor should we miss the ongoing bipartisanship. In a situation which is hard to imagine now, Holt invited not only academics, policy-makers and implementers, but also the leader of the opposition, Arthur Calwell, who addressed the conference:

> May the [immigration] programme continue to prosper, and may the critics, most of whom know better than they say and do, cease their carping. Unfortunately, there are some people itching to get busy with pen and paper to prove by addition, subtraction and multiplication . . . that migration is economically unsound, and that if Australia has 11,000,000 by 1960 we shall all be camping under gum trees and perhaps eating each other. (1951, p. 13)

We can see many features of current immigration policy in this 'pre-multicultural' era: the drive to a new Australia; the idea that the nation had a responsibility to refugee populations; and the notion that Australia itself might benefit economically from the policy. We also note a contrast with debates today, in the open and optimistic support for this early program, which was much larger per capita than anything in recent decades.

Let us not doubt the scale, pace and nature of this moment of change. By the end of the 1950s, the 'White Australia' policy was swept away. In the early 1960s, a group of activists under the banner of the Immigration Reform Group published *Immigration: Control or Colour*

Bar? (1960, 1962). Their book pushed a strong case for a radically new basis for immigration policy, one that dispensed with the 'outmoded dualism' of the old immigration policies (1962, p. 104). Their texts show how far there was still to go, but also how strong a multicultural perspective there already was.

This story is very different from the consensus view, which pivots around an almost mythic date for the foundation of Australian multiculturalism, 1972, with Al Grassby, architect of the ALP multi-culturalism policy, as hero. We have already indicated the value of Grassby's work, but we don't accept a flattened history written in these terms. As one instance, David Cox wrote in 1996 about policy history under four broad headings: 'Early post-Second World War Years: Assimilation' (1996, pp. 4–5); 'Changes in the 1960s: Inte-gration' (1996, pp. 6–7); and 'The Multicultural Era Arrives' (1996, pp. 8–10; cf. Foster & Stockley 1988, pp. 24–37).

The optimism of Keating-era writers has gone, but the structure remains. However, now there is another mythic date, 1996 and the election of the conservative Howard government: the end of multiculturalism. For many critics of multiculturalism, recent history (since 1996) blends with older shameful histories (colonialism, the 'White Australia' policy, stolen children, failed reconciliation). For them, multiculturalism was always a flawed idea and a worse reality. Paradoxically, the harshest criticism of it from left and right emerged in the Keating era, when a negative spotlight was turned on to all multiculturalism's claims and achievements.

We believe this view has serious gaps. Some dramatic progress in multicultural policy and reality occurred during times of apparent conservatism, the Menzies and Fraser years. For the same reason, we can *expect* lasting improvements in multiculture to emerge in conservative Coalition governments (alongside some more steps backwards). But many Australians do not expect the Coalition to be associated with such policies. This can too easily become self-fulfilling prophecy.

Another problem is a generally negative reading of most of the stages in this history. 'Multiculturalism' has not lurched from failure to failure. Whitlamite multiculturalism did *not* arise because inte-gration 'failed'. On the contrary, the policy succession was possible precisely because of the *success* of preceding policies in responding to an emerging multiculture. By success we mean only this: despite the harshness of the immigration policy of the 1950s, the massive transformation of Australian political and cultural life of the 1960s was built upon it. Despite the struggles of migrants in the 1960s under integrationist policies that now look draconian, 1970s multiculturalism was built on that era.

What is noteworthy about all three policy stages is that they oversaw a process of rapid cultural and social change that was accomplished without a single shot being fired. As a society whose population trebled in less than half a century on the back of immigration from all sources, Australia has become a more prosperous and more diverse society than ever before—and that is a tribute to all Australians.

Principles of multiculture

We have written this book around a series of guiding ideas:

* Australia's multiculture includes all its diversities, majority and minority, of ethnicities, classes, genders, ages, sexualities and regions, dispersed across an often functional but sometimes dysfunctional whole.
* Australia's hard-won policy achievement ('multiculturalism') in controlling racism and discrimination was never the whole story of multiculture, but its value should never be doubted. It came from above, in the form of directives that were often resented, but it also found a mighty resonance in Australian hearts and minds.
* Tendencies towards multiculture in Australia have always coexisted with opposing tendencies to separate, in different proportions, and a 'perfect multiculture' is not a realistic aim—now or ever. If reforms like multiculturalism are critiqued too negatively by those who wish they went further, the critiques may make things worse.
* A multiculture is both a product of and a strategy for coping with a chaotic, far from equilibrium world, so it is full of contradictions and surprising changes. Among the most surprising of the changes has been the emergence of Australian multiculture itself, as a new form arising from an unjust, divisive society. But that change could equally well be reversed, over a short time.
* All modern societies contain diversities within and across their borders. Multiplicity and diversity are not enemies of national

cohesiveness, security and sense of purpose, but the opposite, as the history of Australia has shown many times.

* 'Multiculture' is not opposed to or the same as democracy, but the two are inseparable. A multiculture is the only condition under which the kind of democracy Australia prides itself on can function as a free, dynamic, open system as its supporters claim. The ideals of democracy are needed to make multiculture a living, functioning political and social reality.

* Indigenous Australians have always been an integral part of Australia's multiculture, and long-standing targets of racism and discrimination. Their creativity and generosity in negotiating a new vision of Australia are an intrinsic part of Australian multiculture, full of lessons for all other groups and cultures within Australia.

2. Borderwork

Rethinking Tampa

In 2001, a small incident reputedly changed the course of a federal election. When Arne Rinnan, Norwegian captain of the cargo ship the MV *Tampa*, embarked on the second last voyage of his naval career, he had no idea that he was sailing into Australian history. The so-called *Tampa* affair exploded at the end of August 2001, when this conscientious skipper responded to the distress signal of a sinking ship, and followed international law to offer assistance to the passengers. It turned out that these were mostly nationals from outside Australia, mainly from Afghanistan and Iraq in the Middle East, who were attempting to seek refugee status in Australia. Captain Rinnan asked permission from the Australian government to land the rescued passengers at the nearest landfall, as prescribed by international law. This was Christmas Island, part of Australia out in the Indian Ocean. But the federal government refused to allow Rinnan to land. The stalemate continued until Rinnan transferred his human cargo onto the Australian HMAS *Manoora*.

Onshore, an election campaign was about to begin, in which the government—the Coalition led by John Howard—was trailing in the polls. Only a week earlier, a controversy about three rapists of Lebanese background had been raging in the media. Under headings like 'Victim Tells How Rapists Taunted Her "You deserve it because you're an Australian"' (Toy & Knowles 2001, p. 1), what we will describe in this chapter as a 'moral panic' was unfolding. The government's response was in tune with the sense of crisis. Soon afterwards, two separate opinion polls themselves became news as the *Australian* and the *Herald/Age* group provided similar results. Journalists Dennis Shanahan and Megan Saunders announced a surge in support for the Howard government, giving the 'Coalition an election-winning lead' (2001, p. 1), while Michelle Grattan et al. announced 'Howard's *Tampa*-Led Recovery' (2001, p. 1).

At the time, this incident was treated as a litmus test to establish the real condition of Australia. The election outcome was treated by all sides as a sign that the country had shifted dramatically to the right, voting 'no' in a de facto referendum on multiculturalism. In this chapter we will look more closely at this incident to see whether this indeed is the only message we can take from what happened. We have the advantage of perspective over those earlier commentators. Years have passed, and this election has receded into the past. The *Tampa* affair is an ideal object to study in order to understand 'hot spots' of multicultural controversy in Australia—recent enough to have living connections with the present, yet distant enough to give us hindsight and perspective.

In the 2004 election, the 'refugee issue'—such a vote-winning election issue three years earlier—went off the boil. There were no dramatic new policies. The government did not raise the stakes on the issue, or claim floods of 'illegal' immigrants. On the contrary, in the words of one commentator: 'The Howard Government appears to be quietly shifting tack on its treatment of illegal entrants to Australia.' (Morris 2004, p. 9) And then, beneath the headline 'Compassion Back in Fashion as Australia Throws Refugees a Lifeline at Last', we read that 'thousands' of refugees on the cruel temporary protection visas would be actually allowed to stay 'permanently' in Australia (Banham 2004, p. 1).

So what happened? The Howard government was re-elected in late 2004 with a majority enabling it to implement whichever programs it chose, with control of both houses of parliament. It then gained the power, if it wanted to do so, to enact a series of harsh measures that would create a new 'Fortress Australia'. Yet in the first half of 2005, a series of embarrassing cases emerged that revealed that the government detention policy was in a shambles. A German

Australian, Cornelia Rau, was discovered in a detention centre when she should have been receiving psychiatric treatment. A Philippine Australian, Vivian Alvarez Solon, had been deported, again by mistake. In June 2005, a small group of Liberal backbenchers achieved a breakthrough:

> John Howard has agreed to dramatically liberalise the immigration detention system, admitting it is 'one of the many failings of this government'.
>
> Bowing to pressure from Liberal MPs, Mr Howard has agreed to release families with children and to offer a new deal to long-term detainees and refugees on temporary visas. (Dodson & Kerr 2005, p. 1)

The history of detention still has many chapters in store for us, but the story so far has all the characteristics of a far from equilibrium situation. The same cause (the border theme) acted very differently after only a three-year gap. In mid-2005, a seemingly all-powerful government bent before the pressure exerted by four lowly back-benchers. Of course, there were many particular reasons why this happened as it did, but that is our point. The trajectory of multiculture is not simple, linear or predictable, and seemingly massive borders can be created and removed in a trice.

Moral panics and borderwork

One important reason for looking again at the *Tampa* affair is that it helps us understand the processes of multiculture in far from equilibrium conditions, when the system is in crisis, rather than when things are running smoothly and people aren't paying attention to them. Media sociologist Stanley Cohen (1980) wrote a classic study of what he calls **moral panics**, which makes good sense of the *Tampa* affair, using a wealth of empirical detail to illuminate how far from equilibrium conditions function in society. Moral panics happen in any society where there is insecurity, and a mass media system that can focus that insecurity on a single issue. They are moral *panics* because the public response to the feared threat is completely out of proportion to its reality. They are *moral* panics because the outrage is linked to a perceived breach of a moral code. We note here a contradiction that is a sign of far from equilibrium conditions: the claimed concern for morality typically licenses behaviours that would normally be regarded as immoral. With the *Tampa* affair, for instance, the moral code shared by the majority of Australians was thrown out of the window. The panic response to a threat was a morality override, enabling laws to be passed that would otherwise have been seen as harsh and unjust. For this reason, we might say that 'moral panics' could equally justly be called 'immoral panics'.

Cohen (1980) also emphasises what he calls media 'amplification'. Such processes are called positive **feedback loops** by communication theorists. A feedback loop describes any open system where responses (feedback) increase the volume (positive feedback) or calm it (negative feedback). Amplification like this is both the product and cause of a far from equilibrium situation. It turns normal tensions into runaway schismogenesis. Moral panics show how potent these positive feedback loops can be. The more a supposed crisis is discussed, the 'hotter' or more 'amplified' it becomes.

Cohen also notes the role of what he calls **folk devils** in moral panics. He describes how societies, even in biblical times, create 'scapegoats'. The **scapegoat** is an important figure for social analysis, and it has been analysed by many writers, among them René Girard (1986), whose ideas we look at briefly in Chapter 5. For our purposes, a scapegoat is someone who, despite sometimes being apparently the 'same', is symbolically marked as different and then punished for that difference. Scapegoat figures are symbolically made to carry everything that is rejected by the society, and they are a symptom of symmetrical schismogenesis. Symbolically, too, the scapegoat's punishment and expulsion purify the group. In practice, of course, whoever is on the receiving end of this treatment suffers real rather than symbolic harm.

In a moral panic, one class of people is constructed as a 'folk devil', regarded as capable of all evil so that the home society can feel good. In the *Tampa* affair, in a famous claim that was later proved false, refugee mothers were accused of throwing their children overboard, thus losing all rights to be regarded as human beings with human feelings and human rights. The two issues—exaggeration of difference and protection of borders—fused in a potent mix, as they typically do in moral panics. If the issue is 'youth out of control', they cannot easily be excluded from the nation, so imprisonment ('and throw away the key!') is the typical solution. In the case of

Borderwork and multicultural Australia

asylum seekers, they were first imprisoned before being ejected over the border and held offshore.

In far from equilibrium situations, everyday issues become deeply confused. In the panic over *Tampa*, there was such border anxiety that expensive and inefficient solutions seemed like common sense. One was the so-called 'Pacific solution', where a small number of far from dangerous asylum seekers were held at huge cost on the island of Nauru, thousands of kilometres away from Australia, as though they could contaminate the country if they were any closer. In less fraught times, such a 'solution' would seem ridiculous. Yet at this time, the desire for crisp borders overrode rational analysis.

The idea that there should be no borders is equally untenable. Even in a society that is functioning well, there are limits and borders to be maintained, differences to be respected. A 'moral panic' is a moment of crisis of borderlines, but borders are still functional and necessary in normal times. Borderwork is basic to human societies. It happens in everyday life in a rich variety of ways, which help us to connect the public (events like *Tampa*) with the private feelings and values around which people organise their lives. The anthropologist Fredrik Barth analysed what he called the 'boundary maintenance' work that takes place between ethnic groups. He focused on 'the ethnic *boundary* that defines the group, not the cultural stuff it encloses' (1969, p. 15). The feminist Barrie Thorne adapted the idea to 'borderwork' in gender relations, where she found that contact between girls and boys can also go either way, reducing a sense of gender difference or reinforcing it (1993, pp. 64–65).

Borderwork in the *Tampa* crisis was as complex as the border concerned was made to seem simple, and was fed by crises at many different levels. At the international level, the September 11 attacks created a generalised sense of anxiety. At a lower level, we mentioned the 'Lebanese rape case', where the borders supposedly under threat were those protecting women's bodies and the family unit. The passengers were seeking refuge because of actions in parts of the world far from Australia, mainly in Afghanistan and Iraq. They looked for homes in Australia, so far away from their homelands because of the instability of the world in which they lived, and problems they would have faced with other hosts closer to home.

Balanced against these situations, where the threats seemed to justify higher borders, other kinds of borderwork were taking place.

We should not neglect these, because out of them grew cosmogenesis. These were sources of restabilisation: border crossings not invasions, friendships built rather than fences erected. For instance, the *Tampa* affair was itself a multicultural event, the intersection of a Norwegian and an Indonesian ship carrying Middle Eastern passengers, in international waters far from Australia's coast. It had ramifications well beyond Australia itself (although we cannot treat them here). The international maritime law Rinnan obeyed came from a global body, recognised by Australia as it is by Norway, set up to regulate problems on this scale. There was no real need for panic in this case. The complex network of links and boundaries already in place would have been enough. But pragmatic efficiency was never the point.

'Breaking down walls?'

The Berlin Wall, 1983: Breaking through to the other side?

We used this photograph, taken by John in 1983, as a cover image for our course. It shows the Berlin Wall at the height of the Cold War, built by the DDR (East German Republic) to 'protect' its citizens from the temptations of the other side.

The photograph captures the beginning of a famous reality-denying speech by the president of East Germany two decades earlier as it was being built: in English 'No one has any intention of erecting a wall!' The graffiti artist painted a jail door on to the wall, and

Borderwork and multicultural Australia

wrote DDR on the 'grille'. It seemed a mere gesture of defiance, as reality-denying as the president's words.

Who would have thought that this wall would come down? Certainly not John in 1983 as he stared at the concrete and barbed wire that divided streets and suburbs in the worst kind of social division. What did this graffitist hope to achieve against all that concrete? It must have seemed pointless.

Yet in 1989, the wall was demolished piece by piece. We used this photograph as a symbol of hope. Shot on the cheapest camera available on a whim ('Hey Ton! Go and open that door would you—I want to take your photo!'), it speaks volumes of the power of hope. Walls only stay if we want them to. The time and the place are specific. But the message is for us all.

Borderwork that works

How do we judge the success of a borderwork policy? For a linear mind, borders work if they keep everything out. But reality is more complex than that. Borders are meant to increase security and allow desirable flows to continue otherwise unimpeded. If borders decrease security and make life worse, then the borderwork is not a success, even if nothing passes it.

Medieval Europe, for instance, built massive fortresses which dotted the land, yet it was a dangerous place and dysfunctional society, made less safe by the obsession with strong walls. Paradoxically, a defensive mentality can create enemies, not just keep them out. This still applies today. For instance, a work devoted to analysing Australia's defence had a title, *Threats Without Enemies* (Kettle & Smith 1992), which says it all: we don't need a real enemy to want a defence force.

In Chapter 1, we introduced the idea of fuzzy logic. Let us think about border security in these terms. To recap, in complex and dynamic conditions, the more precise the criteria the less relevant or meaningful they will be for purposes of control. The crisp thinking so typical of responses to moral panics is not only useless, it is dangerous. This is a startling proposal, yet it explains the Australian case rather well.

For instance, a system of identities is essential to see who should pass and who should not. A rigid, crisp set of identities produces a bureaucratic nightmare with refugees, who often lack the right papers precisely because of what they are fleeing from. The current crisp

Australian system classifies people as 'unauthorised arrivals' or 'asylum seekers' in the first place, before they progress to the category of 'refugee', staying in holding camps, with crisp borders, for as long as that takes.

In fact, this system is too dysfunctional to work on any scale, and in practice Australia relies in most cases on a parallel system which is fuzzier. For a long time, people who arrived by boat were treated crisply, but those who arrived by plane were processed by a fuzzy system. Even today, many categories of 'unauthorised' visitors or over-stayers are treated under a fuzzy system, with different kinds of visas and different kinds of treatment. This system leaks profusely, where the other is almost watertight—yet there is no panic, no sense that things are out of control. So when a group seeks to 'crisp up' its borders, to make them more definite, a common pattern is that they become less, rather than more, effective *as borders*.

How, then, should we rate the government's borderwork? The immediate political success is not in doubt: these are policies (ironically largely devised by the ALP when it was in power) which some—including the prime minister, it would seem (Dodson 2005, p. 1)—believe to have delivered an election victory to the Coalition. As a purely administrative arrangement, there are some grounds to rate the system a success, since there were no more illegal immigrants arriving by boat. But in spite of this measure of success, there are other purely administrative criteria by which it rates less highly. The period of maintaining the system as an impermeable structure via a system of detention centres was brief, and the total numbers were always small. A crisp set of borders is unsustainable over a long time, as a system, without consuming huge resources and turning the whole nation into a prison. This is what the East German government did, of course: it *is* possible, for a while. But the consequences are severe, as the East Germans ultimately learnt.

Paradoxically, the system succeeded as far as it did partly because it was not in fact the real system, but rather a system managed partly through exceptions. The minister responsible for immigration has what is called a 'discretionary' power to intervene in cases when the system fails. As minister, Philip Ruddock (and after him, Senator Amanda Vanstone) frequently used this discretionary power to override outcomes he thought were really unfair. The fact that he was not reluctant to use this power suggests the need was there. This discretionary power always worked in favour of the applicants, usually after the court or appeal tribunal process had rejected their application.

Yet a national system dependent on the acts of judgment of a single person is not efficient or sustainable. Mr Ruddock had to be both a crisp and a fuzzy gatekeeper, single-handedly restoring flows cut off by his own rigid system. This made him seem contradictory, but the contradictions came from the system itself. To rely on one person to have the main responsibility to correct a whole system is inefficient, in management terms, but even these concessions are better than none at all.

How to not take sides

At the time of the *Tampa* affair, our students were agitated and confused, not knowing what to think as statement and counter-statement circulated, and some of our best students were the most confused. We saw our task as teachers as being to give them ways of coping with such confusion. Part of the problem, we felt, was the way people took sides, and tidied up reality to fit one or other of them. But the reality is that there are always more than two sides to a story, and there are shared elements in many apparently opposed positions. Such a debate structure is schismogenic, for a university class or a nation. When a debate is schismogenic, it splits people from each other, reducing anyone's chance to understand the complexity of the whole.

In this situation, we found it helpful for students to use three-body analysis. First, it organised the various positions, to avoid the usual unproductive oppositions that would otherwise have taken over (pro- and anti-border controls, 'racists' versus 'wimps'). Then it reminded us to look always for the dynamics that linked each to the others, sometimes in surprising and unpredictable ways.

We illustrate this by taking three writers from the immediate historical aftermath of *Tampa*, each representing a still significant point of view. First, the view that dominated letters pages and opinion columns strongly supported the government's hard line. This view is typified by right-wing columnist Piers Akerman. Akerman defended the victorious Howard voters against charges of racism:

> Tired of being told you're a rednecked racist because you don't believe illegal immigrants should be permitted to break the law and get away

with it? Well, take heart, you're in the majority, your views are those of the wider community and you have the sympathy of influential people in Europe and the US. (2002, p. 14)

Akerman is notorious as a populist of the right, so it is unsurprising to find that he splits the political world into 'us' (we won the election) and 'them' (they didn't). He doesn't invite these opponents to take his argument seriously, but he has a point that they should acknowledge. He is surely correct to point to the value of democratic processes, and his ingenious attack refers to 'international opinion' to bring in the idea of a global audience which opponents of the *Tampa* policies often invoked. Neither the 'Australian people' nor 'the world' should be invented as a simple, homogeneous fiction, a single entity speaking only one thing (what the speaker already thinks). It is true that the international community—like the Australian community—was deeply divided on this issue.

The second position opposed Akerman's perspective. These left-wing proponents did indeed call their opponents racist. They recognised that events were not unfolding as they would wish, but saw no reason to change their basic views or values which supported progressivist multiculturalism. Many of them wrote not from letters pages, but from institutional positions. Anne Summers, for instance, wrote an important book on Australian history before becoming a senior policy adviser to the Keating Labor government. In an invited commentary, she argued:

> Those thousands of middle-class educated people who flocked to the [Australian Labor] party because of Gough Whitlam . . . were part of the transformation of Labor from the narrow-minded, bigoted and frankly racist party of Arthur Calwell's day. (Summers 2002, p. 12)

Summers laments the weak 'me-tooism' of Labor under its then leaders, Kim Beazley and Simon Crean, arguing that the Whitlam period transformed an older, deeply racist structure. 'Progressivists' like her were shocked by events of 2001, such as the *Tampa* affair and the election victory based on it. They are as schismogenic as Akerman, but this fact in common only makes each hate the other more.

So far this is two-body analysis. A third interpretation of these events, significantly different from both, has much in common with both. This position denounces racism, but from a distinct point of view. For instance, Robert Manne, former right-wing commentator, strongly denounced the racism of the policy. Fred Chaney, a former Liberal minister, was another dissenter. Perhaps the most influential of all was Malcolm Fraser, Liberal Prime Minister of Australia from 1975 to 1983. In one essay, 'Stumbling on a Path of Inhumanity', Fraser opened his analysis:

> Australians are being led in the wrong direction about asylum seekers. Only seven years after the 1930s Depression, Arthur Calwell persuaded the ACTU to accept a major immigration program in Australia's national interest. The ACTU did not put it to the vote. If it had, there would have been an 80 percent majority against it. As the migrant program developed, governments did not poll the community on whether they wanted several hundred thousand Italians or Greeks. If they had, people would have voted against it. (Fraser 2001, p. 12)

Fraser went on to list the same pattern with the migration of Irish Catholics in the 1920s and the Vietnamese 'boat people' in the 1970s. In each case, he asserted, the people would have rejected it automatically and emphatically. 'Governments provided a lead and Australians have accepted that lead. We are a better country as a consequence.' (2001, p. 12)

Fraser has a classic Liberal background, yet here he joined Anne Summers in advocating an elitist form of multiculturalism as something that the rulers of the society must trick their citizens into. The virtuous end seemingly justified non-virtuous means, just as the government used immoral means in the *Tampa* case in pursuit of what it claimed was the high moral ground. This is a problematic argument, profoundly undemocratic in nature. It sees the Australian electorate as inherently untrustworthy, susceptible to the basest forms of racism and opportunism. It assumes that not only were Australians once deeply racist, but they still are. Paradoxically, this argument against Akerman's position accepts Akerman's basic premise.

Three-body analysis does not stop here. Having seen that Akerman's argument resonates surprisingly with the others, we note that he too has an elitist side. It is only 'influential people' who would be 'sympathetic', not a global majority. A tension between democratic processes and independent judgment turns out to be common to all three, to some degree.

So also is a concern for morality. Initially it might seem that Summers and Fraser are the moralists, and Akerman rejects morality. But Akerman's article exists to justify opponents of asylum seekers, not simply because they are the majority (no one disputes who won the election) but also because it is *morally* sound. He may seem to be saying that might is right, but implicitly the charges of racism clearly hurt. He does not say that being racist is good, just that the charge is unfair.

This kind of analysis encourages us all to get outside the specific position we are most used to. It helps us to see the complexity *behind* issues, to be able to ask good *questions* of each. It is not a key to the main debate, but something more useful, for those who want to do more than take predetermined sides. It does not remove all disagreements or differences, but it sees patterns of connections and oppositions out of which a more common alternative understanding can grow. This is how a three-body analysis can deconstruct apparently fixed binaries, bringing out the complexity in all of the positions, including even the apparently most simplistic.

And the facts are . . .?

Faced with a swirling mess of claim and counter-claim, our students wanted more than just a means to sort out arguments. They rightly wanted to know just what the 'facts' were. Each writer says or implies things about how the world is, and it is always valuable to try to check out these claims using some outside sources. This is where statistics have a role to play. Reputable agencies such as the Australian Bureau of Statistics (ABS), or world bodies such as the United Nations (UN) and various non-government organisations provide a wealth of relevant data. But this information needs to be selected fairly and interpreted carefully.

In highly charged situations, this is not always a straightforward business. For instance, take Akerman's claim that, by world standards, Australians are not racist. Akerman here was picking up a claim made by Howard in his policy launch of August 2001 that Australia is one of the most generous nations towards refugees. He maintained that Australia would 'retain a generous approach' to refugees by continuing 'on a per capita basis to take more refugees than any country in the world except Canada'.

The demographer Thuy Do quoted this, then assembled data from good international sources to show that this claim is only nearly true for countries with a formal refugee resettlement program. However, many countries accept refugees even though they do not have a formal program. Looking at this larger list, Do shows that, of the 40 top countries in the world for taking refugees, on a per capita basis Australia comes in at number 39 (Do 2002, p. 41). Compared with 31 other industrialised countries, Australia comes eighth. Not so good after all, it seems.

Even if the 'facts' come from good sources, as in this case with both Howard and Do, they turn out to be open to different selections and interpretations. In practice, each points to a different part of a complex, contradictory truth. Across the planet, there is indeed a high degree of ambivalence towards the worldwide 'refugee problem', just as Akerman claims. Many of the countries that take more refugees than Australia are close to war zones, trying to cope with a flood of refugees without the necessary resources. If they take more refugees than Australia does, it is not necessarily because they want to.

Amongst industrialised countries, there is a similar pattern of ambivalence to that existing in Australia, as Akerman indicates. In these countries, there are many people who strive to do something about the problems of refugees—some more, some less, as in Australia. In the comparison, once *all* the *relevant* facts are *interpreted*, it is clear that Australia *does* do more than nothing, but that more could easily be done.

Was Fraser right?

Many politicians on both sides assumed that support for asylum seekers would be electoral disaster. But was this 'fact' really so? The independent member for Calare, Peter Andren, contested it. Laurie Oakes, in *The Bulletin*, said: 'the gutsiest speech was made by . . . Peter Andren . . . [from the] rural seat of Calare where bleeding hearts on the issue of would-be refugees from Afghanistan and the Middle East are almost certainly in short supply'. Andren: 'The only trouble was, the bulk of my constituents don't read *The Bulletin*' (p. 18). He goes on:

I had written my local newspaper column and clearly explained my stance . . . Despite my confidence in my electorate . . . the fervour of this issue on the national stage, the misinformation and propaganda, had me concerned. Part of me thought that I didn't want to represent an electorate if it reflected views so out of kilter with my own, despite the fact the national polls were also showing that the vast majority disagreed with me, too. (2003, p. 20)

And win decisively he did: 'I felt vindicated. I felt proud of my people in Calare, my voters and my team.' (2003, p. 36) Explaining his position actually changed people's minds as a survey of 250 Andren-voters later indicated. (2003, p. 37)

Andren's sustained support for this cause after the 2001 poll, and his strong opposition to the war in Iraq (a somewhat different issue, but one again opposed to both government and opposition positions), did not damage his result in the election in 2004 either: once again, he won in his own right. What if Andren had been prime minister, or leader of the opposition in 2001? He wasn't. But maybe the Coalition victory did not prove as much about the Australian psyche as Andren did.

Borderwork over time: A sketch

In Chapter 1 we told the neglected history of the surprisingly early emergence of Australian multiculture. Here we will balance that story with its complement, the roots of the schismogenesis that erupted into the *Tampa* affair. Readers may wonder what we are doing: 'Make up your mind,' they may say. 'Is Australia basically multicultural, or basically racist?' It is both, to a degree. One merit of a fuzzy logic approach is that it allows us to capture the contradictions which really exist in a situation, without being forced to choose one or the other half-truth.

We will concentrate on the decade 1991–2001. The decade's bookends were detention centres. Detention centres differ from prisons in that the people in them are not criminals. Sometimes they are run by the same people as prisons (when the system is put to tender for private operators). But, unlike prisons, the people detained have committed no crime. Australia had many detention centres in this decade, and our students were surprised at how many there were, and where they were located. The Port Hedland centre was opened in 1991, inaugurating the decade, and the short-lived, highly expensive 'Pacific Solution' centres (in Papua New Guinea and Nauru) opened in 2001. In the intervening years, centres came and went (such as the centre at Woomera in the Australian interior). Some that existed prior to this time kept operating as normal (like Villawood in western Sydney).

But let us begin our story at the beginning of the decade. The backdrop to the Hedland centre's opening in 1991 was a new refugee assessment system introduced in 1990 by Mr Gerry Hand, Labor Minister for Immigration. In it, we see the stirrings of the 'borderwork' that was to bear its political fruit a decade later. Mr Hand said:

> What we had to do was set up a system which could stand the scrutiny of people in terms of its fairness and its consistency. It is a horrendous area to administer because everyone becomes emotionally involved. I never made a judgement as to whether they were or they weren't refugees. What I always said was: 'I'm going to make sure they have a fair go to prove their point'. (*People and Place* 1993, pp. 1–2)

Note the 'humanising' tone by today's standards. The apparent empathy quickly disappeared, even in this interview. For Mr Hand, 'fairness' involved a number of things: 'You can't just come to Australia, land on the beach and wander ashore like the invaders did 200 years ago. There is now a proper process of entry and if you don't come the right way you will be put in custody. That's the rule.' (1993, p. 6) But the tone is ambiguous. If we compare this with debates of more recent years, we may recognise the schismogenic tone of moral outrage in the language used ('proper process', the 'right way', and 'you will be put in custody'). At the same time, his phrase 'the invaders' sees the current dominant Anglo-Celts from an Aboriginal perspective as all 'illegals'. The borderwork is already underway, and it is creating a split within the minister himself.

The Hedland centre was commissioned in 1991 to deal with those who arrived by boat. This and the other new centres were all put in remote locations. The rationale for detaining unauthorised arrivals in this way was 'to ensure that they do not enter Australia until their claims to do so have been properly assessed and found to justify entry'. (Joint Senate Committee on Migration (JSCM) 1993, p. 21) This same policy and language are still used in debates today.

Let us make this point very clearly. 'Border security', as it is now called, has *always* been a bipartisan policy. It *still* is. It was founded by the ALP in 1990–91, developed by them through a succession of reports and reforms, and taken over by the Coalition when it entered government in 1996.

Labor Senator McKiernan as chair of the JSCM declared the principles of the policy, which still operates. His slogan was: 'Defend, Deter, Detain'. Defence of the borders involves repelling or detaining refugee boats. Deterrence involves seeking to frighten would-be asylum seekers from trying their luck in Australia. Detention prevents those who get through from being deemed to actually be 'in' Australia.

A crucial premise in this logic is the illogical link with issues of defence. McKiernan argued explicitly that the detention centres were part of our *defence* system (as opposed, say, to being part of our population program or welfare system): 'I believe it is the government and its authorised delegate bodies that should determine who should be admitted to Australia. To concede that right to foreign nationals would be a direct attack on Australia's national security.' (McKiernan 1995, p. 4) These words were echoed in the Coalition's election-winning slogan on border security in November 2001.

This borderwork was conducted over a decade of Australian history. At first, it went virtually unnoticed. Politicians chipped away with a new language about asylum seekers that stripped them slowly of their status as worthy applicants, constructing them instead as 'illegal' or 'unauthorised arrivals' or 'queue jumpers'. It took a decade to really take effect, but the positive feedback loop that started inconspicuously at Port Hedland built into a mighty force that, in Frankenstein fashion, came back to bite its architects in the Labor Party. But with moral panics, once a chain of positive feedback cuts in, it develops a momentum of its own unless active efforts can break the circuit.

Borders are commonly erected out of a need for control at every level—personal, familial, national; to control others, or to defend against their threat to the self. Beyond a certain point, the will to control can produce a sense of being more out of control, generating further problems, requiring further efforts at control. This paradox can be seen at work in multiple instances at many levels in the responses to the problems of multiculture in Australia.

We take a number of lessons from this history. One is that when political groups frame a situation in terms of crisp borders and vague threats, the same dangerous logic can take hold, no matter which political party is in power. Conversely, these ideas have never formed a total policy framework, for either party. Whatever some may wish or fear, Fortress Australia does not exist and is not a realistic possibility. Nor would an Australia thrive that tried to erect high boundaries, and to police crisp categories. The real issue, recognised to some degree by both parties, is how best to live with and as a multiculture, open to the world, managing flows and gates with an easy grace. Australian citizens and politicians alike need to learn lessons about borderwork, and the value of permeable boundaries and fuzzy categories.

The invasion has happened—why are people laughing?

We are indeed now 'all together' with a shared destiny, whoever 'we' might be. A short account of *Pizza* star Paul Fenech evokes urban Australia now:

His shows are full of chockos—Australians who don't appear to be holding a walnut with their butt cheeks: 'everyone who's a bit loose, they're the chockos' . . . Now he's doing the great multicultural comic triumph: a wog doing bogan skits. 'Forget what the government thought about it (multiculturalism) but the fact of Australia being a classless society ultimately created more camaraderie—nobody can really say they're better than anybody else,' Fenech reasons. 'And the funny thing is that now, in terms of humour, the bottom of the barrel is your bogan—your fringe-dweller, white Anglo-Saxon Australian.'

The idea that we live in a classless society might be mythic, but Fenech and Stevenson think their style of joke is now firmly part of mainstream Australian culture—are they wrong? (Stevenson 2003b, p. 13)

From little things, big things grow

We have used the term 'borderwork' to mean a continual process involving barriers—physical, social or mental—and also categories of persons who are to be included inside those borders or excluded. Borderwork, we have seen, includes not only erecting, maintaining and policing borders of different kinds, but also *continuous redefi-nition* of categories of person as outsiders, at the same time setting and resetting *limits* (rules and ways of speaking) for that defined outsider. But borderwork can also aim to relax boundaries, find connections and dream of a more humane society, as part of cosmogenesis.

In the wake of the *Tampa* affair, there were many signs of a reaction against the detention policies. It is easy to minimise the importance of these compared with the high profile of the policies themselves. They can be dismissed as the unrealistic sentimentality of a few middle-class 'bleeding hearts', politically irrelevant to any main-stream definition of Australia. But people's attitudes were challenged by the bureaucratic brutality, which made them feel uncomfortable. Once fears receded after the 2001 election, campaigners opened up some effective lines of questioning, especially around the humanity of keeping children in detention.

There were other, smaller gestures too. In 2003, a petition written by an inmate of Villawood Detention Centre read as follows: 'We the imprisoned asylum seekers of Australia, respectfully appeal to the people of the world to hear our story, understand our plight, and come to our assistance.' (Anon 2003, p. 1) Many Australians heard such appeals through missives like this one, or from eyewitness accounts, or saw them on television. They felt at the time that this was something that concerned them directly, in their own very sense of being. And many responded:

> I entered the reception area of Villawood Detention centre at around 4pm on Tuesday afternoon before Christmas . . . The biggest visual impact is the wire. There is an inner perimeter fence of cyclone wire about five metres high with several strands of barbed wire at the top. The exterior perimeter fence is cyclone wire topped by razor wire. Beyond a high fence, Lei, Ussa, and Ina were waving to us with smiles. 'We can't come through yet, because the "mahsta" isn't finished,' Ina called to us. 'Mahsta' is how I would have written the word, not because of Ina's pronunciation but because I had not yet come to terms with one of the facts of life in detention. Ina was talking about the *muster* which takes place several times a day . . . and night. (Pryor 2002, pp. 11–12)

Jackie Pryor, white, Anglo-Celtic middle-class woman, an editor of *eremos*, an interdisciplinary journal with religious affiliations, wrote

Borderwork and multicultural Australia

here simply as a concerned member of Australian society. Villawood, as she pointed out, is one of the better internment centres in Australia. It is close to the facilities of Sydney. The scene she describes, of picnic tables and chairs, grass and trees, gives a good sense of the combination of harshly defined perimeters within which a small, heterogeneous multiculture seeks to exist.

For reasons unrelated to the writing of this book, John also visited Villawood. It is something he would encourage others to do, if only to see what is being done in our name as Australians. Perhaps the strangest thing about the visit for him was the way that we, the visitors, have our social world turned inside out, as *we* are welcomed by those whom the government has decided cannot be welcomed among 'us'. And then, what of those within, too depressed by endless periods of waiting to come out at all? Once one enters this world, the personal stories, anguish, hope and despair leave an indelible mark. The harrowing experiences of the visit become a kind of self-ethnography, where the subject of inquiry becomes one's own government, oneself.

This is also the experience described by Pryor. Doubts cloud the experience at every turn:

> After Ramadan, some women brought in a huge feast to share. I asked one of them to tell me truthfully whether or not a visitor such as myself was of any use. She reassured me that it definitely was because, she told me, detainees readily get the impression that Australia does not, therefore Australians do not, want them, and do not want to have anything to do with them. (Pryor 2002, p. 14)

We quote Jackie Pryor at length because she writes not from an academic or official position, not even as an activist, but as a concerned member of a community—in this case, the Anglicans. Pryor, like us, is an Anglo-Celtic Australian, but that means many different attitudes and affiliations that we may not share. Whatever these differences, though, there are many points of possible connection, all valuable.

The contribution of people who simply turn up, or make a gesture, is often disregarded in multicultural literatures. Yet, just as we have seen and questioned the bipartisan borderwork that generated the current wave of angst, so too we must pay tribute to those who sought to dampen the feedback loop, in the only ways they knew. These people have also been present since the outset. On Sunday,

12 April 1992, well before a Howard government was even considered a serious possibility, a small group of protestors gathered outside the recently commissioned Hedland detention camp. The protest went largely unnoticed because there were no arrests or confrontations. The local paper, the *North West Telegraph*, reported:

> A candlelight vigil was held outside the Port Hedland Processing Centre last Sunday evening to acknowledge and share the turmoil of the illegal arrivals housed in the centre. A banner with 'We share your anguish' written in Cambodian, Chinese, and English expressed the message of more than 200 people who attended the vigil. (Barrett 1992, p. 3)

The Uniting Church and the Catholic Church both had representatives, alongside local citizens. Since the opening of these facilities, such events have become commonplace. Such people were already being dismissed by advocates of detention (by Mr Hand, among others—1993, p. 3). The contempt for 'bleeding hearts' is a widespread trope in Australian political discourse; the lawyer upstarts, the women with candles, the priests and reverends are all, strangely enough, presented as a risk to those who fan the moral outrage. Don't these very people stand for values in Australian society?

They, too, perform a kind of borderwork. It is all too easy for academics (like us) to devise concepts (be they 'moral panics', 'borderwork' or 'schismogenesis') which lead to a view of society as inherently negative. Criticism is something we academics are trained to do, and it can be valuable. But it cannot be all—otherwise people are left with nowhere to go, no pathways forward. It is easy to complain; to find solutions is harder.

In this chapter we have suggested that, while the challenges that confront us all are great, not all the borderwork we do is negative. It is true that as we write we are in the wake of more than a decade of governmental borderwork, the chief effect of which has been to reduce asylum seekers to the category of illegal or unauthorised entrants. But this is not the only borderwork that has been going on in this time, nor is it the worst phase in our history. Many families in Australia have rallied to support those who are detained. Every time someone fills out a visitor's application form to a place like Villawood, a border is crossed, questioned, changed. These daily acts are also borderwork: they restore links and create the promise of a new kind of society in the future.

Borderwork and multicultural Australia

VILLAWOOD IMMIGRATION DETENTION CENTRE		Confirm No:	VF 1901
		Issue No:	2
		Date of Issue:	12/11/01
		Page:	Page 1 of 1

APPLICATION TO VISIT DETAINEE

Date:	Time:

VISITOR DETAILS (18 Years and over)

(Mr/Mrs/Ms/Miss) Surname:	Given Names:

Address:

Postcode:

Phone No. (Home):	(Work):

Date of Birth:	Relationship to Detainee:

WARNING: Introduction of contraband/non approved items into the Centre can result in denial of current and future Visits.

Signature:

Children (Under 18 Years)

Name	Age	Relationship to Detainee

DETAINEE DETAILS

Surname		Given Name:		DOS:	
Surname		Given Name:		DOS:	
Surname		Given Name:		DOS:	
Surname		Given Name:		DOS:	

Office Use Only

Stage Number:			Tag No.	
ID	Type		Number	Expiry Date
Primary				
Secondary				
Visit Denied: Yes / No	**Commetns:**			
Officer Name:		**Signature:**		

Villawood visitor's application form

Defending the Australian parliament

New ramparts for Parliament House

Earlier in the chapter, we displayed an image of the Berlin Wall as an example of borderwork. The East German president denied he was building a wall, even while it was being built. Once erected, it was solid and permanent, and many people died trying to cross to the other side.

We conclude this chapter with a reflection on this image of the newly defended Australian parliament. Are the threats really so great? What about the costs to the functioning of a democracy? Will this borderwork be permanent? Should we try to do what we can to bring these walls down?

Borderwork and multicultural Australia

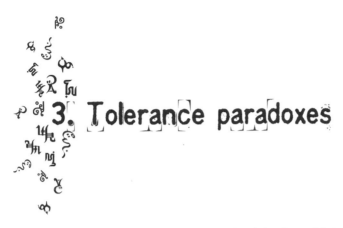

3. Tolerance paradoxes

In a debate about education in 2004, the federal Health Minister, Tony Abbott, remarked that:

> Australians were 'tolerating the intolerable' because of political correctness. 'There is a tendency in some schools to ignore what might be described as traditional values, to pretend that all value systems are equal, and I just don't think that's true and I don't think the Australian people think it's true,' Mr Abbott told ABC radio. He said the only value 'politically correct educators' really supported was tolerance. 'It's a good value, but sometimes I think that in modern Australia we end up tolerating the intolerable,' he said. (Metherell 2004, p. 4)

Tolerating the intolerable: is such a thing possible? In terms of standard logic, it isn't. Something intolerable cannot, by definition, be tolerated. And yet it is.

We call any situation that looks like this a **tolerance paradox**. Despite saying it is intolerable, Mr Abbott says we actually *do* 'end up' tolerating it (or others do—he himself doesn't think that we should). It seems impossible, but his statement is not nonsense: it is a paradox. Often, as in this case, there are further paradoxes just below the surface. For instance, he and his prime minister, two of the most politically powerful people in Australia, present themselves as fighting against 'political correctness' (or, in this case, politically correct educators). How could this be? Could a bunch of school teachers be so powerful? Additionally, although this is not quite a paradox, Mr Abbott does not actually *reject* tolerance as a value; rather, he seeks to slightly weaken its force in society in relation to other—unspecified—values.

Tolerance paradoxes imply a special kind of borderwork, one that is often highly intense. Despite their apparently neutral appearance (they seem to have a merely 'logical' or 'linguistic' nature), they frequently betray uncertainty. Sometimes they mask the hostility of outright schismogenesis. Once the knots of paradox are loosened, we often find they are not paradoxes at all, but rather are unresolved layers of society. Whichever form they take, these difficult pressure points are valuable indicators of borderwork.

Borderwork is not always hot and noisy. Sometimes it can be subtle. It can be quietly corrosive or it can be healing (or both). It can also be very deceptive, even if those engaged in it don't mean it to be. Tolerance paradoxes are a kind of borderwork that is especially like this. Let us put it this way: because they *appear* to be the products of reason or of language, tolerance paradoxes *seem* to lie outside the borderwork contexts that produce them. Yet they are always highly charged with meaning, and they always have histories. For this reason, it is important to restore to them their proper social and cultural contexts—these help us to make sense of them.

In this chapter, we will be looking at the role of paradoxes and how to cope with them when analysing claims and counter-claims in hot debates, especially those that pivot around that word 'tolerance'. Wherever in society we find this complex buckling of language and sense, these paradoxical uses of words, we can be sure there is a complex context, a far from equilibrium situation.

'Multiculturalism' and 'tolerance' in discourse

Both 'multiculturalism' and 'tolerance' are highly complex words, full of minor and major contradictions which make them difficult to interpret in isolation, outside the contexts in which they are used. For instance, the federal Coalition government, when first elected in 1996, had an ambivalent attitude to multiculturalism since it seemed associated with their political opponents. Even so, it never repudiated the word 'multiculturalism', and the term 'tolerance' was used freely throughout this period. Towards the end of its first term of office, analysts detected a change. 'Multiculturalism' seemed to grow in official favour. But, even as official documents talked more about diversity and multiculturalism, they retreated from using 'tolerance'.

A little of this can be seen in the history of a paper called *A New Agenda for Multicultural Australia,* beginning from its publication in December 1999. This was an official government publication, reflecting government (rather than merely bureaucratic) policy. In it, the word 'tolerance' was downplayed, but still used. The foreword by the prime minister talked of Australia as an 'open and tolerant society' (DIMA 1999, p. 3). The document itself stated that government policies and principles are based on 'tolerance, humanity and mutual respect' (1999, p. 6). The document used the word several more times.

In 2003, a new paper was released, *Multicultural Australia: United in Diversity,* bearing the subheading *Updating the 1999 New Agenda for Multicultural Australia: Strategic Directions for 2003–2006.* Once again, the prime minister's message referred to 'tolerance'. But now the text itself did not use the word. In its place, we find other words: harmony, diversity, respect, acceptance, cultural enrichment (DIMA 2003, p. 6). This text is authored by a government whose leading members have at times expressed reservations about the values of multiculturalism and tolerance. This goes beyond party politics: at least part of the reason for hesitation in the case of tolerance is the complexity the term entails.

When people use apparently loaded terms in this way, we say they are participating in a **discourse**. It is not immediately clear in the above text that the language *is* loaded. That is why the usual idea of discourse is not enough. The word 'discourse' can, of course, mean a speech or text. But in the field of social analysis, discourse refers to ways of speaking that actually *construct meaning* in the world. This idea, drawn from the work of Michel Foucault (1972), looks at how things like 'tolerance' or 'multiculturalism' create social meanings. That is, discourses construct subject positions (for instance, tolerators) but also objects (the tolerated), and they make some choices available, but close off others. Discourses *happen* in social situations, and these are also crucial to any attempt to make sense of a text.

In official texts on multiculturalism such as the two above, we need to pay attention to a lot of apparently small things. Meaning does not just come from what is said, or from what the sentences or speeches 'really mean'. Instead, we look for signs and cues that indicate what weight the key players are giving to these statements. In the case of policy statements, indicators like nuance, emphasis and absence are all part of what we should look for when we read a text.

So the kind of shift in words we have noted over three or five years signals a possible shift in policy. In this case, for instance, the description of 'multiculturalism' is still a full, comprehensive statement, much as it was for the previous government. But the slight shift in terms, along with changes in departmental responsibilities, reduced funding, conditions attached to the funds, and so on combine in a total package of contradictions around both 'multiculturalism' and 'tolerance' which sends a signal: the government still supports these policies, but not as much as before, and not in quite the same way.

A gap between grand-sounding policies and actual practices is usually seen as hypocrisy. In one sense it is, and perhaps all governments are hypocritical in this way. But we need to do more than simply note hypocrisy, condemn it and pass on. In this case, it is equally important to see that a government which began by not 'believing' in multiculturalism still felt obliged to restate it as a primary principle of Australian society. Yet it subtly downgraded the key principle of 'tolerance'.

Discourse analysis turns up these loaded terms, suggesting there might be tensions surrounding particular social fields (intercultural tolerance, support for multiculturalism itself). The word 'tolerance' is not used innocently in these exchanges, and we as readers need strategies of our own that extend beyond the manipulation of words that we find in documents such as those we discussed above. For the paradox—and promise—of tolerance goes far beyond what we have traced so far. We need to understand the competing tendencies at work in it, to see our place in it, to see what possibilities there are for us as social players.

The roots of 'tolerance'

The word 'tolerance' has a long history and, as with everything important in culture and society, history contains many clues and patterns that can help us to understand the complexity of the present. The meaning of the word 'tolerance' comes not just from modern contexts, but also from its earlier history.

Borderwork and multicultural Australia

The word comes from the Latin *tolerans,* itself from *tolerare.* This word in turn came from a more basic root, *tollere* (from an Indo-European root). The core meaning over this long history is to carry, bear, lift up. The Greek god Atlas, who carried the world on his shoulders, took his name from this root. Latin *tolerare* had this meaning at its core, referring to a range of activities: to carry (heavy weights) and hence endure (or 'tolerate') pain and hardship, and also support in another sense, that is nurture (sustain offspring).

Across its range of meanings, it always included a sense of effort, often driven by duty, whether from below ('tolerating' hardships) or from above (taking on the burden of agreeing with the people). These are still part of the meaning of the word. From this, we get a historical explanation for a number of different meanings: tolerance implies 'putting up with things we don't like' and also a sense of work or 'effort'. We note that in most of its senses it refers to a quality that may be necessary, but not always enjoyable. We also note that it is a relative term. There is a limit to the weight anyone can carry. 'Tolerance' will always only go so far.

The term 'tolerance' in political discourse is usually tracked back to England and the seventeenth century. In 1689, the English thinker John Locke published his *Epistola de tolerantia (Epistle on Tolerance),* in Latin and English, in which 'tolerance' is, as the title implies, a lynchpin in a whole political program. He asks of the:

> consciences of those that persecute, torment, destroy, and kill other men upon pretence of religion, whether they do it out of friendship and kindness toward them or no? And I shall . . . believe they do so, when I shall see those fiery zealots correcting, in the same manner, their friends and familiar acquaintance for the manifest sins they commit against the precepts of the Gospel. (1966, pp. 125–26)

Locke has come to be seen as the major thinker of a tradition known as 'liberalism', influential in Britain and the United States, as well as elsewhere. A major set of political/ethical ideas (personal liberty, private ownership, pluralism) are seen as descending from his work.

These ideas formed part of wider fields of politics and theology. The fact that these ideas were formed in Christian Europe gave it a particular colour. John Milbank, a modern philosopher, pointed out a potential problem arising from this fact. His argument went like this. These ideas provide the basis for some of the key terms—'dialogue', 'pluralism' and the like—for describing encounters with other religions, along with the ideas which have guided these interactions, such as social justice and liberation. Yet they are themselves a specifically *Western* form of discourse, which 'pluralistically' dominates all the non-Western discourses (1990, p. 185).

For Milbank, this involves a historical paradox. The triumph of the ethos of pluralism, dialogue and tolerance is no more than the triumph of the West itself, he argues. The West celebrates its ability to recognise other religions and cultures at the very moment that it is obliterating them, burying them under the weight of its influence and philosophy. Indeed, Milbank argues, the very idea of a *dialogue* of faiths and cultures is not only a Western, but a Christian, structure.

This is a striking point. It is true that tolerance (as well as pluralism, etc.) *does* have a Western history. But the value of terms like the 'West' (perhaps even of Christianity, given its own pluralities) is that they admit a range of positions, and they are fuzzy categories. Milbank's observations on the nature of dialogism are astute, but they do not weaken the value of dialogue, especially if more than two positions are engaged.

In addition, the things 'the West' (like any major cultural system) brought to world culture do not all form a single whole. The nations from which came ruthless ivory and slave traders also contained people who developed new conceptions of self and soul, and founded a remarkable human rights tradition (see Stackhouse 1999, pp. 23–24), based on a vision of abstract justice and the things we are talking about in this chapter: tolerance and all its paradoxes. The idea that it was the 'same people' who did all these things is the same fallacy that multiculture disproves.

Moreover, tolerance is not a static thing that came into being fully formed in a stroke of lightning. It is still being formed; *it depends on us*. The word had a meaning when Locke took it up and reworked it for his audience. This was not just an English audience, as can be seen in Locke's choice to publish first in Latin, the common language of European elites. And his text not only contributed to the transformation of this word, but also the foundation of liberalism. Tolerance was a multicultural achievement, English and also part of a wider European system. French thinkers like Voltaire developed it in the eighteenth century. The idea of tolerance was co-created in Europe for reasons that themselves reveal further paradoxes.

Locke's version of the concept in fact arose as a specific intervention *against* the culture of his time. It is worthwhile looking at the circumstances surrounding Locke's intervention. This was the time of the English Civil War, when the monarchy was overthrown by the militant Puritans led by Oliver Cromwell. This wheel turned again, and the monarchy was restored; however, struggles continued. In 1689, when he published his text, Locke had returned to England from exile in Europe, forced by threats of persecution by Catholic King James II.

We hope this history makes the context clear: Locke lived in dangerous times. He released his letter just after his side had returned to power. His appeal was addressed to the new rulers, among whom he had an influential voice. Crucially, his words spoke for the experience of the excluded, a voice from below to those above. His primary targets were the new masters of England, urging them not to use their power to be intolerant. He was also trying to mobilise his fellow citizens on behalf of tolerance. This form of tolerance, unlike most earlier uses, was multi-directional: from citizens to government; from governments to citizens; from citizens of all categories to each other. Even at this weakly democratic moment, tolerance was motivated by ideals of personal liberty and political justice for individuals and minority groups.

Paradox is again evident in all of this. Locke's use of the principle of 'tolerance' did not show that England was a tolerant culture, but rather the opposite. He wanted his fellows to see how dangerous their intolerance was, *to see the value of tolerance*. That is a paradox that applies to all policies. There would have been no need for a policy of multiculturalism if Australia had already been multicultural. Yet Locke would not have been so persuasive if there had not already been a groundswell in the nation recognising the need for precisely this change in direction. Locke's principle helped to change things for the better, no less because it did indeed express an impulse that was already potentially there.

Does tolerance have limits?

Up until now, we have been looking at historical paradoxes (a tolerance-imperialism, a tolerance with a genesis in historically intolerant circumstances). We now look at what appear to be 'logical' paradoxes. Many have criticised Locke for an apparent logical paradox, concerning the limits he imposed on 'tolerance'. For instance, he advocated tolerance for some religious groups, but not for 'atheists'. There were many other exceptions he proposed. Where does one draw the line? And if one draws a line, does that not mean the end of the principle of 'tolerance'?

We reply, *no*. The principle of tolerance, like many ethical principles, needs contradiction at its core, and it is no less valuable for that fact. If we get back to the concept behind the word—the idea of carrying a burden—why should a person not be able to say 'enough!' to a load? The key to its use is that 'tolerance' is a fuzzy category that has limits built in. In many ways we could say that it is the principle of fuzzy thinking applied to ethical and social life. It is the kind of ethical principle that is *not* absolute, true in all circumstances without the need for any further ethical thought by anyone, but the contrary.

We will illustrate with a contemporary example, which shows the continuing value of Locke's principle, as a principle. Discussing the contradictions that can arise in practice, Kalpana Ram (1996) refers to a typical issue that emerges in relation to immigrant women in Australia, where the principles of feminism seem to clash with the principle of respect for the culture of others. She takes the case of immigrant women from cultures where marriages are normally arranged by the family. She probes the issues arising if these women refuse to enter into such marriages. Such women are defying their 'culture', so should the dominant culture show its 'tolerance' of the other culture by supporting or enforcing these arranged marriages? Or would this 'tolerance' on the part of the dominant culture reinforce the power of the state over the various ethnically diverse components? (Ram 1996, p. 135).

This is the kind of issue students often raise in our classes, and it is hardly a rare or hypothetical situation. Our response is not that 'toleration' has reached a point at which it collapses in self-contradiction, but that this is indeed a complex situation, whose complexity comes from social life, which is not to be understood or resolved by a rigid use of a single, simple, invariable principle.

And there *is* a limit. Tolerance has built-in limits. We have only to reflect on what tolerance is by thinking about what it *does*. We saw before that tolerance supports a democratising framework of justice concerned to protect liberties—whether personal or of the minority group. Given this, it is not surprising that a conflict between an individual and a group interest can arise.

In this contradictory context, tolerance does *not*—under its own terms—support patriarchal oppression that infringes the personal liberties in the situations our classes graphically conjectured. Far from being a failure of tolerance, this sort of example shows how the tolerance contradiction works. And work it does. In Australia, as elsewhere, aspects of tolerance and limits to tolerance are not just advised, but enforceable. In a principle that has been refined somewhat since the seventeenth century, tolerance implies not just rights, but duties—on all sides.

The attack on 'tolerance'

If 'tolerance' is a contradictory and paradoxical principle, how can the concept be useful in searching for a balanced, harmonious and comprehensive stance? A good challenge to our position is provided by the work of Ghassan Hage, an Australian intellectual of Lebanese origins whose book *White Nation: Fantasies of White Supremacy in a Multicultural Society* (1998) caused a tremendous stir when it first appeared. Hage, a fine product of Australian multiculture, argued against multiculturalism, attacking the core idea of 'tolerance' as a sham. He is intolerant of tolerance, an 'ethnic' opposing the multi-culturalism that many have been seen as a charter for an inclusive future. As he was aware, his position could be seen as closer to a populist right-wing attack on multiculturalism (like that of Pauline Hanson in the 1990s) than to that of those on the left who supported it.

We take issue with some of his arguments and conclusions, yet we also see *White Nation* as a major achievement, so important that we used it for some years as the set text for our subject. It sought to revalue what had, until the mid-1990s, been a decade of mostly self-satisfied official multiculturalism, which overlaid a wide and varied community unease. Hage did not try to counter that unease. On the contrary, he gave a voice to a perspective on multiculturalism from below which expressed reasons for the unease.

For him, there were continuities between multiculturalism and older policies, and he criticised what he saw as 'white fantasies' about the way social space is ordered. Privileged and underprivileged whites alike, he argued, shared this fantasy—a belief that they had the special right to 'manage' non-white migration. Even the apparent goodness displayed by those who 'worried' about non-white migrants was seen by Hage as a mark of their fantasy of power, not actual compassion. It showed that the function of 'worrying' for the national well-being was theirs alone (1998, pp. 42, 125). Hage's book develops a thesis on the nature of imagined national space and how we possess—or are excluded from—its national-cultural capital (1998, p. 54). Central to his argument is a critique of the idea of tolerance.

Hage writes as we have done of the 'paradoxical history of tolerance'. He sketches a history in which he argues that 'tolerance' discourses arose initially, but separately, in the Islamic world (1998, p. 80). For him, tolerance is a structure that comes into being in intolerant societies for practical reasons: to regulate outsiders rather than include them. From this, the tolerance paradox is this: owing to its genesis, tolerance—including the Australian version—will always be a feature of an *intolerant* society.

Versions of history always have differences, but often—as in the case of ours and Hage's—they can be recognisably similar yet still come to very different conclusions. At the core of this difference is our respective treatments of paradox. For both him and us, tolerance and intolerance are linked. Intolerance is the site where the principle of tolerance was born, which still sometimes nourishes it. For Hage, this paradox delegitimates tolerance—how can it be tolerance if it coexists with intolerance? But for us, this sort of reasoning is reversible: how can it be intolerance if it coexists with tolerance? Clearly a different approach is needed.

Behind Hage's negative judgment lurks a crisp, binary logic applied to tolerance: it is either a pure and homogeneous essence of tolerance, or it is unworthy of the name. For us, tolerance is a contradictory, fuzzy principle, existing as more and less, not as a thing in itself. Differences between more and less matter in everyday life. Christians and Jews who were 'tolerated' in early Islamic societies knew, like Jews who were not tolerated in Hitler's Germany, that limited tolerance was better than being killed and dispossessed. There is a range of positions in between—the fuzzy, complex terrain where life is mostly lived.

Hage does not only use history and logic to make his case. He is also a brilliant analyst of discourse, whose acute ear picks up minute

Borderwork and multicultural Australia

traces of attitudes and issues. His book is full of little excerpts of interviews, with many thought-provoking commentaries. As teachers,
we often used this one to set off debate:

Simonne: I really feel at home here . . . I like the multicultural feel.
Interviewer: Hmmm.
Simonne: You know, I originally came from around Manly. I mean, I love
it there . . . I liked living there because of the ocean. But, ah, it's too
conservative . . . You miss out on what makes Australia such a nice place.
Interviewer: Is . . . ?
Simonne: You see a mixture of people here, you see the, the, the Indian
culture or, down the south end of Newtown, it's the Fijian Indians and
then you, you see the Asian people and ah, and ah, I like going to the
deli and . . . ah visit George's. (1998, p. 97)

Hage's remarks on this are scathing:

One notices here how a homely feeling, what makes Australia such a
nice place, is generated by diversity. At the same time, we see how talk
moves from specific locales to the level of the nation. Underlying this
homeliness is a fantasy of a national order based on a clearly positioned
otherness: Indians are here; Koreans are there . . . and in the centre of it
all is the White Australian bestowing her tolerance. (1998, p. 98)

The conclusion that tolerance is bound up with intolerance is ingen-
iously drawn from the fact that an empowered figure like Simonne
can choose to 'enjoy' diversity while others, Hage assumes, do not
have this choice. (Why not? we may ask.) Hage does not pick out
Simonne's genteel, middle-class adjective 'nice', but it would have
made his point. This seems to be a person who filters out what is
disturbing or challenging—the reality of poverty and violence, for
instance—in a pleasing fantasy of harmony. Paradoxically, she main-
tains an illusion of power, whereas John Howard and Tony Abbott,
who are genuinely powerful, present themselves as powerless
victims of the 'politically correct'. We could ask, here: who is *really* the
more powerful?

Simonne is a white Australian, displaying her tolerance. Hage uses
dirty as well as clean analytic tricks to skewer her. The name he has
chosen for her, Simonne—with its unusual spelling—is pretentious by

a subtle cultural code. He chose the pseudonym well, to 'protect' her identity, but also to mock her. He is an insider in her own culture. 'Bestowing'—Hage's term—is brilliant demolition, presenting her as a lady of the manor in the English myth. The verb she uses is 'see', as though this is a series of cultures offered for her gaze, not sites for profound encounters with different histories, cultures, people and problems. However, she knows the difference between Fijian Indians and other Indians, which isn't the case for all Australians. She does place herself at the centre of her world, but so do most people if asked 'what do *you* feel?' Hage presents her as totally confident in herself, but if he had continued to be as sharp here as he is elsewhere he might have noticed signs of uncertainty. Simonne's hesitations suggest that she is eager to please this interviewer, who exerts a power in her space Hage seems unaware of.

Simonne, based on this text, seems superficial in her understanding of the 'culture' in 'multiculture'. Her goodwill does seem to exist (though Hage does not value it), but its limits seem close to her own comfort and self-interest. Many students in our classes from non-Anglo-Celtic backgrounds reacted strongly against her. One powerful response to Hage's book came from a student who had herself migrated to Australia. At the end of the subject, she made a point of saying to us, yes, that is how it is, that *is* what it feels like. 'Toleration' feels like an insult to those who are being 'tolerated'. She *felt* constructed as a burden being carried by these 'tolerant' others, patronised and despised. Simonne is aware of her goodwill, but unconscious of the effects of her status.

Hage cites other powerful examples too, from different points in an Australian spectrum. There's working-class Anglo 'Paul', who fears for the welfare of his nieces and nephews in multicultural Australia (1998, p. 213). From a different place, Hage quotes an unnamed Lebanese 'boy' who 'got agitated during the interview' and lashed out at everything: 'Fucking Australian shit, they're the shit. They're all shit.' (1998, p. 43)

There is anger, stereotyping, name-calling in Australia, but is this the 'real truth' behind multiculture, as Hage seems to think? The reality that makes multicultural Australia a sham? We do not think so. To deny the tensions, conflicts and resentments arising from the many interactions that make up a multiculture would be to retreat into a fantasy of harmony like Simonne's. But other perspectives coexist with hers, deserving to be heard—as does hers. Australia and its multiculture will not come apart if some or many people feel angry about others, and say so.

One problem we always faced with Hage's book as a class text was that it left students of all backgrounds with nowhere to go. Even the student who recognised herself as the patronised object of 'tolerance' was given nothing to do. Those who could see themselves in Simonne were told that what they had taken as a right was not one. Apart from a negative feeling about the whole business, they were given no sense of what kind of multicultural Australia Hage wanted instead. It may be that these criticisms are not fair—like criticising Hage's rhubarb for not being an apple. His book is, after all, a critique—hence perhaps the need for works like ours, that seek to build, not just criticise.

The multiculturalism paradox

'Does multiculturalism cultivate intolerance and beliefs and justify the slaughter of innocents?' asked Roy Eccleston, just after suicide bombers killed more than 50 people in London in July 2005.

Immediately after the London bombings, one senior European-based intelligence official lashed Britain for failing to realize it had tolerated the intolerant for too long.

Commentators from across the political spectrum have expressed fears in recent days that multiculturalism is the problem, not the solution, for a safer Australia in an environment of Islamic terrorism (Eccleston 2005, p. 13).

Another commentator took an even harder line. The US analyst Joel Kotkin argued: 'Sadly, many metropolitan leaders seem less than prepared to meet the terrorist threat head-on, in part due to the trendy multiculturalism that now characterises so many Western cities' (2005, p. 9).

These critics say that multiculturalism has allowed the problem to build up, and now it blocks the only correct response, a range of 'hard measures' which will impact on the civil liberties and safety of all citizens.

It's interesting that for Kotkin, multiculturalism's problem is that it's 'trendy'. His cry for a savage response to terrorism is now even more trendy. Does that make it bad?

Not long after Kotkin wrote, English police licensed to kill shot an innocent Brazilian, wrongly suspecting him of terrorism. Kotkin's 'harsh measures' did not advance the war on terrorism, or make London a safer place. Quite the contrary in fact.

We argue that multiculturalism should be seen as part of the very fabric of society itself, a communal resource. In Australia, as in Britain, the prime minister was able to mobilise a moderate majority of the Muslim community, a force that can be invoked precisely because of multiculturalism. As Ameer Ali, head of the Australian Federation of Islamic Councils, says: 'We have to re-educate them. And when the majority brings pressure on the minority groups they have to change' (quoted to Eccleston, p. 13).

Which is the more effective response? Risking shooting innocent citizens, or talking to and trusting Muslim leaders? They report that the source for the terrorists' anger and alienation was not too much tolerance, but the war against Iraq, which they saw as unjust. It's not so clear that multiculturalism was the problem. Maybe it does indeed make Britain and Australia safer, for all citizens, Muslims and others.

Tolerance as civic duty

Hage treats the tolerance of the whole 'white' dominant group as their privilege, which they are free to exercise or not. Another Sydney academic, David Burchell (2000), disagrees with him on this point. He returns to the scene of origin of tolerance, Locke's *Letter on Toleration*, which he connects to the Latin meaning of *tolerantia*—specifically to a traditional use in which the meaning of 'endurance' was primary. He compares this with the same attitude that citizens had to the demands of their sovereign, to matters like taxes or other civic duties: not something to like, just to be endured (2000, p. 7).

From this he argues that tolerance is both a part of 'statecraft' (the process of running a nation and managing its population) *and*, because of this, a responsibility of citizens. He goes on to remark that there is a difference between the respect citizens owe each other and what they owe their government, and that tolerance plays a part in both (2000, p. 7). Tolerance, in this view, implies reciprocities of rights and duties, between communities or between individuals and governments.

While Burchell is as cynical about the way 'statecraft' is deployed as Hage is about the 'surplus value' of multiculturalism, he reminds us that

Borderwork and multicultural Australia

tolerance is not like charity, that those who *participate* in it are not so much bestowing it (to use Hage's word) as *benefiting* from its existence. Hage argues that to be part of a tolerant society, one must feel 'enfranchised', in the sense of having a formal stake in the society, a vote. But as in the social contract, another of Locke's ideas, one cannot simply choose to 'withdraw' one's tolerance, however powerful one may be, for to do that is to withdraw from society altogether. This political fact lies behind the resentment such powerful figures as Howard and Abbott have for 'political correctness', since it refers to the consensus values that are part of the contract that puts them where they are.

In this view, tolerance becomes a threshold. A tolerant society is one that facilitates the reciprocities of mutual relationship. At the individual level, it is left to each person to act accordingly— which can make it seem, as Hage thinks, that the tolerance is freely 'given'. But in this respect, tolerance is a bit like taxation. One might resent writing the cheque, but one must write it all the same.

For Hage, multiculturalism is a fantasy, about imagined ethnicity and national space. His book is mostly about an imagined world. Like Hage, we believe that fears and fantasies matter, and have real effects. Burchell is more concerned with a social world of complex rights and obligations, which also is influenced by the world of feelings. Resentment against multiculturalism indicates that those people feel disenfranchised, and that has political effects. Whether this is felt by white citizens or in a different way by migrants, this is a failure of the multiculture at the levels of legislation, aspiration and experience. Conversely, the multicultural 'feel good' factor Hage so obviously despises (which is not, in our experience, confined to 'white' Australia as he suggests) might appear trite, but it is an important sign of enfranchisement. Simonne's 'celebration' might be temporary or foolish, but it is her life, her right as a citizen, a strand in Australian life.

We suggested in Chapter 2 that it is too easy for academics to mock the feelings or naiveties of people. If official multiculturalism supports the bedrock on which people's hopes can be built, this is for us valuable and important. Hage calls the fantasy he despises a 'managerial' one. He says that 'good' and 'bad' nationalists alike claim the exclusive right to talk about immigration and immigrants. He sees such conversations as bad or arrogant. This is a forced binary, as impoverished as many such binary choices in social situations (this or that, black or white) typically prove to be.

We agree that there should not be a class of those who talk and those talked about. But this is a simplification. Some migrants are indeed left out, so are many citizens. The forces of disadvantage for migrants have been and can be powerful: trauma, language, education, culture, wealth can all play a role. But equally the streets of Sydney that Hage and Burchell walk in are, in our experience, also alive with successful stories of multiculture—the 'multicultural real' he only ever alludes to. It exists in the shops and homes of the Fiji Indians Simonne may only 'see', or Greek George's deli which she 'visits'. Without quotations from such as the despised Simonne, multiculture itself would not enter his text: only the demon multiculturalism, and its fantasy supporters.

Tolerance is the bedrock of this system. The fragile idea was floated some time in the seventeenth century, as a minimum threshold. Multiculture relies upon, and also helped in some original sense to engender, a system of tolerance. The last three decades in Australia have shown how far beyond tolerance it is possible to go. It is certainly true that we should not stop at tolerance. But nor should we ever think of rejecting it, or minimising its value.

The democracy paradox

Democracy, tolerance and multiculturalism go together naturally, right? Many Australian citizens would assume so. World history is full of acts of intolerance so murderous they disgust ordinary citizens in other nations. We Australians comfort ourselves by saying that such things have nothing to do with us. These only happen in totalitarian societies, symbolised by Hitler's Nazis, Stalin's Russia, opposed by the free world in World War II. Or they are a throw-back to primitive times, the tribalism of Rwanda or backward Serbs and Croats, not what Western-style democracies like Australia would ever do.

At least one important political theorist disagrees. In a fascinating and disturbing analysis, the British sociologist Michael Mann criticises most of these assumptions. He calls the twentieth century the most 'genocidal' in history, with more than 60 million people killed in acts of 'ethnic cleansing' (1999, p. 18). Hitler and Stalin were the most murderous, but there are many others. And the histories of Western democracies, including Australia, are full of foundational acts of 'ethnic cleansing' (1999, p. 26). In these histories, 'democracy' has not moderated genocidal impulses, he says: it is often the core reason (pp. 26–27).

We will try to do justice to his argument not just because he names Australia at particular points in the essay, but because his essay offers a challenging interpretation of relevant history. He begins with a link between genocide and modernity, repeating Leo Kuper's claim, as founder of modern genocide studies, that modern states exercise exclusive sovereignty over territories that were always in practice culturally plural and economically stratified, and this fact alone 'created both the desire and the power to commit genocide' (1999, p. 19). This opposition between power and unity of nation and state, and cultural and economic diversity, is a fundamental equation. In this scenario, diversity—what we call multiculture—precedes the drive to unity of the nation state, which first devalues diversity, and then removes it as a problem.

As one might expect, Mann is highly critical of Hitler's Germany and Stalin's Russia. But he also has severe things to say about settler-societies like Australia. Looking at these societies, he sees a common historical trend. The early colonies tended to become more 'democratic' than the metropolitan power, but those excluded were also often treated *more* harshly than in metropolitan societies (1999, p. 26).

Mann includes Australia in his survey, but does not make a detailed study. His ideas offer an antidote to any complacency we might feel about this multiculture. We find instances of schismogenesis in Australian history in all the terms argued by Mann, especially against the Indigenous people, in the forms of dispossession from land, enforced migration, forced assimilation, exclusion from the body of society and murder (1999, p. 22). All this was accompanied—irrespective of the good intentions of some settlers—by assaulting their culture, destroying its objects, separating those objects from living practices, and denying that the people whose culture it was could understand and value it properly.

We finish with another paradox. The history of ethnic cleansing shows that 'cleansing' in one territory can create 'dirt' (or multiculture) in others. Inadvertently, British colonial policy created Australia as a potential multiculture by 'cleaning up' its own refuse, hurling people from all sorts of backgrounds together, and largely leaving them to their own devices. This produced the schismogenesis Mann describes so unrelentingly. It also provided a context from which a multicultural nation arose from such unlikely beginnings.

Mann's story is the essential other side to the history of tolerance. His history shows how and why tolerance is so crucial, today as in the past. Tolerance is not just niceness, a Simonne enjoying ethnic food: it is the core logic and practices that oppose racism. His history makes even more compelling sense if we set it in a framework of far from equilibrium conditions. He does not draw attention to the fact, but many of his cases of ethnic cleansing include a surrounding sense of crisis, in which schismogenic solutions, when they first appeared, could seem relatively harmless and 'sensible', before they exploded out of control. Tolerance, by contrast, emerges from below as well as from above, as in the exemplary case of Locke. It is not inevitable—as too many grim stories of genocide show us. Yet once it has come, it is well worth preserving.

The 'PC' tolerance paradox

A study conducted by 'The Truth Report' found out what we already know: many people are sick of having to watch their words:

> More than two thirds of Australians are fed up with political correctness. A survey of 1200 people . . . found more than 70 per cent of men and 65 per cent of women are tired of having to watch what they say. Those aged 18 to 24 and over 50 were most likely to be annoyed. (Lawrence 2003, p. 36)

This has a context: according to 'AustraliaScan', the September 11 and Bali attacks have made people more determined to 'call a spade a spade' (2003, p. 36).

The term 'political correctness'—often shortened to 'PC'—is widely used as a term of abuse in political debates. In arguments it is a dangerous term, because it labels a whole argument and dismisses it without having to say why it is wrong. It contains a paradox that only makes it stronger and more difficult to argue against. It accuses the opponent of being *correct* (politically). What do they want of them? To be incorrect? Obviously not: its force is *rhetorical*, not critical. But this does not mean we can dismiss it or laugh it off: 'PC' is a highly loaded term, and is the nub of powerful and contested discourses of rights and identity.

The words 'politically correct' signal an obvious paradox. PC suggests a desire that society be simpler, as if Australia once were a straightforward place. Even more paradoxically, the sentiment resonates in some of the least privileged parts of the community. Decades of global and local economic restructuring have brought benefits to many and changes to all—not all of them welcome. Sociologists, political scientists and economists call such patterns *globalisation*, a term we defined in Chapter 1. In a global context, PC is part of an international economy of ideas, all with local accents and dimensions. PC is not just an Australian phenomenon, but part of something wider: like the multicultural Australia it is part of, it is affected by ideas from elsewhere, and yet in its always local playing out of these, it makes a contribution to this worldwide system.

People in Australia who joke angrily about PC seek to reduce social complexity to simplicity by treating it as a kind of scapegoat-abstraction. In some ways, PC and the society of which it is part *have* become more complex, with many kinds of borderwork producing new barriers to effective communication. These include, most obviously, proliferating litigiousness based on individuated victimage, leading to ever greater legal 'protection' for institutions and professionals of all kinds—and complexity for those that deal with them. But we should remember, in this respect, that PC refers to things like protocols on discrimination or vilification. These exist to protect disadvantaged people from being abused. PC is an abstraction, and it seems an easy target. But the target is ultimately those it seeks to assist. So how does PC come to get blamed for complexities which are well beyond its purview? Perhaps the best thing to do is look at *how* the term is used, and then *by whom*.

If we think about how it is used, we see that PC exists in at least three different ways. It refers first to the suite of policies against abuse, discrimination and vilification, as a shorthand. This usage is not derisive, but it is rare because those involved in a dispute tend to call it by its name. Second, it refers to the consternation in the community about yet another bureaucratic imposition, yet another interest group, yet another problem. This sort of usage is usually derisive, but needn't be. It needs to be addressed because it reflects community feelings of being excluded from the 'national conversation' about tolerance and its limits. Third, it refers to the strategy of manipulation by interest groups or politicians, seeking ends sometimes unrelated to the imagined terrain of PC itself. This might best be called anti-PC rhetoric, such as happens when the most powerful political figures in the country use it as a term of derision. By naming it, we do not have the scope to neutralise this latter trick of argument, because it is used so easily and with so little thought against so many valuable positions. But we do want to bring out some of the logical mistakes it rests on in relation to tolerance itself, because these are the things that make it *seem* plausible.

Having identified its three uses, we can say that the aspect of PC that most needs addressing is the second one: the view that is in the community, and the view that is linked to a tolerance paradox. The underpinning reasoning is not self-evident. It looks like this: tolerance is an attitude or value, which by its nature is something *freely given*, so laws cannot *require* tolerance. In this view, tolerance required cannot be true tolerance, so the laws shouldn't do it.

But this is just the old problem of crisp thinking. 'Tolerance' concerns both attitudes *and* behaviours, physical and symbolic. It is the latter (behaviours) that can be subject to legislation. As Mann's history shows, murderous intolerance and systemic discrimination have been legitimated, promoted and enforced by many governments in the past, as in the present. If intolerance can be made worse by some legal measures, it can be countered by others.

When laws ban violence, it is easy to justify them. But what about discrimination? Or vilification? We can ask you to think of it this way: laws against discrimination are part of the borderwork of a society. Discrimination is an act, not a thought; vilification itself involves more than just an attitude. That is, the borderwork being governed involves actual behaviours and certain kinds of speech acts or communication. If governments intervene only minimally—at the level, say, of violence to person and property—a vicious circle can come into play. A well-grounded fear by a scapegoated community can coexist with subtle discrimination by a dominant community accustomed to inflammatory rhetorics that are allowed in the name of free speech. That is, if excessive restriction of speech endangers social sympathies, a 'hands off' approach fosters schismogenesis, which can burst into the open as soon as the social equilibrium is disturbed.

To be sure, not all the problems of 'PC' come from the crisp logic of its critics. A campaign to purge the language of all 'racist' expressions can use equally crisp and schismogenic logic itself. Just like any other kind of excessive borderwork, it will produce its opposite: more racism, such as that unleashed by the anti-'PC' movement. This is not to 'blame' PC on those who, with perfectly good intentions, framed rules for a just society. On the contrary: the very spirit of this book is to move away from things that end in blame. The point is to offer a vision for people to aspire to, not to focus on the limits that must be imposed. Tolerance need not be only a system of limitations. Part of its promise is an open and accepting society.

Another 'tolerant' white Australian?

Another good childhood friend was Angelina Leschenko. What kind of name was that? It was a Russian name, and we spent a lot of time together during Primary School . . . Her house was different to ours. There were polished timber floors, instead of the lino in our house and the carpet in our lounge room. They played Russian folk music. There were unusual pictures on the walls and beautiful Russian embroidery on the cushions and table runners. Her family ate different food to us, and at Easter they made beautiful coloured and polished eggs. Real eggs—not chocolate like we had.

This was during the 1950s and 1960s, the time of the Cold War—the time when Russians were generally considered suspicious. 'They might be communists!' I didn't care . . . We were such good friends. We never had any trouble with one another and over the years we discovered that different was just that, *different*—not wrong. (Christine Langshaw, in Duarte 2001, pp. 39–40)

Was there an undercurrent of superiority in the young Christine? Or older Christine (the one telling the story)- is she just inventing a multicultural younger self, using Angelina as part of her own story? Or is this how a multiculture grows, out of ordinary friendships and interactions?

Tolerance and multiculturalism

Tolerance is not an easy idea. However, part of the problem for tolerance has also proved to be a strength: its roots in a world movement. The Holocaust became a symbol of genocide that aroused revulsion in the world community, causing it to do something about it. This period saw the emergence of the United Nations, and a series of international conventions aimed at promoting the good citizenship of nation states, responsible members of a global multiculture (one planet, inhabited by many different peoples, all of equal value, all with rights).

Australia, along with many others, signed these conventions, which gave them a certain (but fuzzy) binding force on successive governments. For instance, in 1951 Australia ratified the International Refugee Convention, and in 1967 it signed the supplementary protocol. Since 1945, Australia has admitted over 600 000 refugees on humanitarian grounds (Jupp 2002, p. 32), who with their families now constitute around 5 per cent of Australia's population.

But against these positive developments, there has been a global downside. According to the UN High Commissioner for Refugees, at the end of 1951, the total number of refugees recorded was 2 116 200. By 1991 this number had risen to 17 022 000, falling to 12 148 000 by 2000 (Maley 2002, p. 2). These grim figures show that systemic 'ethnic cleansing' still continues on a grand scale. Movements of refugees and asylum seekers have aroused intense debate throughout Europe. Governments introduce harsher policies to meet supposed threats to their (relative) ethnic purity, making 'tolerance' as vital as ever.

Yet, as Maley has noted, many governments try to maintain their commitment to tolerance in words only, attempting to make themselves look good while actually weakening actual levels of tolerance in their society (2002, p. 6). One instance is the Australian government's use of league tables of 'generosity' on its behalf, while pitching its policies so as to blur the value of tolerance itself. In a sense it does not intend, the Australian government, like most others, has been 'politically correct' in what it claimed to do, but politically expedient in what it actually did.

So it is important, but not enough, that 'multiculturalism' is still a consensus policy in Australia, and more important that Australia's multiculture is still strong in spite of attacks on it. Statements like the following, in government discourse, should be both valued *and* looked at sceptically, as an image that may not truly be at the heart of government actions but which still invites a majority support, and is therefore in that deeper sense politically correct:

> The term Australian multiculturalism summarises the way we address the challenges and opportunities of our cultural diversity. It . . . accepts

and respects the right of all Australians to express and share their individual cultural heritage within an overriding commitment to Australia and the basic structures and values of Australian society. ('What is Australian Multiculturalism?')

This statement of the spirit of tolerance also declares its limits, in the vague, open reference to 'mutual civic obligations'. But this part of the statement does not contradict the spirit of tolerance. As we have seen, at every turn contradiction is part of the concept itself.

4. Anglo-Celts in multicultural Australia

Not me?

When we teach classes in 'Multicultural Australia', there is always a defining moment, when we ask students to share their stories, and talk of their own ancestries, links, languages or heritages. This is the web that makes up Australian society, we tell them. Among the many rich and moving responses, we always come up against what seems like a powerful stumbling block. Typically a student, young, white and male, mutters with a look of consternation: 'Oh no, not me. I'm just Australian'. The simple adverb 'just' qualifying the word 'Australian' says it all. It turns what they could also say, 'I'm an Australian', into something they resent having to say. 'Just' says they feel at the end of the queue of stories of multiculturalism. It says: no story, no other plan, no other homeland, no other language.

Defining oneself by what one does *not* have is a strange thing to do. It's a definition by a lack, which implies a sense of something missing in relation to the dominant discourses of a society. The shame of the dominant culture at its dominance, the sense of being excluded from the story of multiculturalism, is crucial to understanding how to create an inclusive multiculture. We know that multiculturalism as a policy has been criticised, from the point of view of minority groups, as a strategy of 'diversity management' by the dominant. The price of this power, it seems, is the exclusion of the so-called powerful from all culture and identity—even their own. This is surely the strangest borderwork of all—and the hardest to understand.

But we must understand it. Our shame-faced students are integral to Australian multiculture, and that fact itself is crucial to their identity, whatever their origins. They are defined by others, if not by themselves, as 'Anglo-Celts'—a term which, for new migrants, captures a sense of the homogeneous essence of the dominant group.

The shame at being 'just' (Anglo-Celtic) Australian, far from being a step forward for Australian multiculture, acts as a barrier. Why would they want to 'lose' their identity to affirm someone else's? And how can newcomers learn how to share in *Australian* multiculture if Anglo-Celts are silenced from telling their stories and their culture?

In practice, Anglo-Celtic Australians, like the students whose interventions have taught us so much, do not know and value their own roots as deeply as they might. Anglo-Celtic cultures do not have to be downgraded to make way for an Australian multiculture; rather, the contrary should be the case. Understanding Anglo-Celts better is basic to our approach to Australian multiculture. Anyone who believes they are 'just Australian' has forgotten or lost earlier histories, which hold powerful stories of multiculture relevant to our times.

First thoughts on Anglo-Celtic Australia

Let us start with this crucial term. What can 'Anglo-Celtic' mean—this hyphenated term which fuses these two groups into a single mass? Is the term historical? Ideological? Descriptive and demographic? Or, like multiculture itself, does it define a way of seeing, a perspective? Let us look briefly at the term before looking at the issue in other ways.

Demographers, in practice, tend not to use the term 'Anglo-Celtic' in statistical analyses, referring more precisely to languages, or places, of origin (for instance, the Australian Bureau of Statistics says 10.2 per cent of Australians still consider their ancestry to be ethnically Irish) (ABS 2001). But even some political scientists presume it to be the neutral basis from which to consider 'ethnicity' or 'race' in Australia, even if they do not state this as such. This leads to the Anglo-Celts being invisible, without a structure, the reference point from which other cultures are examined. In a recent book, for instance, political scientist James Jupp (2002) makes only passing reference to 'Celts' in Australia (five entries for the Irish, fewer for other Celtic groups).

In giving a historical background for his analysis, however, he remarks casually that Henry Parkes 'warned Italians not to congregate together because it would delay their assimilation. He dispersed them throughout the colony as a condition of settlement and he was hostile to Irish Catholic immigration and advocated its limitation.' (2002, p. 21) He notes that such attitudes were common at the time of Federation. In practice, there is much to understand and unravel about how Celts merged into the hyphenated Australian hegemony. How did a schismogenic social order that discriminated against Irish Catholics become a multiculture? Has the process left any traces on what is now the dominant culture in Australia?

Commentators on multiculturalism now treat this dominance as a basic structural fact, and this is why the term 'Anglo-Celtic' has come into use. It names and gives value to a position for the 'mainstream', in a simple, persuasive two-term structure: 'us' against 'them'. In *The Teeth are Smiling*, Ellie Vasta cites the historian Geoffrey Blainey attacking multiculturalism because, for him, 'Sadly, multiculturalism often means: Australians come second.' (quoted Vasta & Castles 1996, p. 55) Commenting on this, she remarks quite rightly on what Blainey's remark implies: 'Clearly, by "Australians" he means Anglo-Australians and not the millions of naturalized immigrant Australians who have benefited from the integrative characteristics of multiculturalism. This argument is racist and nationalist and has a strong populist appeal.' (1996, p. 55).

Yet when Vasta says 'Anglo-Australians', we think she probably means Anglo-Celtic Australians. We cannot be sure because she doesn't find it necessary to say, but she doesn't include any note to say where this significant group has gone. Nor does she explain what the term 'Anglo' actually means, because it is being used as a purely *structural* term, in a two-body system that mirrors Blainey's.

Hage, whom we looked at in the previous chapter, offers a better critical understanding of the term in his *White Nation* (1998). He sketches its place in history and shows how it works today. He acknowledges that the fact it exists in the critical vocabulary shows a useful but still inadequate attempt to reflect on society. But he argues

Borderwork and multicultural Australia

that it describes and reflects a 'fantasy' history of struggle between British and Irish forces, a 'mystification' that replaces a much more plural and complex class-riven reality (1998, p. 57). So far so good: this is a rich sense of a many-body reality. It is important to recognise that the 'Celts' did not exist as a living culture in 1788, only as Irish, Scottish and Welsh (and Cornish, and Bretons), and even these groups were divided by class, religion and region. But then he sweeps aside the many bodies, and even the two bodies, to be left with just one: the 'Whites' (1998, p. 57), sufficient to describe the entire scene of the 'struggle'. He sees modern multiculturalists (what he calls 'cosmo-multiculturalists') occupying centre-stage by deploying this self-conception (1998, p. 204).

These accounts of 'Anglo-Celtic' Australia—whether they come from critics like Blainey, Vasta or Hage, or demographers like Bob Birrell—share one unstated assumption: there's little to learn about real multiculture from Anglo-Celtic history. We believe otherwise. Australia started as a multiculture, a many-body system. The Anglos were a multiculture, and so were the Celts.

Australia developed as it did because it started in this way. A three-body analysis which refuses to blend the Celts into an Anglo-Celtic blob is a crucial step in keeping a sense of diversity and complexity alive, then and now. We cannot, in this analysis, unpick all the threads of the 'Anglo-Celtic' multiculture (even in an origin-name like 'England', there are endless cultures within cultures, all of them fissured by gendered, classed and geographical historics). But a three-body analysis allows us to see this plurality as inherent to the 'Anglo-Celtic' weld whose contested histories are so often bracketed out of multicultural studies.

The original scene of colonisation of Australia was already profoundly plural and schismogenic. It contained violent hierarchies, and different social orders (classes within English society, different categories of female migrants) meshed with ethnicity in ways that were decisive at the time and afterwards.

Let us not doubt how deep the divisions were. We need to remember that Australia was colonised during one of the most revolutionary periods of European history, and the Irish played a major role in those revolutions. In Ireland itself, the bloodiest uprising took place in 1798. This rebellion failed, as did subsequent attempts. But the 1798 uprising was in the name of a united Ireland, and a republic inspired by revolutionary France. Thousands were massacred in Ireland's west, and many of the ringleaders were transported to Australia.

Their legacy lingers in the republican movement, something many young people today regard with bewilderment. The sectarianism itself lingered even until the 1950s. British administrators did not always take it seriously, but there were conditions for rebellion, even in Australia:

> The pool of sympathisers was formidable, as the number of Irish convicts transported for sedition since 1794 had now reached 235. Added to this were the earlier transportees, the disaffected Scots, Englishmen and other Irishmen, making the sum of potential rebels considerable. (Silver 2002, p. 46)

In the event, there *was* an uprising in 1804, ironically named 'Vinegar Hill' after a larger one in Ireland. The disparate groups never added up to a political force, but they did form a culture of resistance (one that included English as well as Irish) which has become part of the general Australian culture.

The Irish and other Celts, along with the English poor, started life in the colonies near the bottom of the pile, but they did not stay there. Still a minority, now partly absorbed into the 'mainstream', there is much to learn from the Irish and other Celtic experience for anyone seeking to see and *create* new pathways in modern Australia.

Today the Anglo-Celts are seen as the 'non-multicultural' part of Australia, with no difference between Anglos and Celts. We suggest a more complex and nuanced reality. If the conflict and diversity of English and Celtic groups helped to create Australian culture in the early days, then in order to understand what Australian culture actually is, we need to restore the problematic, ambiguous history of this early multiculture. Imaginatively de-assimilating the Celts is a vital step in disassembling all later reductions of historical and cultural diversity. We have begun by undoing that term 'Anglo-Celt', questioning its hyphen.

What to do with identities?

How can Anglo-Celts think about their identities in a multiculture? We start with a form of fuzzy logic that anyone can use, from whatever culture. According to fuzzy logic, identities are always partial, true only to some degree, coexisting with other categories that are also true to some degree in multiple identities. Crisp black and white identities may seem reassuringly clear and definite at first, but they quickly become inadequate if they are forced on to individual histories. We will illustrate how our readers, Anglo-Celts or others, can put these concepts to use productively.

Think of genealogies. Genealogies have become very popular amongst Australians, especially Anglo-Celts, who seek out their ancestors using the resources of genealogical societies and libraries. These searches are a cultural phenomenon which is significant in itself, both about those who make them and those who are indifferent. Both responses point to profound attitudes to identity. Those who search for ancestors in the past look to that past for identity anchors. Those who 'aren't interested' tend to emphasise their identity as 'Australians', created in the here and now.

This interest in origins is problematic if it is guided by crisp logic, seeking a single ancestor or bloodline. A full genealogy, on the other hand, will always reveal the many strands that make up any one person alive today. Nor does genealogical research contradict contemporary Australian identity. It is surely possible to be *both* fully Australian *and* a person whose ancestors came to Australia from England and/or Ireland, Wales or Scotland.

Like all genealogies, Anglo-Celtic family histories get more complex the further back they go. To illustrate, we take the case of Bob's genealogy. Bob Hodge's name sounds solidly English (though there were Scottish and Welsh Hodges). But following his family tree back three generations, we get a different picture. His father's father was English, with a Welsh mother. His father's mother was the Australian-born daughter of two Irish people. So this father was literally Anglo-Celtic, or more exactly Celtic-Anglo: 75 per cent Celt and 25 per cent Anglo.

Bob's mother was the daughter of an Australian-born mother with both parents Scottish, and an 'English' father whose mother was English but father of Irish origins. This mother, then, was also Celtic-Anglo, in exactly the same proportion: 75 per cent Celt, 25 per cent Anglo. Bob, the Australian-born son of these two, preserved the same proportion, so he too is a Celtic-Anglo, 75 per cent Celt and 25 per cent Anglo. That is, he is *both* Celtic and Anglo—more one than the other, but both of them to some degree—on both sides.

As we track this genealogy, we see one absolute law. Each generation doubles the possibilities. We all have two parents, four grandparents, eight great-grandparents, sixteen great-great-grandparents, and so on. The past becomes a jungle of possibilities, even if little is known of some members. There is bias built into the English name system, which follows the father's line (it is easier to track the same name). But each marriage introduces a new name into the search.

As we go backwards, we are at the apex-point of an inverted pyramid that expands forever. As a rough calculation, in 350 years everyone has around 16 000 ancestors, not just one Founding Father (or Mother):

> The world is a closer-knit place than it seems . . . American researchers created elaborate mathematical models of human migration to come up with this estimate [3500 years ago] of when our most recent common ancestor existed. 'While we may not all be "brothers", the models suggest we are all hundredth cousins or so', said Joseph Chang, a professor of statistics at Yale University. (Smith 2004, p. 3)

And this is only genealogy. A genealogy is based on bloodlines. But how strong are *they* in creating identity? Bob was raised in Australia of Australian-born parents, not in England, Ireland or Wales. He is *Australian* in that respect: an Australian Anglo-Celt, very different from an English Anglo-Celt. Already, in these terms, no Australians are 'just Australian'. They are fuzzily Australian-*and*. Nor are the Anglos in Australia just 'Anglos'. A restriction to bloodlines may be convenient for settling matters of inheritance, but in explaining 'identity' (what he is 'the same as') it is far less useful. This requires us to think about how we 'imagine' ourselves as Australians.

Nation and identity: Imagined communities

In order to move beyond the terms of genealogy, we deal now with **imagined communities**. In an argument that influenced both history and the social sciences, Benedict Anderson (1991) claimed that nations were 'imagined' as communities, grounded in shared language rather than antiquity or blood (1991, p. 145). We tend to think of nations as having existed since 'time immemorial', but Anderson argues that nations emerged only in the last few centuries.

We mistake the kind of thing they are because they are talked of that way, and because of this we can call them 'imagined'.

This process is of tremendous importance in shaping modern identities and sense of belonging. Most Australians have not met most other Australians, yet we feel we are all part of a single community, with common interests and histories. This 'Australia' in a sense is a fiction, yet it is a powerful fiction with many real consequences.

Identity, including national identity, does not emerge in a vacuum. Devices like newspapers and television and schools have played a role (1991, p. 37). Institutions like the family, school and the media are important sites where identities are taught and constructed. The electoral process is another major agent in constructing the imagined community. It produces a body that speaks on behalf of 'Australia'.

This single fictional entity—in this case 'Australia'—is typically constructed in crisp terms, as though it were a single, homogeneous entity. The devices that create the fiction (which is not to say that it is a lie) are institutions like those we have just named. They provide many opportunities for productive paradox, for contradiction. In the rest of this section, we focus on one institution which is involved in this process of constructing and circulating national identities: the museum.

Museums are publicly funded bodies, one of whose roles is to represent the national identity, the national story. In the past, that story seemed taken for granted, as a monocultural narrative. In multicultural Australia today, the story has to be more diverse and complex. We can see this with a controversy that broke out over a new national museum, the National Museum of Australia (NMA), which opened in March 2001 in Canberra.

As the national museum, its version of Australian history, culture and identity was an immediate focus of commentary and criticism. Barely two years after it opened, the government commissioned a report on the museum and its exhibitions. The impetus for the review came from conservative critics who objected to the 'politically correct' interpretation of history they saw in it, which with a conservative government in power became 'politically incorrect' by the paradoxical inversion of this term that we examined in the previous chapter.

The committee of review noted that visitor numbers were high— 1.7 million in the museum's first two years—and they concluded that 'political or cultural bias is not a systemic problem at the NMA'.

But some such judgment lay behind their specific objections, as summarised in a newspaper report:

> Primary themes in the nation's history are absent from the National Museum of Australia, which has failed to adequately tell the story of the country. Explorers such as Captain James Cook, Matthew Flinders, Burke and Wills, and outlaw Ned Kelly are either under-represented or absent, according to a review of the two-year old museum. (Safe 2003, p. 5)

The absent heroes here are all males, all white, all Anglo-Celts. The implicit objection is that the core Anglo-Celtic narrative of the nation is not represented fully enough in this definitive public statement.

Yet the members of this exclusive club are not identical. The list begins with an English captain, but ends with an Irish outlaw. The first died 'heroically', on another journey of discovery, but the last was hung. His Irishness, in 1880, was still an acute problem, contributing to his life and death and to his later fame. His myth is a monument to the antagonism of Anglos and Celts. Of the explorers in between, Flinders mapped stretches of the Australian coastline, but Burke and Wills got lost—partly because, like most Australian explorers, they did not defer to the expertise of Aboriginal people whose lands they were 'discovering'. Even this set of five names projects a complex history, full of conflict, failure and achievement.

We do not believe that these stories should be erased. Nor do we feel the stories should be told so as to show only the warts. The need is for more recollections, more plurality—not less. One dimension of these other stories is carried by a subtext in the *Australian* report (Safe, 2003). There is no mention in the article that the museum's director, Dawn Casey, is Aboriginal, but she is photographed, with her Aboriginal features there for all to see, with a text below: 'Wake-up call: Ms Casey in the Garden of Australian Dreams, which the report says should be removed from the National Museum of Australia'. Ms Casey should 'beware' (as events soon proved she needed to be, when her contract was not renewed). 'Dreams' connects with the Aboriginal concept of 'dreamtime', which she needed to abandon in the harsh light of this politicised day.

But Casey herself is a story of Australian identity, a living one alongside these other dead heroes. She is Aboriginal, but her names signal other possible identities, from the Anglo and Celtic heritages she also has. She is fuzzily Aboriginal, Anglo and Celtic, and as well as these she is a distinguished Australian, the former director of a museum which defined Australian identities for *all* Australians.

There are many lessons here about Anglo-Celtic identities and the complex ways they really operate in multicultural Australia. Pride can be a positive feeling, and so can compassion, and they do not need to exclude others. For instance, we authors are male, yet we can take joy in Dawn Casey's achievements as a fellow Australian who is also Aboriginal, though we aren't. Non-Anglo-Celtic Australians, men and women, likewise can be intrigued and moved by all these stories of people from long ago who are not only different from them, but also different from 'Anglo-Celts' they see around them today. The crisp story of national identity—that we can only identify with those who are officially 'like us'—is psychologically implausible when faced with the reality of human interconnection.

Captain Cook: A hero for multicultural Australia?

The 'discoverer of Australia' occupies pride of place in any list of 'Great Australians', though he couldn't be Australian himself. How can his story weave into a multicultural foundation myth?

First his origins: his father came to Yorkshire from Scotland, so Cook is not just Anglo, but Anglo-Celt. Northern England was an Anglo-Celtic meeting point of sorts, and it reminds us that even in the 'homelands', there is still a plurality of cultures. Cook was a 'typical Englishman', who went on in an unlikely way to become an Enlighten-ment hero, a case of the emergence of 'the different from the same'.

The striking features of the rise are further enhanced when we consider his class position. Cook's father was a farm labourer, and James had to work his way up by his own merits, in the class-based oppression of eighteenth century England. He sailed merchant coal ships in the North Sea before switching to the Royal Navy, starting at the bottom. He rose quickly, but was not officially 'captain' when he mapped Australia—just 'master and commander' of a converted coal ship.

Cook also had other roles. In 1770 he was part of an international (multicultural) team in different parts of the world, accurately measur-ing the rare passage of Venus, its 'transit' across the sun. He played a

role in medicine, too. Scurvy, caused by vitamin C deficiency, decimated sailors on long sea voyages. Cook sailed to Tahiti, New Zealand and Australia in a three-year journey without losing a single sailor to scurvy because he had a clean ship (with plenty of vitamin C). In 1775 he won the Royal Society's Copley medal for his paper on scurvy: in modern terms, this was like a Nobel Prize in medicine.

But then there is his death, speared by natives of Hawaii. Did he provoke them? Was he a symbol for Europe's complicity in practices of exploitation? Or was he just unlucky? We do not know, but does that make him less interesting as part of Australia's foundation myths?

A Kelly tour

Critics of the NMA demanded that Ned Kelly's story be told more prominently. Fair enough: let us do exactly that. In this section we report a 'tourist' trip John undertook for this book, the aim of which was to discover, or invent, a multicultural tourism aimed to take apart the 'Anglo-Celtic' story of Australia. The trip was also a reunion with his Irish father, also a Queenslander, who had long wanted to see southern Australia again.

The tourist experience, properly interrogated, is basic fieldwork for anyone interested in Australia and its multiculture. Tourism is not only a major industry, it also plays a key role in circulating and redefining images of nation and identity, part of a complex, three-body system that includes museums and the education system. Parties of schoolchildren visit museums to see physical traces of what they have been taught, the same story yet already slightly different. Then, as tourists, they may visit the actual sites where these stories once took place: again, the same, yet different, giving a pleasure that is both educational yet more than that.

Our trip began in Benalla, a mid-sized town in rural Victoria in what is now packaged as 'Kelly country'. For a few years in the 1870s, this is where Ned Kelly and his gang (four men in total) operated as 'bushrangers', holding up the occasional bank, robbing the occasional coach, evading a massive police effort to capture them until they were finally cornered at a hotel in Glenrowan. Why should it matter? Partly because they were so few, four men against a whole police force who were made to look foolish by their failure to catch them. Partly because this episode came at the end of a period when Irishness was a distinct ethnicity, as ambivalent as 'Middle Eastern' has become today. Partly because he expressed a continuing spirit of rebellion.

Kelly country is not far north of the site of the Eureka Stockade, a rebellion by miners on the Victorian goldfields in 1854, many of them Irish, though there were others from many other parts of the world. A republican flag, a white image of the Southern Cross on a blue background, flew briefly above a poorly defended camp before the police prevailed. But many of the reforms the miners demanded were granted, and in 2004—the 150th anniversary—a Eureka flag flew in Parliament House in Canberra.

The visitors' guide *What's on in Benalla* (2003) offers points of interest to the tourist: the raceway, the art gallery, the Dunlop memorial. The guide also tells us: 'Remember, you are starting from Benalla, headquarters of the Kelly pursuit. Countless police parties set off from here in search of the gang. Today, you will follow some of the roads they travelled . . . Good luck, enjoy your search.' (Jones 2003, p. 25) These words introduce a 'journey' across ten sites compiled by 'writer and Kelly historian Don Farmer', who advises us that the 'time taken to complete the drive is very much down to personal preference, but as a guide . . . allow at least six hours for the trip' (Farmer 2003, p. 25).

The first thing we notice in this text is that it is not one place. The map on the facing page is titled 'Benalla Bushrangers Scenic Drive' (Farmer 2003, p. 24). This is a strange drive, a search that re-enacts a hunting. Tourists might have different reasons but, like the troopers of the 1870s, they start from Benalla and they are looking for the Kellys. The quest has a military feel to it. Yet the activity itself consists of viewing things. The views are sometimes memorials, sometimes views of things the bushrangers (and troopers) viewed. This is a search for meaning. Tourists are asked to decide on guilt or innocence over and over again. We are put in the position of troopers, judges or juries, representatives of lawful citizenry, as well as outlaws. We acquire the multiple identities that together make up the story and the experience.

We are driving in a car, not riding horses, which distances us from the police and bushrangers—who were, after all, *fighting*. They are remembered because they were fighting a series of symbolic meanings. Benalla itself has few memorials, only a museum and a bootmaker's shop where Kelly was involved in a punch-up with police. The guidebook then takes the visitors to the hills.

A giant Ned Kelly in Glenrowan. Photograph by John O'Carroll

Driving in this region in early summer, we see apparently benign hills covered in yellow and purple flowers. There is no mention of these in Farmer's guide, and no labels on the landscape to say that the purple flowers are *Echium plantagineum*, Paterson's curse, a Mediterranean plant named for an unknown Paterson who liked its colour. We add this small moment to our experience of the trip, its message a sobering join of culture and nature, beautiful but toxic (it kills horses, but seemingly not cattle). It breaks the spell of the Kellys to remind us of the ongoing impact of settler-invaders on these lands, on these peoples.

We go north to Glenrowan, the site where the Kelly gang was defeated. Here we find also the key element in Ned Kelly's iconography, his famous armour. This armour has been made iconic by the painter Sidney Nolan (another Irish Australian). The simple cylinder with a slit for the eyes is one of the best known images in Australian popular culture, expressing the mysterious essence of Kelly and the Australianness he symbolises.

Borderwork and multicultural Australia

What we see in Glenrowan is not the armour itself, but a giant replica, a 'Big Kelly' in the postmodern Australian tradition of the 'Big Banana', the 'Big Pineapple' and the 'Giant Merino'. This bigness comes from modern Australia, not Kelly's Victoria. It is not authentic, and is not trying to seem so. Yet the two meanings combine here in the actual Glenrowan: the heroic but small-scale past and the huge but tacky and self-mocking present. This is an experience that can only be had here, by a tourist in this particular place, seeing this iconic hero of Australianness as superhuman yet ridiculous, laughed at and revered.

In Glenrowan, the icon seems to come straight out of official histories. Visitors (including, on this occasion, a group of intrigued Japanese tourists) are invited to see it as representing mainstream Australian culture. But the figure holds a gun and a hidden projector produces troopers who seem like mannequins, mown down by the gigantic figure. The simple narrative is like the famous image of King Kong, clinging to the Empire State building, swatting at the attacking planes as if they were flies.

Marxists argue that oppositional symbols are co-opted into dominant systems very quickly. Is that what is happening here? This image of Kelly is detached from the historical struggles he engaged in, in which he opposed the same establishment that now demands that he be given pride of place in the NMA. In this stripped-down form, he can stand for the mythic underdog Australian, the 'battler' in popular political discourses, whose welfare is close to the heart of politicians of all parties. In the intervening century, the Kellys have been changed from ambivalent criminals, victims, rebels and so on into national icons whose Irishness is no longer an essential part of their identity. Or isn't it?

The next site we visit is Mansfield, and 'The Monument', which commemorates troopers killed in action against the Kellys. From here, after the cemetery and another small site on the way, we reach site five, Stringybark Creek, where the Kellys shot three police (Farmer 2003, p. 27). Here, alongside the Kelly signs, is a relatively new memorial to the three troopers.

And next to the memorial is something else: fresh flowers. Someone had actually driven the 30 kilometres to place them here. Alongside the two opposing memorials, is a different, more transient memorial: *someone still cared.* They cared in a way that was not

The meaning of flowers: Stringybark Creek memorials. Photograph by John O'Carroll

simple. For every tourist journey, there is a moment like this. It is the moment when one realises, almost despite the plaques, that there were many lines of division, then as now. Many impoverished Irish suffered racist indignity. Some did not. Some who did responded violently. Others joined the police force. Many of them had divided ancestries too. There were Catholics and Protestants, of course, but also some were landed and wealthy, and others were seeking to make a living in Australia.

A multicultural Kelly?

There are many stories about how Ned Kelly got the idea for his famous armour. Some attribute it to a book titled *Lorna Doone* (Balcarek & Dean 1999, p. 222). But at the Burke museum in Beechworth we can find a stranger thread of history. Amongst the carefully arranged historical exhibits and simulated shopfronts of yesteryear, there stands a Chinese suit of armour. Made from interleaved metal plates, with a helmet and metal mittens, the suit was 'Brought from China with a consignment of costumes, banners, and ceremonial weapons . . . in the carnival procession held in Beechworth on

Borderwork and multicultural Australia

November 1st 1873' (museum postcard). Some speculate that this inspired the armour. Among the many stories, there is one that the Chinese-influenced Joe Byrne witnessed the Beechworth parade, and drew the germ of the idea from the experience.

Meshed into the Kelly gang legend is the backdrop of multiculture. The reduction of the story to a fight between the 'Irish' and the 'English' on Australian soil is too simple. There were troopers of Irish descent, as well as rebels. Irish Catholics were on both sides of the divide. Equally, the theatrical representation of Kelly moving against an oppressive Anglo backdrop leaves out the complexities, be they ethical, political or cultural. In Gregor Jordan's 2002 film *Ned Kelly*, Joe Byrne speaks fluent Chinese, which was entirely possible. One of the gang lowers his gun when he realises that the target is not a trooper but an Aboriginal man.

Whether or not these stories of Chinese and Aborigines in the heart of an Australian (Anglo-Celtic) myth are factually true, they carry an important message about Australian multiculture. The Chinese were also in 'Kelly country' in the nineteenth century, complicating the simple opposition between the Irish and the English. Aboriginal people also played a role in the story of the Kellys told by Superintendant John Sadleir (1973), the Irish-born police officer who oversaw the final capture of Ned Kelly at Glenrowan. Sadleir was the other kind of Irishman, who escaped from poverty in Ireland to join the police force instead of becoming a bushranger. He had great admiration for Indigenous abilities, especially black trackers. He tells how a group of six black trackers brought down from Queensland so terrified the Kellys with their prowess that they changed their whole pattern of life immediately on their arrival:

> The effects on the movements of the Kellys were remarkable; in a sense indeed much beyond what was desired. Hitherto the bushrangers made their appearance pretty frequently, fearing only to be seen by the police. Now their fears were lest they should be seen by any private person who might lay the Queensland boys on their tracks. (Sadleir 1973, p. 211)

One Irishman working for the establishment, catching another who has become a legend, both in awe of Aboriginal skills: it is the kind of complication that multiculture so often gives to simple, 'crisp' myths of repression and heroism.

A recent story about the indigenous AFL footballer Michael Long looked briefly at his 'Irish links', and perhaps shed light on how multi-culture happens in reality. Long's great-great-grandfather John Byrne sailed from Ireland in 1849. Some of the stories involved official marriage, but others certainly did not (Rintoul 2005, pp. 24–25). Not only did Stan Byrne 'not marry Jessie Kurowiny, nor did he recognise their children'; worse yet, he instigated their removal to a mission (2005, p. 25). One of those children, Agnes, would one day be Michael Long's mother. This too is a story of 'Celtic' Australia.

All these stories—be they happy or sad, tragic or uplifting—are stories told from particular points of view, not objective truths. Aboriginal people also had their stories—again not objective truths, but part of a multicultural fabric woven around the Australian myth of Ned Kelly:

> According to the Yarralin people from the Victoria River District, Ned Kelly was the first white man to come to the area. He was a friend of the Gurindji Aborigines and taught them how to cook damper and make tea, his small damper and single billy feeding all the Gurindji. Ned Kelly also went with angels on a boat and created a river when all had been salt water. The second man to arrive was Captain Cook, who stole the land, shot many of the Aborigines and also shot Ned Kelly. (Holland & Williamson 2003, pp. 27–28)

This story at first may sound merely bizarre. But its broad-brush rendering shows the kind of sense-making that is at stake. Its Ned Kelly and Captain Cook are both mythic figures, as important as the critics of the NMA could desire. In this myth, Ned is a 'white man', yet he is also an Aboriginal creative spirit: both white and Aboriginal, in this 'Dreamtime' story. Captain Cook remains fully white, standing for all the whites who did indeed steal the land, shoot many Aborigines, and finally hung Ned Kelly. The story is, perhaps, not so bizarre after all. It weaves cultures into a story of identity, an Anglo-Celtic-Aboriginal story and identity that Australian multiculture can value today.

Postmodern bushrangers: Harry Power's Lookout

Harry Power, the bushranger who 'taught' Ned Kelly, is less famous today than Ned. One difference between the two may be that Power

grew up in Ireland, and as a migrant was not convertible into an 'Australian icon'. Described as an illiterate Roman Catholic, he was transported for 'stealing a pair of shoes' (Passey & Dean 1991, p. 1). Power's Lookout performs the same task today as it did for the bushranger: we can look over the landscape and have a commanding view of the surrounding hills and valleys.

Power's notoriety led by a complex route to him finally being hired as a tour guide. In Australia, as in England, old rotting hulks of vessels were used as floating prisons. While on one, 'he received 18 lashes for trying to escape'. Forty-five years later, after a life as much in gaol as out of it, Power took a job as a tour guide on a ship that had once been his prison quarters. The prison hulk *Success*, moored in Port Phillip Bay, was converted to a floating museum where people came to see what was described as a 'living hell' for prisoners. Power—the infamous bushranger and former inmate—was its star attraction. (Information taken from Parks Victoria sign at Power's Lookout.)

We often think of tourism as a mass, post-World War II phenomenon, but this situation reminds us that fascination with horrifying or tragic sites is not new. It says. 'This is what we were'. Yet it also says: 'We don't do this kind of thing any more. The "we" who did this is no longer us.'

Just Australian: An Anglo–Celtic culture nevertheless?

In the mix of cultures in multiculture, is there a definable Anglo-Celtic *culture* as such? If so, how did it emerge and what are its prospects? We have argued that there *is* a multiculture, with the Anglo-Celtic multiculture an essential component. Most writers on multiculturalism would not agree. We find plenty written about the distinctive cultural traits of cultures that have made Australia home, but little *cultural* analysis of the always-implied 'mainstream'. Myths, yes: whole books are written on a stereotype, a white, rural male who probably never existed in that form, and is harder to find today. But what about Anglo-Celtic, multicultural Australians today—men and women who are not caricatures, yet do have a distinctive way of life?

'Just Australian' is where we might usefully begin anew. Can we not see in this often-repeated statement a certain wryness, a certain style? We know it has been mythologised, but does this mean it does not exist? Not in our view. The stereotype is itself a shorthand for a wider code. To be Anglo-Celtic Australian has long implied a pattern: understatement, irony, modesty. It also implies a suspicion of ideas, and an anti-dogmatic uncertainty, captured by linguists in the still-to-be-heard rising intonation at the end of statements typical of the 'Aussie' accent. It expresses a class perspective, and a deep experience of ethnic differences, yet it now crosses classes to some degree, uniting them while not removing the category of class itself.

In their fascinating book *Accounting for Tastes: Australian Everday Cultures* (1999), Tony Bennett and his colleagues look at intersections especially of class, gender, educational attainment and age. Asking questions about what it means to prefer one food over another, or one colour scheme for a house to another, they draw up a matrix of factors to make sense of contemporary Australia. Their book suggests how complex the relationships are, so that—for instance—while 'taste' cannot be said to be 'directly expressive of social groups', values can nevertheless be associated with 'particular infrastructure' (the pub culture, for instance) (1999, p. 104). Yet this does not lock us in forever, because later in the book they remark that there is no single 'binding scale of cultural legitimacy', instead suggesting a 'plurality of scales of value in many of which age or gender or regional location, rather than social class, play a dominant role' (1999, p. 269).

Anglo-Celtic Australia reflects these complexities. Bennett and his colleagues did not look at issues of ethnicity in any detail (although they did briefly consider the issues of Indigeneity and migrancy). In saying that Anglo-Celtic Australia needs to be seen as a multiculture, we need to see that it is not singular, that its signs are complex. But how can we describe this complexity adequately?

Think again of the accent, that badge of 'Aussie honour'. Some years ago, in *Myths of Oz*, Bob and his co-authors wrote that the Australian accent should be viewed ambivalently, not just as a sign of 'slackness' on the one hand, or of brave defiance on the other (Fiske et al. 1987, p. 173). Rather, it is a complex sign that masks a lot of social meaning, be it a case of manipulation of the accent for commercial purposes, or the layers of class and location that are revealed each time we open our mouths.

Some may contend that we are looking at it only as it fades from view, that even the rising intonation which characterises the accent is no longer to be heard in the tones of the urban young. But the idea that it is dying might itself be illusory. It is probably quite resilient, turning up not only in caricatures such as those found in TV series about suburban life, like *Kath and Kim*, but also in popular films like *Wog Boy*, whose Australian Greek hero is as much a larrikin as the Anglo-Celts who once oppressed him in the playground. In fact, recent research by Felicity Cox at Macquarie University suggests that, while the extremes of the Australian accent are becoming less common (that is, the 'ocker' extreme at one end and the more 'formal' extreme at the other), the accent itself is becoming even more strongly entrenched around a sort of middle ground (Connolly 2005, pp. 1, 5). The 'multicultural larrikin' has escaped from hegemonic control, and 'strine' culture is adopted by the children of migrants as a language they can speak and innovate with as their perceived right. And (as was pointed out in *Myths of Oz*), because this is a living culture, we can expect the same complexities of power and solidarity to be operative in everyday life.

Yet little of this is visible in research into Anglo-Celtic Australian culture in the field of multiculturalism. Books on multiculturalism typically treat the Anglo-Celtic dimension of multiculture as a cata-logue of faults. In Hage's *Against Paranoid Nationalism* (2003), a scathing polemic on John Howard's Australia, the list of faults makes up most of the book. Hage is consistent in that he sees multiculturalist tolerance as a very white (i.e. 'Anglo-Celtic') idea, and also as totally inadequate. Vasta and Castles' *The Teeth are Smiling* (1996), perhaps the most important book on multiculturalism in the 1990s, also constructs the mainframe of the argument (essays by Castles, Vasta and Collins) in terms of the political economy of mainstream (Anglo-Celtic) Australian racism. Earlier works, like *Mistaken Identity* (1992), are even stronger in these views.

In all these works, there is a taken-for-granted Anglo-Celtic mainstream which is seen as being everywhere and always pathologi-cal. Seen as having little cultural interest, it is analysed in structural terms. Economic class issues and patterns of globalisation are traced, with other complex aspects of culture downplayed. Of the above commentators, only Hage dwells on the striations within: he writes of a 'class imaginary of colonial racism, a racism that is still very alive and well today' (2003, p. 113). But class layerings are only one aspect of what is always also an ethnic history. This is why we have focused at length on key aspects of Anglo-Celtic history in ethnic terms in this chapter. The phrase 'Anglo-Celtic' hides a wealth of culture-history.

The focus on such history does not involve discarding broader economic contexts, however. One of the shortcomings of traditional views of globalisation is that it tends to privilege economic and political factors over cultural and social ones. But it is not a question of either/or. In this respect, one useful development has been the notion of 'multicultural citizenship'. Stephen Castles, one of the authors of *The Teeth are Smiling*, has co-authored a refinement of the idea of globalisation to pose questions like these:

> Globalization, the increased mobility of people and the burgeoning of new forms of communication make myths of homogeneity unsustainable. Cultural diversity has become a central aspect of virtually all modern societies. Assimilation is no longer an option because of the rapidity and multidirectionality of mobility and communication. More and more people have dual or multiple citizenship. Other people lack citizenship in their country of residence ... Answers to the question, 'Who is a citizen?' are becoming increasingly difficult. (Castles & Davidson 2000, p. 127)

For them, the need for 'cultural' rights (including access to mainstream culture and maintenance of minority languages and customs) is a constituent *of* citizenship (2000, p. 126).

For us, this is a useful nuance. But we think it can go further. As the title of our book makes plain, things always happen *somewhere*. In this case, what is at stake is the borderwork that happens according to local logics in an always multicultural Australia. That is, we see multiculture as *happening* differently depending upon the borderwork conditions under which it locally (and yet always also in relation to a wider context) arises. This location is not just spatial (globalisation tends to be a profoundly spatial model of the world system); it is also *historical*. In this regard, we gain powerful insights into Australian multicultural formations by looking back in time.

Hence our interest in the specificities of Anglo-Celtic borderwork, now and in the past. Within the constellation of cultures in the greater Australian multiculture, it continues to change, and Anglo-Celtic peoples continue to migrate to Australia. In practice, the pattern of migration has remained stable in some ways, despite the changing profile of cultures: '23.3 per cent of Australians were born overseas— much the same proportion as in the year of federation, 1901' (DIMA

2000, p. 1). The mainstream that emerges from these figures is dynamic and malleable, like the culture itself.

'Just Australian' reflects a culture that has seen its population treble since World War II, and grow fivefold—that is, 500 per cent—since Federation in 1901, when the population stood at just 3.774 million people (ABS 2002). During this time, it has retained a sense of place and purpose, while devising new, ingenious solutions to communications, geographical isolation and radical workplace change. The latter has been particularly traumatic. Since 1977, the population has increased by almost 50 per cent (DIMA 2000, p. 105), while entire sectors of the workforce have been restructured into oblivion (Fagan et al. 1994, pp. 49, 79–80). The changes have benefited new generations of workers, but older colleagues have been relegated to the scrap-heap.

Economic globalisation has fostered local discontent and resentment, as victims of economic transformation see others—sometimes migrants, sometimes not—appearing to thrive while their own fortunes fail. At these times, critics are quick to point to intolerance and hatred, often a case of misdirected anger. There is no easy solution to these complex issues coming from what we see as potential qualities of Australian Anglo-Celtic culture.

Commentators are fond of exploiting the difference between the 'myth' (the image of the stereotypical Anglo-Celtic Australian) and the 'reality', as though the pure forms of the first are now sadly lost. Here is one such comment:

> Australians are now the hardest workers in the developed world . . . We're not nearly as rural as we fondly imagine. Australia is second only to Belgium for the highest proportion of the population living in urban areas—91 percent. And we're tops on the proportion of population living in cities of more than 750,000 people. (Gittins 2004, pp. 1, 10)

The shock that Australians (these are modern, multicultural Australians now) are so hard-working is contrasted with the 'laid back' image of the myth. This myth has, as part of its structure, a 'bush' or rural component that never corresponded to wider reality. But maybe there is not such a contradiction. The relaxed style which is 'the Australian way' was *itself* always part of a reality that had to include hard work. Incoming waves of migrants of all backgrounds had in common a migrant work ethic: it is nothing new, no lapse from an original (Anglo-Celtic) 'laziness'—and, of course, no lapse from a nineteenth century colonial outback Eden.

Remembering such history is an ongoing task for the present, because the way we explain the past tells us a lot about ourselves. Commenting on the way First Fleet re-enactments have fallen out of favour since the spectacles of 1988, Jonathon King (2005) tells us of the Timbery family, descendants of the Indigenous people who were on the other side (2005, p. 12). He also reminds us of the words of Charles Perkins. Perkins, a strident advocate of Indigenous rights, made many fiery speeches about the problematic status of settler-culture in Australia. Yet he also said:

> You whitefellas have gotta have your own dreamtime stories. If you bury 'em, you'll have no past, won't know where you have come from and won't know how to find your way into the future. (cited in King 2005, p. 12)

The core Australian values have been derived from all its peoples, formed by a history in which Anglos and Celts played a significant role. That culture needs articulation, both in terms of its history and its present. In that history, no one is *just* Australian.

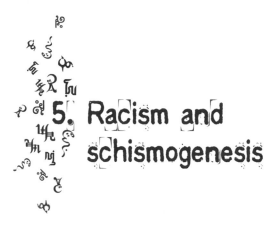

5. Racism and schismogenesis

'Racist taunts draw blood'

A series of assaults on international students at the University of Newcastle has been linked to a propaganda campaign by a far-right militant group.

Herbert Gatamah, a Kenyan student studying engineering at the University of Newcastle, north of Sydney, was last week attacked outside the University bar by a gang of six men, one of whom allegedly tried to choke him.

'They cursed me and my friends, they called us monkeys,' Gatamah told the *HES*. 'They told us I'm not welcome in this country.' (Robinson 2004, p. 41)

At present, even as we write—even as you read these pages—individuals and families in this country are suffering attacks like this. Australians are dimly aware of this through academic studies that make it into newspapers or through particularly terrible assaults or events. We, as teachers, have heard students share things that happened to them. They reminded us that racism exists in all walks of life, in every Australian city and town. The idea that we might one day be altogether rid of it is naive.

Racism is surprisingly difficult to define. There are many theoretical debates about its true nature. Yet there is little doubt about what its effects are, and these are the best clues to an acceptable definition. In social reality, then, **racism** can be defined as discrimination against a person or group of people, on the assumption that the entire group shares genetically common characteristics. On the one hand, it seems the opposite of multiculture, the grim alternative facing every society rejecting diversity, so our position ought to be obvious: to condemn racism in all its forms, to mount a continuous assault on all its manifestations, however subtle, until they are all rooted out and nothing is left but multiculture. Yet multiculture and racism have a complex relationship with one another, and after a point a take no prisoners attack on racism is not the same as multiculture. Responding to the incident described above, Jeremy Jones, president of the Australian Jewry Executive Council, noted: 'It doesn't take many people to cause a lot of pain to members of the community who are singled out for harassment and vilification.' (Robinson 2004, p. 41) But he then recommended against censoring these students: 'The most important thing that can be done, rather than combat the groups, is for strong assertions by the overwhelming majority of students that if you attack any group within Australia you attack all of Australia.' (2004, p. 41)

The dilemma for Australia today is to recognise and tackle the disproportionate pain caused by racism, yet to affirm—as Jones does— that Australia today is not fundamentally a racist nation. But Australia has been a racist nation, and could become one again. Racism has not gone away. What racists do damages others and the societies they live in, causing suffering and distress to many. Yet 'racism' must be understood, not angrily dismissed in a mirror image of the way racists typically refuse all dialogue. In this chapter we will rethink racism in the broader framework of schismogenesis, as one important way that societies come apart, as a pathological response to complexity. The 'logic' of racism turns out to be a form of crisp logic that does not always refer to 'race', and isn't always a simple response to difference.

Racism is personal

However we define racism, we need to remember how traumatic the experiences we are discussing really are. Racism is an abstract noun. But it is also something that *happens* to people, through the actions of others. In this respect, we believe that schismogenesis offers a new way of understanding racism. As we saw in Chapter 1, there are two

Borderwork and multicultural Australia

orders of schismogenesis: the complementary and the symmetrical. Structurally, people are familiar with complementary varieties, because these refer to groups which are *different*. But, as we will see later in the chapter when we discuss the 'difference myth', many aspects of racism reflect fear of *sameness*, of group symmetries.

Let us take a recent case. Western Australians may remember the racist attacks on a number of Chinese restaurants in Perth in the late 1980s. The problems were apparently resolved when a right-wing nationalist movement leader, Jack Van Tongeren, was brought to trial. But recently there were new attacks:

> Ethnic communities were reeling yesterday from an unprecedented spate of racist attacks linked to the neo-Nazi group that firebombed Perth restaurants in the 1980s. Businesses across three southern Perth suburbs were early yesterday morning plastered with swastikas and racist slogans and posters produced by the racist Australian Nationalists Movement. (Taylor & Shadbolt 2004, p. 6)

Van Tongeren, only two years out of gaol after a twelve-year sentence, explained his group's stance: 'I prefer my own kind, there's nothing wrong with that.' (Taylor & Shadbolt 2004, p. 6) The statement is at once self-justification and concealment. The concealment defends a right that is not being questioned. It argues the right to have preferences, when no one has contested *this* right. By contrast, current Australian law does *not* enshrine the right to vilify others, or burn their property.

There is a deeper kind of work going on in this apparently simple assertion. The statement is defensive, as if the speaker were the victim. We note a strange symmetry in the race for sympathy between perpetrator-as-victim and actual victims of attack. Members of nationalist movements by definition align themselves with an imagined nation, so they ought to see themselves as mainstream. Yet this mainstream claims victim status. René Girard has argued that social and cultural meaning is sometimes supplied not just by scapegoating imagined others, but also by casting oneself as the victim of their perfidy.

Van Tongeren's position contains other interesting paradoxes. Photographs show he has features which could be identified as 'Asian'. Are his 'own kind' fellow 'Asians'? His surname is Dutch, and his ideology derives from Nazism, a German movement. He is a multicultural package denouncing multiculturalism, denying his own complex identity. This extreme case illustrates an important general point: militant racism denies complex realities about selves as well as others.

As teachers, one task we set our class was to reflect on how racism is experienced. In 1991, the Human Rights and Equal Opportunity Commission (HREOC) reported on racist violence in the wake of the Gulf War, 'directed at persons on the basis of the ethnic identity attributed, rightly or wrongly, to them by those perpetrating the violence' (1991, p. 137). From what our students told us a decade later, this definition is still relevant. In fact, more recently a report into the experience of racism found that 'racism in Australia was rising and people were becoming more used to it' ('Racism Rise' 2004, p. 15).

In our teaching, to help focus on these experiences, we ask our students to read from the HREOC appendix. Here is a story from that report:

> An Adelaide woman says that recently people in the street outside her home called her and her children 'wogs' and bloody ethnics, spat on them and threatened to harm them. People, she said, also jumped onto her property and tried to break her car. She and her children were very scared and couldn't sleep for days. She was too scared to give any details about the offenders. (1991, p. 423)

We asked our students to imagine what it might be like to be in that woman's shoes, night after night. Not only has she her own fear to contend with, but her children also wake in fear at night. Does she stay or does she move? Would it be any better somewhere else? Would the authorities help her, even if she did report it? And most important: is this the kind of society our students would want to live in? Put in this way, all were clear: No, they wouldn't!

Racism often produces paradoxical effects:

> In addition to the attacks on schools and restaurants described earlier, several incidents have been reported in which deliberate damage has been done to motor vehicles driven by women in traditional Islamic dress. In one case in Melbourne, a female motorist deliberately drove into a vehicle driven by a Muslim woman, and then verbally abused her, accusing her of being an Iraqi terrorist. (1991, p. 156)

In case we doubt the emotional impact of the incident, the report goes on to remark that the 'victim of this attack now feels unable to leave her home and commented: "It is now unsafe for us to live here and I feel scared all the time. I am a prisoner in my own home, too afraid to go out."' (1991, p. 156) But let us note the paradox: a woman drives her car into another woman's car and calls *her* the terrorist! As with Van Tongeren, there is a symmetry between attacker and victim. And in this case the focus of the rage is not race as such, but a potent mix of religion and ideology built around the idea of terrorism.

There is another thing common to all these cases. HREOC is supported by the government to investigate these cases. Van Tongeren served time in prison. Racism indeed happens, in working-class suburbs and swanky urban precincts, in workplaces and schools, and the Adelaide woman would not be alone in doubting how energetically the police would protect her. Yet the state does not sanction such actions, and nor does the community. This difference should not be forgotten if we compare the Australian situation with other famous cases like Nazi Germany.

Schismogenesis: Rethinking difference

As a model, schismogenesis calls attention to the fact that cultures, societies, polities and even economies are first and foremost *anthropological* entities with belief structures about the world. Like anthropologists, we should be sceptical about the explanations the culture itself proffers about the way the world 'really' is, relying instead on broadly observable patterns of behaviour in the best tradition of the exploratory social science hypothesis. This approach points out obvious patterns that criss-cross human group behaviour all around the world, and it does so without making a prior value judgment. The advantage of schismogenesis as a model of human behaviour is that it is schematic and suggestive, rather than detailed and restrictive. It is compatible with many other ways of examining the issue, including much theory about the nature of racism in the modern world. But it offers help in making broader sense of racism, as well as in devising strategies for combating its reach.

To start with, then, when we teach how racism works as a schismogenic process, we make use of a powerful, semiotically oriented essay by Colette Guillaumin (1988). Her title, 'Race and Nature: The

System of Marks: The Idea of a Natural Group' summarises its argument: that there is no scientific foundation for such a thing as a natural group (like a race) in any society. Instead, such groups are always produced by a semiotic process which is social in its origins. Her essay offers a three-step process in the semiotics of racism. First, she says, take a cultural group which will have evolved socially. Then identify some physical traits or aspects of that group, some features that seem common. If necessary, as with the cloth Star of David for Jews in Nazi times, attach the mark to the group yourself (1988, p. 31). Then call that group a 'race' by attributing the cultural features you associate with that group to deep biological patterns (1988, p. 33).

This is a chilling and plausible account of a classic form of this process. Yet we also note some interesting features that break with mainstream understandings of racism. First, this process does not need 'race' as such. Since it is so abstract, it could work equally well with religion (as it does) or many other qualities. Second, 'difference' as such plays an ambiguous role. If a quality can be found on the surface—in skin colour, for example—that is used. But if it is less clear, as with Jews in Nazi Germany, then differences are manufactured, and these work equally well. *Similarity* is as likely to be the raw material for schismogenesis as observed difference. Finally, the connection with biology does not seem basic in the cases we have looked at. Any theory will do, however lacking in foundation. The Melbourne woman who ran into the Muslim woman had a theory of global terrorism which did not have its origins in any science.

This brings us to the logic that drives this process, and makes its wild connections plausible. Its crisp logic has two categories, 'us' and 'them'. 'They' are all the same, and not 'like us' in one fundamental way; whatever the other similarities, they are 'other', not to be treated the same as 'us', not trusted, not human. Yet this simplistic logic contradicts many other ideas formed by complex experience. It is not just the crispness, but its coexistence with fuzziness, under specific conditions, that drives schismogenesis—which can, at its most extreme, take the form of genocide or other forms of destructive discrimination. Yet, even as the worst atrocities are happening, at another level members of the group really 'know' better. Cosmogenesis, as we have claimed repeatedly in this book, is always also present in the scene of extreme racism—not always as a healing force, but sometimes as a source of deeper, angry confusion.

When we treat racism in terms of schismogenesis, what does it mean to say that this makes us pay attention to the *anthropological* aspects of human behaviour (rather than simply attributing dominant causality to a single factor, such as economic circumstances or scientific knowledge)? It means first of all that it is never so simple. It means too that we can set aside certain sorts of deep causal inquiry in favour of observation and analysis. This turns up the surprising fact that difference is not itself an inherent driver of racism, and that the system of marks Guillaumin (1988) describes *does* have a potential anthropological basis.

Earlier in this chapter we mentioned René Girard, a writer who has explored the 'myth of difference'. Most social scientists look at racism as an issue of difference, presuming that we dislike those who are different. But this view does not hold up, he says. The fiercest racism seems reserved for those who are most *similar* to us. Girard (1986) explains how the logic of racism works. For Girard, we exist in cultures that overplay difference:

> No culture exists within which everyone does not feel 'different' from others and does not consider such 'differences' legitimate and necessary. Far from being radical and progressive, the current glorification of difference is merely the abstract expression of an outlook common to all cultures. (1986, p. 21)

The problem arises when the sense of distinctness is threatened:

> The various kinds of victims seem predisposed to crimes that eliminate differences. Religious, ethnic, or national minorities are never actually reproached for their difference, but for not being as different as expected, and in the end for not differing at all . . . We hear everywhere that 'difference' is persecuted. This is the favorite statement of contemporary pluralism, and it can be somewhat misleading in the present context. (1986, p. 22)

The problem is not that 'they' are different; rather it is that 'they' are just a bit too much *like* 'us'—'they' live next door, take 'our' jobs, go to 'our' schools.

Girard focuses on the role of the 'scapegoat' as a social mechanism for dealing with explosions of schismogenesis. The scapegoat is a victim chosen to allow a society to focus its fury on a small target, so that it does not tear itself apart in a frenzy of symmetrical schismogenesis. The process is not conscious, as it intensifies and polarises violent impulses against a randomly chosen victim. The performance of expelling this victim, which symbolises what divides them, 'can and does reunite them in fact at a certain point by virtue of a rapidly emerging mutually endorsed enmity directed at a common enemy' (Fleming 2004, p. 47).

We make the point again: difference does not lead only to hostility or neutrality. Simple ideas of identity imply that we like everyone who is like us, and dislike everyone else. But the reality is different, as Girard points out. We don't only dislike people for being too like us; we also like others precisely because they are different, complementing our own strengths and weaknesses.

The United Nations and the coalition against racism

In understanding racism and multiculture in the world today, it is important to look beyond racist crimes against humanity to see the transformative force of the cosmogenesis described above. Here a crucial event was the foundation of the United Nations (UN) in 1947. This organisation has no army of its own to enforce its will, and depends on financial support from the nations it exists to regulate.

Two experiences coloured its foundation. One was the first global war in human history, proof that the old ways of managing conflict were dangerously inadequate. The second was the Holocaust, the genocide perpetrated against the Jewish people by Hitler, legitimated by a racist ideology. The two lessons were aspects of a single remarkable new wisdom. Explosive racism, explosive war—schismogenesis at its most extreme—threatened the very existence of humanity. The UN, a cosmogenic response, offered shared possibilities, shared futures.

With all its flaws—and it has many—the UN has helped transform the world into an environment where multicultures can be fostered, where racism is mitigated, where schismogenesis is reversed. The 'anti-racist' mission of the UN, and the memory of the Holocaust, motivated a tremendous era of *affirmative* change. Colonisers decolonised within a new framework of expectations, immigration policies slowly dropped some of their more racist elements, coercive assimilation policies gradually weakened. A new internationalised values system emerged—even if, as ever, it was opportunistically broken or weakly adhered to. These entailed a new way of seeing, a new world-view.

It is important to recognise that these changes came from below, from individuals and nations, and if this had not happened then the UN would have just been another pious and ineffective focus of rhetoric. To illustrate these deeper, more subtle changes, we can look at two short documentaries from the early 1950s, included in a DVD compilation of archival films, interviews and reflections on postwar Australia released by Film Australia in 2004. Many of the films are propaganda, advertising the merits of Australia to potential migrants. But two films, *Double Trouble* (1951) and *Mike and Stefani* (1952), stand out (Film Australia, 2004).

In *Double Trouble*, two new migrants walk into a bar and ask for a telephone in their native tongue. The others in the pub respond: 'foreigners', 'can't speak English', etc. A voiceover comments: 'Uh-oh, *that* makes it a bit different. They're foreigners—can't speak English' (1952). There follows a scene where two of the 'Aussies' are transposed to a European country, where they end up unwittingly bringing out the fire brigade because they called from an emergency phone box. The voiceover comments at the end: be helpful, it won't hurt.

Mike and Stefani is an excruciating film to watch, even today. After showing Mike and Stefani's years of painful separation, in labour camps and refugee camps, we see them interviewed by an Australian immigration official. The interrogation seems cruel and endless. At one point, we hear the applicant mutter in English: 'I must be quiet' and 'So many questions!' After the process ends, the official calls out, 'Next one!' as if he were processing cattle.

These two films show traces of the UN transformation that was taking place all round the world, including Australia. These films, with their critical and compassionate stance, ask people to think about their attitudes, to imagine how they might feel if they stood in the other person's shoes. Buried in the heart of an immigration bureaucracy, they are surprising empirical evidence of the ways of seeing that were becoming possible in the post-UN world.

In Chapter 1, we reported an occasion on which the Minister for Immigration, Harold Holt, and Arthur Calwell from the Labor Party both spoke at a conference on the new program. That conference also took place in 1951. From the outset, Australia played a positive role in this international movement. Bert Evatt, later leader of the ALP, was an influential member of the body that set up the UN. The official removal of the 'White Australia' policy in 1958 was an important sign of the new Australia.

The signal changes of the mid-twentieth century reflect not just local pressures and motivations, but also global ones. We have seen how globalisation is a complex process: it describes the sweeping interdependency of peoples and nations that has arisen in economic, political and social frameworks. The UN itself reflects something of the change, as it too is a global organisation. It has affected local conceptions of what is and is not acceptable. Whatever the failures of its political processes, its characteristic biases or even its membership, we can say that one of its most important successes has been in changing the way people all around the world now think about both multiculturalism and racism.

In Australia, the development of multiculturalism policies from 1972 was an affirmative statement of the new values of a UNESCO-framed world. In 1975 the Labor government passed the *Racial Discrimination Act*, which was supported by the incoming Fraser Liberal government. The current legislation is the *Racial Hatred Act*, a 1995 amendment. In it, we find the legal description of racism. The Act says it is 'unlawful to offend, insult, humiliate or intimidate another person or a group of people because of the race, colour, or national or ethnic origin of the other person or group'.

This more or less bipartisan framework is administered by the Human Rights and Equal Opportunity Commission (HREOC), an independent national statutory body set up in 1986, one of whose reports we have quoted. This body also has the responsibility to give effect to Australia's other obligations under the international conventions and declarations it has signed. HREOC is both the child of the UN and its mirror image within Australian society.

Human rights includes the rights that racism tries to deny, alongside many others. Because it is a fuzzy category, it can grow as new crises emerge that are not obviously racist, but involve issues of common justice. **Equal opportunity** expresses the basic conditions for a just society, a multiculture that includes all groups, all 'cultures'. In this way, HREOC has turned the merely negative battle against racism into a vision of justice for the whole society.

Is the United Nations out of date?

Some powerful people, like US president George W. Bush and Australian prime minister John Howard, have complained about UN conventions. These complaints are part of contemporary debates, so we address them here as our students ask us to do in our classes. In the wake of September 11, 2001, some argue that the world has changed so much from the 1950s when the conventions were formed that they are now out of date.

One focus of attack is the Geneva Convention. This international agreement preceded the UN, but performed the UN role of managing conflicts. It began in the nineteenth century as a way of managing prisoners wounded in war. The original agreement in 1864 was extended several times, including in 1949 and 1977. After the attacks of September 11, 2001, the United States invaded Afghanistan. In the ensuing conflict, captured enemy would normally have been held under the Geneva Convention as prisoners of war. Instead, they were held at Guantanamo Bay, a US military base in Cuba. By redefining the prisoners as 'enemy combatants', not 'prisoners of war', these prisoners were denied rights they were entitled to under the Geneva Convention. Two were Australians.

The reasoning that 'things are different now' was flawed. Certainly, a nation as powerful as the United States can defy international opinion. But this is nothing new. This possibility has always coexisted with this weak, dependent body. Nor was racism absent from the strategy. Collapsing 'terrorist' with 'Muslim' allowed these people to be treated, as in racist ideologies, as not fully human. When methods developed by US authorities for prisoners from Afghanistan (some of them outsourced to contractors) were then applied in Iraq, a prisoner-abuse scandal broke out. Shocking photographs were published for the world to see, showing prisoners sexually humiliated, along with hooding, and other 'controlled' means of torture. Was this worldwide outrage 'out of date'?

Science and racism

The core event for the modern understanding of racism is undoubtedly the Holocaust, in which millions of Jews were killed simply because they were Jews. This shocking event taught the planet a lesson it has not forgotten and should never forget. Yet this event should not be seen through the crisp logic of schismogenesis, in which every racist or offensive act is labelled 'Nazi', treated as though all racists and racist societies are the same. The Nazi state can be defined as a **racist state** not because of attitudes its leaders had, but because *those attitudes were enshrined in law and largely adhered to by the people*.

The Nazis also justified racism by an appeal to science. Before the war, explanations of human history, society and culture were sometimes offered in terms of theories of race. Racism was a permissible hypothesis: it could be called science. Writers like Goldberg (1993) go further. For him, a form of 'racial knowledge' was developed that still forms the basis of many forms of knowledge today. He argues that this 'knowledge' affected 'established scientific fields of the day, especially anthropology, natural history, and biology' (1993, p. 149). Crucially, this way of knowing (racism) was 'historically integral to the emergence of these authoritative scientific fields' (1993, p. 149). But after the war, the UN expressed the revulsion of the 'civilised' world in outlawing these ideas. 'Racism' came to be identified as false science.

In 1950 and 1951, UNESCO convened a group of scholars to prepare an authoritative statement on race which instantly became a defining document, with great rhetorical force. The 1950 statement declared that there was 'general agreement . . . that mankind is one: that all people belong to the same species, *Homo sapiens*' (in Snyder 1962, p. 173). The sting in the tail for those who believed in race was explicit: 'Unfortunately, however, when most people use the term "race" they do not do so in the sense above defined [in article four]. To most people, a race is any group of people whom they choose to describe as a race.' (1962, p. 173) In 1951, these statements were modified slightly because, contrary to the appearance created above, there were few biologists on the first UNESCO committee (1962, p. 173). But the message was the same: 'races' do not exist in the sense that they had been popularly imagined as having existed. 'Race' itself is not relevant in social or cultural analysis. Put bluntly:

National, religious, geographical, linguistic and cultural groups do not necessarily coincide with racial groups, and the cultural traits of such groups have no demonstrated connection with racial traits. Americans are not a race, nor are Frenchmen, nor Germans nor *ipso facto* is any other national group. Moslems and Jews are no more races than are Roman Catholics or Protestants. (Snyder 1962, p. 180)

With this assault on race as a social determinant, 'racialism'—or the scientific study of race—came to an end. Anyone who made such claims after this era was regarded simply as a racist.

Only six years after the UNESCO statement, Crick and Watson decoded DNA and launched a new era of genetic research. Our students rightly ask us: how does the UNESCO statement stack up now? The short answer is: quite well, but with qualifications. DNA analysis can now track back groups to a putative ancestor, one of the basic assumptions of the old racism. But the same analysis shows that any modern descendant has many genes not present in the ancestor, owing to the multiplicity of gene lines that have fed into the modern group. It is even clearer now than then that there are no 'pure' races corresponding to the 'English', 'Chinese' or any other major group in the present Australian population—as was already evident in 1950. Genetics has a contradictory message about individuality. On the one hand, each individual has a unique DNA identity, so that not even brothers and sisters are exactly the same. The relevant term is degree of 'match'—how close two DNA samples are, not whether they are identical. But on the other hand, as was known already in 1950, the DNA shared by all humans is far greater proportionally than it is different. The human genome project maps the set of DNA sequences that underlie a common humanity which is the scientific equivalent of the 'human nature' that was an ethical principle for UNESCO.

So does 'science' support the case against racism? The question in this form should make us feel uncomfortable. We feel this argument was posed in a context, but that aspects of it have outlived their usefulness. UNESCO rebukes the vague way 'race' is used to include 'any group of people'. This suggests that what is at stake is really a more fundamental process: that of schismogenesis. Schismogenesis applies to any process of social splitting, to any discrimination. In this light, the scope for appeal to DNA (or biology *per se*) is weakened. Anti-Muslim behaviour is demonstrably schismogenic; this is what matters. Also, it is much easier to describe in these terms than in terms of racism or biology.

In any event, how much science do the members of Van Tongeren's group know? And do they care? It is even pertinent to ask: was Hitler, who ruthlessly subordinated science to politics, much shaped by the science behind his racism? In practice *his racism invented his science,* not the other way round. By overstating how bad the science behind racism is, building it into the dominant definitions of racism, critics have narrowed the target. Only one head of the hydra of racism is named bio-science. Cut it off and the remaining heads are still dangerous, untouched by the definitive demolition.

The 'White Australia' policy

In the next chapter we deal with state racism against Aboriginal Australians in history. Here we deal with the notorious 'White Australia' policy, which restricted immigration into Australia on racial grounds between 1901 and 1958.

To understand this policy, what it was and what drove its architects, we need to go back in time to 1901. Writing in 1923, Myra Willard remarked:

> Because this policy aimed at the preservation of what seemed best to the Australian people, certain things became so closely associated with it that some of the people came to regard them as forming part of the policy. A knowledge of such a conception of the policy makes more intelligible Australia's determination to adhere to it at all costs. 'To my mind,' said Mr Deakin in 1903 . . . 'the White Australia policy covers much more than the preservation of our own people here. It means the multiplication of our own people so that we may defend our country and our policy. It means the maintenance of social conditions under which men and women can live decently. It means equal laws and opportunities for all . . . It means social justice and fair wages.' (Willard 1967, p. 204)

Deakin is often described as an Australian statesman. Many of his aims are recognised as valuable today: self-preservation, decent standards of living, social justice, equity and opportunity. What has changed for the policy's rationale?

We repeat: much changed after 1945. A major lesson was learnt, and rapidly implemented. When we read Willard's account of the arguments of the time in favour of the set of procedures and policies we call the 'White Australia' policy, we can see why there were fears of disharmony, of unassimilated 'alien' groups within, or changes to the ethnic profile of the nation. The fears ranged from cultural issues to the erosion of wage levels.

These fears turned out to be misplaced. Equal laws and opportunities have not been eroded by multiculture. On the contrary, we cannot but wonder at Deakin's inconsistency, holding such values while also maintaining that an entire group of people were not equal, not to be given opportunities—or would not, for that matter, defend the homeland if it were attacked. What we learnt—what all the world learnt—from 1945 was that discrimination of all kinds was dangerous, far more dangerous than any risk posed by a plural and open society like the one Australia now aspires to become.

Understanding the motives of people at the time does not alter the fact that they instituted a state that was racist in this respect. The immigration policy, combined with forced repatriation of citizens who had become classified as undesirable, was a form of ethnic cleansing. There are huge and important differences from, say, Nazi Germany, and we should not ignore these differences. Yet nor should we back away from recognising that Australia at the time of Federation established itself as a racist state. This is not a fact that anyone can deny. It is far better to understand the trajectory that took it from there to where it is today.

In 2004, discussion about Australian history began about precisely this issue. Were the 'White Australia' policy and those who framed it racist? In fact, the question is not quite as easy as it looks. Media theorist and political polemicist Keith Windschuttle (2004) argues that much of what we see as racism in the past has been misread. Windschuttle divides the apparent racists who argued for the policy into different groups. The militant nationalists who wrote for *The Bulletin* were indeed racists, he agrees, as do all other commentators. He concedes that Australia's first prime minister, Edmund Barton, was 'obviously racist' (2004, p. 293) when he said that 'Nothing we can do by cultivation . . . will make some races equal to others'. But he wishes to defend Deakin, whom we quoted above. For him, crucially, Deakin is an 'example of the principle of cultural relativism . . . the very creed now advocated by modern multicultural theorists to justify cultural pluralism' (2004, p. 294). The claim is obviously problematic.

Windschuttle makes some good points. He reminds us that we should not accuse people of being social Darwinists before Darwin actually wrote his books, and that mid-nineteenth century Australia was profoundly multicultural, with 10 per cent of all adult males being Chinese in 1861 (2004, p. 178). His book shows very well the schismogenic tendencies of colonial societies, still struggling to make sense of themselves in quasi-democratic terms when many of those arriving were from cultures with authoritarian histories and attitudes.

Are we wrong, then, to use terms like 'racism' in relation to patterns from the past? By modern standards of judgment, nearly all these founding figures were racists, though for the moment we will accept that Deakin's reasoning was not technically racist. It is useful here to draw on Bateson's (1972) terms: Barton and others showed complementary schismogenesis, built around racist ideas, but Deakin's argument was symmetrical schismogenesis. Yet the two groups combined to support a single policy which undoubtedly *was* racist. And, paradoxically, the fact that there were two such distinct lines of argument for the same policy strengthened rather than weakened it.

We prefer not to over-use the term 'racist' to describe the complex forces at play, then and now. The 'White Australia' policy did discriminate on racial grounds. In this respect, Australia was a racist state, *literally* so. But then, 'racist' has a different connotation nowadays. Windschuttle is right to question this history—up to a point. These people did not live in our time. But there *were* blindspots in their view of things. Later world history bears out the need for careful analysis of what they said about 'races'. The things they did were profoundly schismogenic, even at the time, and they inhibited the growth of Australian multiculture for half a century.

'Would we pass the test?'

The central plank in the set of processes we call the 'White Australia' policy was the infamous dictation test. By 1958, this was a test of 'fifty words or more in any European language, chosen by the officer administering the test' (Palfreeman 1958, p. 43).

The Australian version of the policy itself was inspired by examples from elsewhere in the colonial system:

Borderwork and multicultural Australia

While drafting the Bill, Cabinet had agreed that it would be in the form of the *Natal Act*, and at all stages in the debate, Barton insisted on retaining what he called the 'Education Test' . . . Barton accepted MacEacharn's amendment replacing 'English' by 'any European language directed by the officer'. This change, which implied racial discrimination, was persisted in by Barton as it met the Labor demand for prohibition, and the general objection that the Bill in its original form would discourage European immigrants. By the time the Bill passed to the Senate, the following points had emerged:

1. The Dictation test would not be applied to 'qualified European immigrants'.
2. The Customs officer would select a language with which the intending undesired immigrant was unfamiliar. (Yarwood 1958, p. 24)

In the early years, a few passed the test (33 in 1902), but between 1912 and 1921, none that were forced to sit the test passed it. (Yarwood 1958, pp. 25, 29)

Despite this, non-European migrants were admitted to Australia in these years. Indeed, up to 1916, almost 20 000 non-European migrants were admitted without being required to sit the test at all.

In all this, a number of things emerge clearly. As Palfreeman (1958, p. 43) puts it, the dictation test was 'a method of exclusion because it is only applied to persons who are not eligible under policy to enter Australia. It is intended that they fail the test, and they are tested in a language unknown to them.'

Our question 'Would you pass the test?' is purely rhetorical: once the mechanism was established, no one passed the test because *that was the entire purpose of the procedure.*

Racism explained to our children

Education in the broadest sense is clearly of primary importance as a site where changes in the attitudes of Australian society must be happening if multiculture is taking hold as we believe, where the intellectual basis of racism and schismogenesis must be challenged. How best do we 'explain racism to our children'? A series of books for general readers, published by French academics, offers one model for how to do this. In *Le Racisme expliquée à ma fille* ('Racism Explained to My Daughter', 1998) Tahar Ben Jelloun introduces the dialogue:

While I was demonstrating, on the 22nd of February 1997 with my daughter . . . I had the idea of writing this text. My ten year old daughter had asked me lots of questions. She wanted to know why we were demonstrating, what certain slogans meant, if demonstrating actually achieved anything etc. (Jelloun 1998, p. 5)

The text itself is in question and answer form:

—Say, dad, what's racism?
—Racism is a fairly widespread attitude, common to all societies, even alas to the point of unremarkability in some countries because no one takes any notice of it anymore. It consists of dislike, even contempt, for persons having physical and cultural characteristics different from our own. (1998, p. 7)

The book then gives Jelloun's views on the effects of racism, and attempts to explain why it occurs. Our point is not whether he is always right—for example, he thinks children are not naturally racist (1998, p. 8), racists are more afraid than others (1998, pp. 10–11), and education can create or break down racism (1998, pp. 14–15). More important is the dialogic form, in which these 'facts' are embedded in a relationship that would be familiar in all its complexity to Australian children if this book were used here. This is a father talking to and at a beloved daughter, whose love, confidence and resistance are expressed in her questions and answers. Young Australians would hear a foreign man—French-speaking, Muslim, intellectual—speaking didactically, as a parent. The girl is both challenging him and learning what it is to be the daughter of this Muslim activist: negotiating a relationship and feeling her way into an identity, as young Australians do in different ways.

This multicultural context is part of the complex meanings coming across, part of its content. We believe that something like this quality is vital for anyone 'explaining racism'. Facts are important, but they have to be embedded in a relationship which makes sense.

We see the importance of this strategy on an Australian website, 'Racism. No Way' (www.racismnoway.com.au), a project ('A Guide for Australian Schools'). This runs alongside the school curriculum, yet allows students to step outside the classroom and use their own online skills, as the cybercitizens so many of them are. The text begins

Borderwork and multicultural Australia

with a foreword by Sir William Deane, then Governor-General of Australia, a popular figure who connected strongly with ordinary Australians.

This context is important in realising how effective the otherwise commonplace words would be for children reading it: '*Racism is cruel and unjust*. It cuts deep and lingers long in individual and community members. And it is not a thing of the past—it persists throughout the world and even in our own country.' (p. iii) In this text, 'racism' is displaced from the centre of attention, not ignored but connected to positive core values. As with Jalloun, there is integrity here, along with a subject position (Anglo-Celt) that would be challenging in its own way, for some students. They would read these words against their own background, their own experience of different kinds of father, different kinds of authority, in this way forming a multicultural link with 'Sir William'.

As such texts go, it is hard to fault its wealth of information (including links to other sources). It is what we as teachers would want our students to know. Yet information alone is not enough to animate hearts and minds, to generate deeper understanding, to catalyse change. The text also includes voices of different kinds in its margins. Mark Williams, for instance, is quoted:

There are no words to describe how racism feels . . . How many of our children are trying to learn in a racist classroom? How does a child reach their full potential and exercise their rights as citizens of this country when they are given messages every day that they are worthless human beings? What if it was your son or daughter? What would you do? ('Racism. No Way', p. 10)

Others speak of the distressing experience of racism, students or even teachers who feel disempowered, disabled by racism, victims or advocates for victims. The most severe problems are those of Aboriginal children, followed by people from NESB (non-English speaking backgrounds). These are views and voices that should be heard themselves, not assimilated into a monologue, however well-intentioned. This text avoids that trap, by giving them their place literally in the margins.

We find this unresolved contradiction between different voices a positive quality in this report. Out of such contradictions they can ask:

was Australia racist? Yes, the answer is clear enough: institutionally and systemically cruel and unjust to many, especially to Aboriginal Australians. Is it still a racist country? That is where matters become more complex. No, laws and dominant institutions explicitly reject racism. But yes, racist acts and attitudes are still too common. Multiculture seems stronger, though it still does not fully include Aborigines, the most disadvantaged segment of the population. It coexists with persisting racism, across many sectors of the populace, even within the same individuals.

Is that what we say? What should we tell our children? What else but the truth as we understand it, however complex or inconvenient it sometimes is. And what will they tell us? We should not forget to listen, in our haste to teach.

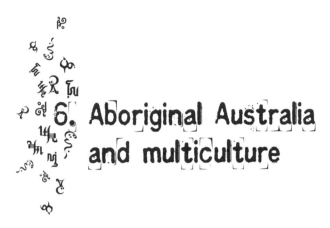

6. Aboriginal Australia and multiculture

Australian Aboriginal people and their cultures challenge Australian multiculture with many paradoxes and complexities. On the one hand, they were present at the outset of the catastrophic colonisation of their lands. Acknowledgment of this has been halting and slow. Indeed, when official multiculturalism belatedly arrived in the 1970s, it did not seem to include Aboriginal people.

In 1967, a referendum was held to change sections 51 and 127 of the Australian Constitution. Prior to 1967, section 51 enabled the Commonwealth government to make 'special laws' about any group of people except 'aboriginal people'; section 127 said that in the 'reckoning of the numbers of the people of the Commonwealth, or of a state . . . aboriginal natives should not be counted' (National Archives 2002). These were racist exemptions. The referendum proposed to remove these exceptions so that Indigenous Australians would be considered in the same way as other communities in Australia. The vote enjoyed widespread support, and the referendum was overwhelmingly passed (a vote of 90.77 per cent in favour) (National Archives 2002; Parliament of Australia 2003).

Now, in the twenty-first century, it is clearer than ever that an Australian multiculture which does not include Aboriginal Australia in its foundations would be so flawed as not to deserve to survive. Australian identity is profoundly dependent on the inextricably interwoven strands of Aboriginality. Untangling these strands is difficult, however. The way Aboriginal Australians are described has been pluralised as they themselves assert a political, social and cultural voice. Terms like 'Aboriginal' have acquired *national* legal status (which we discuss later), just as the ideas of 'Indigeneity' and 'first nations' have *international* significance as part of a worldwide response to ongoing suffering and oppression. Indigenous *regional* conceptions of land and people inform broad designations, such as 'Koori', 'Murri' and 'Nyoongah' populations. These layers remind us that Aboriginal Australia is itself a multiculture, that years of schismogenic policy have not destroyed this, and moreover that this plurality is integral to any future Australian multiculture.

Yet, as the last decade or so has revealed, the way forward is difficult, and there is much to do. The internal layerings of Indigenous Australia mesh—sometimes schismogenically, sometimes cosmogenically—with the rest of the nation. Mainstream Australia needs Aboriginal Australia to give it legitimacy, but how is this to happen in the minds and hearts of non-Aboriginal Australians? And why should Aboriginal people be willing to cooperate after so many years and so much injustice? On which terms? And what should non-Aboriginal Australians offer in their turn?

Our text addresses a double audience, which mirrors a still unresolved tension in multicultural Australia. Many of our readers will not identify as Aboriginal, so we will try to connect our argument with the complex set of feelings, beliefs and aspirations we encounter in our classes, which mirror the wider Australian society. We will also bring in many voices from Aboriginal Australia, as we do in our classes. For too long, Aboriginal people were the objects of others' voices, some well-meaning, others not, but never in dialogue. Today we need more truth about Aboriginal *and* non-Aboriginal culture, and more dialogue in which even partial truths can play a role. Slogans on either side will not help. They often make a complex reality impossible to understand. With this in mind, let us begin with a challenge: Aboriginal Australians who denounce Australian multiculturalism.

Aboriginal Australians against multiculturalism

In 1988, the year of Australia's Bicentenary, the distinguished Aboriginal poet and activist Kath Walker announced that she was changing her name to Oodgeroo Noonuccal: *Noonuccal* the name of her people, *Oodgeroo* meaning 'paper bark' in her language, to signify her profession as writer. She called it her bicentennial gift to the nation, but it clearly expressed anger, repudiating her Anglo-Celtic identity, protesting the way the foundation event was being celebrated.

In the same year, she was honoured in a ceremony by Griffith University in Brisbane, which published the speech she gave on the occasion. In it she begins:

> Blind prejudice to cultural difference is still being indulged in today in this land now known as Australia.
> Australia is still being used as a dumping ground for many other world cultures. Unfortunately, instead of providing a bridge between Aborigines and European Australians, it merely adds to the rift. It must be clearly understood that the Aboriginal nation, yet to be recognized, has little or no enthusiasm for the so-called multicultural society of Australia, for it is unbelievable and a great indictment of European Australians that the Aboriginal people still find themselves once again at the bottom of the Australian socio-economic scale with regard to multiculturalism. (Oodgeroo 1989, p. 1)

This major figure in Aboriginal political life spoke for many Aboriginal people in announcing disillusion with 'the so-called multicultural society of Australia', and she had good reasons. Disadvantage of Aboriginal people continues today, acknowledged by all sides of politics, demonstrated by many expert studies, a scandal now as then. Multiculturalism 'for new arrivals' seemed to compete with the urgent needs of Aboriginal people, giving them an even lower priority.

But Oodgeroo calls this 'so-called' multiculturalism, and she denounces the 'blind prejudice to cultural difference' of Australia. The principles of multiculturalism in practice are central for her. Her problem is only the cynicism of the word as used to legitimate inadequate policy. She has her own vision of multiculture:

> White Australians must accept that it is time for them to be the listeners and the learners. They must accept that Aboriginal and ethnic peoples have their own traditional and contemporary tutors and that they are available here and now. In short, let us learn and understand the logical-grass root cultures of all races in an exchange where all races

stand equal unto each other. Then and only then can there ever be a true multicultural Australia. (1989, p. 2)

This does not deny her earlier position; it describes the conditions of multiculture which are lacking from the 'multiculturalism' she sees. Now she is respectful of other 'tutors' from other ('ethnic') cultures, proposing a careful form of dialogue in which white Australians—now, not forever—listen and learn as they have not done in the past. Yet there is still tension here about multiculturalism that we should not ignore.

Oodgeroo gave this speech in English, at a university, to a mostly white audience. Again it seems a contradiction. Crisp thinkers are fond of criticising contradictions like this in Aboriginal activists, as though contradiction is itself a crime. But what did Oodgeroo mean when she said 'logical-grass root cultures'? 'Logic' and 'grassroots' are normally seen as opposites, or as unrelated. But as readers of this book by now would well understand, grassroots thinking in practice *does* have a logic: tolerant, fuzzy, inclusive, creative.

She goes on to produce more contradictions, all important to our theme. One surprise, from someone so rooted in her own place and people, is her global perspective: 'Grass-root autonomy in every sense, that is, economically, culturally, socially and psychologically, is the only solution to racial harmony. And on this basis it is time to start drawing up a blue print for the global village of the future.' (1989, p. 3) How can she have such an ambitious vision if the plight of her own people in Australia is so dire?

She also praises two kinds of history: Aboriginal ('our ancient history is locked in a cultural memory, which in turn is locked in the alcheringa, or as it has been renamed (incidentally, without our permission) the Dreamtime': 1989, p. 3); and white ('in the meantime, however, we must rely on our white friends to report our history from their perspective': 1989, p. 3). She singles out two authors, Henry Reynolds and Robert Hughes, for special praise, from a movement which, she says, 'will change the very way this country thinks', transforming Australia through 'a new and great Australian philosophy, which has no time or patience for the convenient prejudices of the self-indulgent and illegitimate squattocracy that has been the very meaning of the word Australia for two hundred years'. In the next decade, this historical movement was attacked as anti-white in the so-called 'history wars' which we look at later. It is interesting that this Aboriginal elder sees its function as healing, not war. Oodgeroo goes further than many Aboriginal people would:

> Aboriginal activists will not forge changes in redressing injustices as much as the young white Australian people, who are already outraged at being isolated from the deep wells of wisdom which dot the landscape of an ancient and profound culture. (1989, p. 4)

This statement offers a genuine alliance: a sense of common purpose based on mutual respect, creating an Australian multiculture based on what has gone before, no matter how tough. The rest of this chapter can be seen as a series of footnotes to Oodgeroo's speech. Her experiences of struggle gave her a truly multicultural perspective, committed to diversity and connections.

Aboriginal disadvantage in multicultural Australia

The injustice and oppression faced by Oodgeroo's people in the past are not in doubt. Here we offer a consensus snapshot of the present situation. Dr Bill Jonas, an Aborigine who was Acting Race Discrimination Commissioner, sponsored a 'facts sheet' to lay out some current statistics on Aboriginal and Torres Strait Islanders (1997). Contemplate these figures:

* *Health*: infant mortality is three to five times higher than for non-Aboriginal people; the risk of death for those aged 35–54 is between six and eight times higher than the national average.
* *Education*: only 32 per cent complete schooling compared with a 73 per cent national average.
* *Employment*: the unemployment rate in 1996 was 23 per cent, versus 9 per cent for non-Aboriginal people (about 2.5 times).
* *Housing*: 31 per cent owned a home, versus 71 per cent of all Australian families.
* *Criminal justice*: the imprisonment rate in 1997 was over fourteen times that for non-Indigenous Australians (Jonas 1997, p. 23).

Our students were often shocked by these figures. Many had believed that, in spite of problems in the past, Aboriginal people today were showered with money. Jonas addresses this issue directly. Indigenous people receive no higher social security benefits, he points out. In health they tend to access mainstream programs less; in spite of far higher rates of illness, their funding per head is only 8 per cent higher. In housing, they receive between 9 and 12 per cent less per person. However (our black humour, not Jonas's) they get fourteen times the rate of housing assistance, courtesy of the prison system.

As well as the myth of Aboriginal privilege, there is a myth of Aboriginal irresponsibility—the idea that now Indigenous people are on an equal footing, they are responsible for their present difficulties. This is far too complex an issue to reduce to a fact sheet, and neither we nor Dr Jonas try to do so. On this issue he comments:

> The forcible removal of Indigenous peoples from their lands was supplemented by policies for the removal of children from Indigenous families. The continuing effect of dispossession was recognised by the Royal Commission into Aboriginal Deaths in Custody, which stated: 'Aboriginal people's current circumstances, and the patterns of inter-actions between Aboriginal and non-Aboriginal society, are a direct consequence of their experience of colonialism, and indeed, of the recent past.' (1997, p. 25)

This comment and the issues it raises connect with our own main theme around the construction of an Australian identity and multiculture across time. Culture is inseparable from history and society. The schismogenic culture of earlier Australia underpinned discriminatory laws. A multiculture has to have a material dimension, a basis for fair distribution of resources and benefits. An identity is not just a matter of personal pride, it is also enshrined in laws and constitutions; it is a set of relationships, not just an essence. 'Being Australian' before 1967 implicated *all* individuals in the schismogenic structure that gave them that identity, whatever they thought and felt as persons.

For these reasons, 1967 is a pivotal date. Before Aboriginal Australians were counted in the national population, Australia was *officially* a racist nation. After 1967 there was a change. It is important to insist that, even though the correction in favour of Aboriginal peoples has not been as great as some might think, Australia is no longer officially a racist state. *This matters.* The effects of systemic racism in the past still continue, and racist attitudes can still be found, but it is now an acknowledged multiculture—albeit with work to do.

Why say sorry?

In 1997, Sir Ronald Wilson chaired a Human Rights Commission inquiry into policies of forcible removal of Aboriginal children. Wilson was one of the kind of 'friends' referred to by Oodgeroo, an Anglo-Celtic establishment figure, former Liberal government minister and High Court judge who was committed, for his own reasons, to a more just Australia, and to setting the record straight.

Documentation was difficult and unreliable, and precision impossible, but the report estimated that, from 1910 to 1970, between one in ten and one in three Aboriginal children were forcibly removed from their families by authorised agents. Even the lower figure would be a major human tragedy.

The report also recommended a national 'Sorry Day' to commemorate the tragedies it documented. This seemed a strange recommendation to some, and the day was renamed in 2005. At the time, Prime Minister John Howard refused to offer a public apology on behalf of the Australian people, or to formally institute the proposed 'Sorry Day'. However, many state premiers took up the challenge, issuing formal apologies from their respective parliaments and initiating a 'Sorry Day' in 1998, commemorated annually on 26 May.

In our teaching, we found this episode rich and productive. We asked: why should we say 'sorry'? What does it mean to say sorry? 'Sorry' concerns feelings, 'ours' (and who constitutes the 'we' that says sorry?) and those to whom an apology might be addressed. Feelings are personal, so wouldn't an 'official apology' be phoney? And yet feelings are also a *social* force. Feelings matter, as every advertiser knows. Multiculture without feelings would be empty, even if some feelings (anger or hatred, for instance) seem too strong to be safe.

So what might it mean to say 'sorry', even now that the name of the day has been changed? Here fuzzy logic can help, by seeing two ways of understanding 'sorry'. In a crisp sense, we who *feel* sorry are distinct from those we are sorry *for*, and there is a tight causal link. We must be the cause of the sorrow. It implies a confession of guilt. But it is common in everyday experience to say 'sorry' in a fuzzy sense that does not imply guilt. At funerals, mourners express sorrow without this being understood as a murder confession.

Etymologically, 'sorrow' is akin to 'sore'. We feel pain in others, whether we are the cause or not. 'Sorrow' is first of all the connection around a pain that is understood, felt and shared. 'Sorrow' involves empathy, feeling how others feel, so it is a highly social emotion which creates a social bond. Wilson's report, *Bringing Them Home*, drew on, required and taught empathy.

This makes sense of a subsequent decision about the day itself, and it also helps us see why there is *still* a need to say sorry. When, in April 2005, the decision was taken to rename 'Sorry Day' as the 'National Day of Healing', this did not mean an end to the call for an apology, but that (to take the words of those involved in the decision):

> 'A national day of healing, I believe, is looking more towards the future,' [former Coalition prime minister] Mr [Malcolm] Fraser said . . . Mr Fraser was joined by the author of the acclaimed book *Rabbit Proof Fence*, Doris Pilkington Garimara, outspoken former AFL player Michael Long and Ray Minniecon, Co-chair of [the] National Sorry Day Committee. 'We haven't got rid of Sorry Day,' Mr Minniecon said. 'We haven't moved the goal posts, what we have done is broaden the goal posts . . . This is about helping our people heal.' ('Fraser Says Howard Will Never Say Sorry' 2005).

From this at least, two things are made plain. First, Sorry Day was never about a blame game, but rather was about healing. Second, the need is ongoing. To understand it, we need to see what Wilson's *Bringing Them Home* report (Wilson 1997) taught at the time, *and teaches us still*.

In some ways, the task charged to Wilson in the 1990s involved an impossible brief: acknowledging the strength of feelings of Aboriginal children and parents while being a report for an international agency. It met this dual task by assembling statistics that were hard to obtain, and also quoting extensively from members of the 'stolen generation' themselves.

The stories helped create a *way of seeing* that has profound healing potential. In our view, it matters that the report begins not with judgments or findings, but with a *story:*

So the next thing I remember was that they took us from there and we went to the hospital and I kept asking—because the children were screaming and the little brothers and sisters were just babies of course, and I couldn't move, they were all around me, around my neck and legs, yelling and screaming, I was all upset and I didn't know what to do and I didn't know where we were going, I just thought: well, they're police, they must know what they're doing, I suppose I've got to go with them, they're taking me to see Mum. (Wilson 1997, Confidential submission 318)

Stories communicate emotional as well as literal truths, seeing events from another's point of view. This incident happened in the 1960s. The boy, now a man in his forties, never saw his mother again. The police are not demonised. They told the boy that they were taking him to their mother, and he believed it. It was a lie, but it shows that the police knew well the power of the bond between mother and child, even if they then exploited it. There are no easy villains, but the pain is deep and real.

How ought we respond to this? Prime Minister John Howard responded using crisp logic. He divided himself crisply in two. As an individual, he said, he felt for the families concerned, and regretted their suffering. As prime minister, however, he said he did not believe he or the nation should apologise. Saying sorry, for him, would express guilt and acknowledge liability for compensation claims.

An editorial in the *Australian* on Sorry Day 2004 also showed crisp logic at work: 'Sorry Day, as its name suggested, focuses on white attitudes towards history, but what we need are solutions for the present crisis in which Aboriginal people die 20 years earlier than other Australians' (*Australian* 2004, p. 10). The 'but' is the signal of crisp logic at work. Why must we choose between practical solutions and recognition of pain and injustice? Even in instrumental terms (which are indeed important), education and health programs will not succeed so well without a broader context of reciprocal *care*.

Nor does the idea of Sorry Day focus *only* on white attitudes (therefore ignoring Aboriginal attitudes and experiences). On the contrary, Aboriginal sorrow and grief are also central to Sorry Day. Nor is there a neat division between 'history' and the 'present crisis', as though the past is irrelevant to present problems. On the contrary, a collective act of memory can encompass the shared memories of individuals. In so doing, this creates the potential for inclusion, for multiculture, as a force for change.

Reconciliation

Like Sorry Day, the Reconciliation Project took an institutional form from the recommendations of an inquiry, in this case the 1991 Royal Commission into Aboriginal Deaths in Custody. As with Sorry Day, the 1967 referendum and the emergence of multiculturalism, actions of the state played a crucial role in promoting change, yet in all these cases the reach of the change would have been limited if it had stayed at the level of policy. It is the two in tandem—changes in policies and in hearts and minds—that is the necessary combination to produce a transformation in the culture itself. The Reconciliation movement, we believe, is a change of that scale. Without a reconciliation between Aboriginal Australians and all later comers, Australia and its multi-culture would be forever flawed, incomplete, lacking legitimacy.

The first Reconciliation council, with an Aboriginal chair, Pat Dodson, was set up by the Hawke Labor government with bipartisan support, and continued under the Coalition; however, many projects of the Council, such as a formal treaty and a preamble dealing with Aboriginal people to be included in the Constitution, were opposed by the Coalition government, which emphasised what it called 'practical reconciliation' instead.

This idea of 'practical' action has been a hallmark of Coalition policy since 1996. Yet there has been little 'practical improvement' in the circumstances of Indigenous health, education or other vital statistics in the intervening years. In fact, late in 2004, a report card on Indigenous health suggested a worsening picture. Not only had Indigenous health indicators remained unchanged for the last two decades but, relatively speaking, Australia had sunk to the worst of its class in the world (ABC News, 2004). Given that the Coalition and the ALP have had roughly equal time in government across this period, both stand equally condemned in this respect. And as these govern-ments represent *all* of us, *we* also share in that responsibility.

In 2004, the government abolished the peak Aboriginal body, ATSIC, with bipartisan support. Some in government really do want to improve the realities of Indigenous life in Australia, no matter how belated such a move might appear. If the government does wish to do

something constructive—including this version of practical reconciliation—they will find allies in the Indigenous communities to help
them achieve it.

But 'practical reconciliation' in itself is not new. Pat Dodson,
former Aboriginal chair of the Council for Aboriginal Reconciliation,
for instance, criticised it in its previous forms:

> The complexity of Aboriginal affairs is that we must deal not only with
> abject daily lives, but also with the rights of Indigenous people never
> being acknowledged and agreed. 'Practical reconciliation' denies this
> complexity. Rather, it pulls the wool over middle Australia's eyes that
> the Government is actually doing something. (Dodson 2004a, p. 15)

This shows the fuzzy logic we see as essential in this area. Dodson
rejects a false opposition between 'abject daily lives' and issues of
culture, identity and rights. He pursues a vision of Australian multiculture that has a central place for Aboriginal Australia. In a speech
for National Reconciliation Week, he repeated his vision:

> Our common national journey began with the arrival of Cook and
> Banks in 1770, and we have ambled along for 234 years often hoping
> that one or the other of us would wander off into the scrub. This forlorn
> hope has been recognised by many great people since Cook frightened
> the daylights out of the mob at Botany Bay . . . Many leaders of courage
> and vision have contributed to the dream of reconciled peoples while
> making it clear that justice for Indigenous peoples was integral to the
> achievement of this dream. (Dodson 2004b, p. 15)

His 'typical Aussie' laid-back humour offers an understated version of
200 years of sometimes murderous conflict, yet he also talks of 'many
great people', including unnamed whites and Aboriginal people, in a
single company who have shared 'courage and vision'. Like Oodgeroo,
he has a strong vision of a multicultural Australia.

Dodson argues that the Reconciliation project 'would not
threaten middle Australia': 'It would enable us to take our rightful
place as Australians in an Australia that prides itself upon its democracy, an identity of which we could all be proud, but which is yet,
unfortunately, falsely assumed by most Australians' (Dodson 2004a,
p. 15). The theme plays itself in his profound usage of pronouns. The

first 'us' refers to Aboriginal Australians. 'We' then refers to all Australians, Aboriginal and non-Aboriginal alike, proud in common of an identity that comes from belonging to a democracy. But then the 'we' disappears, as 'most Australians' go their separate way, wanting that identity but not deserving it. Not yet.

The 'history wars'

When academics disagree among themselves, usually no one else takes much notice. But one recent dispute amongst historians spilled over into the media. At its heart was an important issue about the foundations of the nation, particularly the treatment of Aboriginal peoples. The origin of the dispute was a kind of revolution in Australian historiography triggered by one of Australia's leading historians on Indigenous history, Henry Reynolds. His *The Other Side of the Frontier* (1978) turned the historical spotlight on to the Aboriginal side of the 'making of the nation'. Previously, Indigenous Australians were mostly written out of the national story, assumed by default to have basically accepted the takeover of their land, passively dying from diseases or 'breeding out'. Reynolds argued, with considerable evidence, that Aboriginal peoples objected, and resisted, and were killed in large numbers by bullets and other deliberate devices, not just disease. Over two decades, this view has become part of mainstream history.

Two figures disputed this consensus, and turned a scholarly dispute into what could be called a 'war'. In 1996 John Howard declared: 'I do not take the black armband view of history . . . I believe that the balance sheet of Australian history is overwhelmingly positive.' (McIntyre & Clark 2003, p. 3) He wanted to defend the national pride: 'We need no longer be ashamed of our past, of our beginnings.' (McGrath 2004, p. 15) The most prominent academic supporter of Howard's position was a media studies specialist, Keith Windschuttle, whom we looked at briefly in the previous chapter. In 2002 Windschuttle published a polemical work, *The Fabrication of Aboriginal History*.

His introduction gives his basic case. He argues that the current consensus of historians is ideologically motivated, based on bad historical method. In these pages, we are treated to breathtaking attacks on the National Museum of Australia (2002, p. 2), and former

Governor-General Sir William Deane (2002, pp. 7–9). At the very least, it could be said that Windschuttle has courage and confidence. In Tasmania, no one doubts—not even him—that Aboriginal Australians were killed by the military. Windschuttle's focus is not on these deaths, but on the restrained and ethical behaviour of the authorities, as in the circumstances he describes at Risdon Cove:

> The commander in charge was concerned to justify his actions by the threat to his own people. He did not believe he could shoot Aborigines without good justification. The reaction by the colonial authorities, both at the time and for decades afterwards, ranged from regret to repugnance. (2002, p. 26)

We believe that this is a good point, and one which needs to be made. Inevitably mainstream historians have answered back (see, for example, the eminent historian Stuart McIntyre's detailed response on behalf of mainstream history in McIntyre & Clark 2003).

As a first response to this debate, we would say that *even if he were wrong or inconclusive* in his claims, Windschuttle has had a salutary effect on history and on public debate. He has put into circulation a new story about the nation, raising issues that all Australians need to take into account. Let us also say this: there is nothing to fear in such arguments, so long as *they can be supported by evidence,* and *the interpretation makes good sense of the information available.* If he were able to show that the scale and scope of the relentless massacre-story could be softened, all sides of Australian society, including Aboriginal Australians, should welcome it. If the weight of victim-status of Indigenous history could be lightened, and the shame of this history lessened, the chances for the present would be improved for everyone.

But does he really believe there is no need for reconciliation for past histories? Let us trace his account of the so-called 'Black Line' of the 1830s, where a line of whites from east to west moved towards the north, aiming to catch all Aboriginal people in this net and drive them north (2002, pp. 167–69). Let us simply restate *Windschuttle's* own sanitised account, adding nothing. A regime 'drives' people from one place to another through 'intimidation' (2002, p. 169). The success of the process is 'realized' when the victims 'all surrendered' and 'allowed themselves' to be 'shipped off' (2002, p. 169). And this schismogenic picture is supposed to reassure us that things weren't so bad after all!

Other parts of the world have had their own 'culture wars'. These academic contests tell us much about the deep sores in particular societies (they take a different shape in Australia from the United States or Britain). We believe writers like Windschuttle articulate a deep psychological pain in Australian multiculture, a desire that our origins were *other than they were*. One thing that struck us as we read through the succession of legalistic quibbles that he raises in each analysis was a sense of how much he needed to change the story to something more benign—or if that wasn't possible, to get the 'murder numbers' down. His need to show, for instance, that only 120 died in Tasmania, or that not all were murdered, is *psychological* before it is analytical or even political.

Nationally, the damage done to Indigenous communities is undeniable—whether it was intended, whether it was inevitable, whether it came from bullets or bacteria. It is there in *his* record and it is there still as a legacy. Crucially, the damage did not stop in 1847, but continued—as the Wilson report showed—until relatively recent times. In subtle and systemic ways, it continues today. The current situation in which many Indigenous people feel utterly estranged from mainstream society needs to be addressed. Quite simply, Reconciliation and a national apology *are* still on the agenda.

Rethinking histories: Local stories

Not far from the two campuses in Western Sydney where we taught 'Multicultural Australia', there lie the remains (such as they are) of the first 'Native Institutions' in Australia, marked only by a name: 'Blacktown'. Unlike the war memorials we look at later in the book, these sites are largely unacknowledged. They are, nevertheless, important 'white sites'. They were a product of the early settler-culture; they are with us still, even if only in a name that thousands say each day without thinking about what it means.

Blacktown was called 'the Black Town' because of one of the earliest efforts at reconciliation in Australian history: the building of a substantial 'native institution' to cater for educational and health needs for Indigenous Australians. The idea was Governor Macquarie's. A product of the Scottish Enlightenment, Macquarie wanted to turn the penal colony he inherited into a society. This involved him in a range of grandiose building projects. For

Macquarie, even then, the basis for a real society also required a relationship with Aboriginal Australians.

Not that he was the first to think along these lines. Governor Arthur Phillip also sought to build his new settlement in a way that included respect for the Indigenous peoples he encountered when he landed. Robert Hughes reminds us that governors of Australia up until Thomas Brisbane in 1822 insisted on treating Aboriginal people fairly: 'The aim in racial relations was "amity and kindness".' (Hughes 1988, p. 273)

The emphasis on 'amity and kindness', however paternalistic, was usually the well-meaning aim. But as the colony was being established (surviving the ravages of floods in the Hawkesbury, gaps between provisions from overseas and the bootstraps struggle for survival), little more than lip service was paid to these sentiments. In addition, there were other, more terrible edicts passed once conflicts broke out.

Yet let us do justice to what Macquarie did. Macquarie called a meeting in Parramatta of Indigenous and other leaders to discuss ways forward, in particular his idea of a 'native institution'. In modern terms, he set up consultative forums. Dialogue is seen today as basic in managing Indigenous relations, and so it seemed to Macquarie. By this time, the Port Jackson settlement was already over 30 years old. Hostilities in the Darug lands surrounding modern Sydney were giving way to what James Kohen calls coexistence:

> With the end of hostilities in 1816, Aboriginal–Australian relations entered a new phase. Although traditional practices continued in many areas, the Aborigines began to depend more and more on the Europeans to provide them with food, clothing and shelter. With decreasing birth rates and high death rates, the remnants of the clans which once occupied the entire Cumberland Plain began to congregate on a few properties owned by people sympathetic to their situation. The 'Mulgoa Tribe' spent much of the time on the estate of William Cox, while the 'South Creek' tribe were usually camped on Charles Marsden's property near the junction of South Creek and Eastern Creek. (Kohen 1993, p. 68)

Kohen also points out that Macquarie accepted the idea of teaching European methods of farming to Indigenous Australians in 1814 (1993, p. 68).

The Parramatta institution was moved to Blacktown, and the vision got underway. At first, it looked promising. Brook and Kohen (1991) record the initial excitement of the project in the early 1820s, even the use of the official Blacktown postmark emblazoned with stylised images of Indigenous artefacts and symbols (1991, p. 140): 'Nurragingy and those families still living at the farming settlement were excited and full of hope for the future, whilst in the timbered background, the "wild" Aborigines kept a watchful and interested eye on the proceedings' (p. 143). The school was working, the farm established, and by mid-1823 seemed to be well underway.

By 1825, it was all over. A local poet recorded the outcome of the experiment, calling it an 'Ill-fated hamlet', its gardens 'with weeds o'ergrown' (Thompson, quoted in Brook & Kohen 1991, p. 153). A new school replaced the old, but not for Aboriginal children. A new suburb surrounded and displaced the old Black Town, but it too was not for Indigenous Australians. Only the name lived on, recording a white point of view. Where did it all go wrong? Brook and Kohen remark:

> Many pious words were spoken and written relating to the welfare and civilisation of the Aborigines; but after Macquarie's departure, the hierarchy—religious and governmental—showed little genuine concern. Token gestures were much more common. (1991, pp. 152–53)

The gap between rhetoric and real intention is as relevant today as it was then. This name, recording this history, arouses ambiguous feelings. There was not a massacre here, but we can equally well feel sorry for this brief, doomed experiment. It is a reminder again that to be sorry does not always imply that people from Australia's past were better or worse than we are today.

A time capsule

Tranby House is a tourist attraction in Perth, which John visited in 1990. It is a time capsule from the early days of the Swan River colony.

The house itself is elegant and spacious, built by Joseph Hardey (a lay Methodist minister, according to a pamphlet) only a few years after 1829, when the colony was founded. We note the large verandahs in this 'bungalow' design, taken from the Indian colony and well adapted to the hot Australian sun.

Inside, an old diary from 1834 has an entry for 28 October that has its own chill factor:

> Encounter with the natives down at the Murray river where about 25 or 30 of the men was killed, one woman and several children it has been a shocking slaughter I fear more so than was needed.

This was probably the Battle of Pinjarra. The lay preacher, Joseph Hardey, may himself have been the witness recording this. What, in any case, was the writer of these words thinking? Clearly, that it was 'shocking', as we would today. But *why* were some deaths 'needed', in his view?

And what do we think now, looking at these traces of a violent past? Wouldn't sorry be the *least* we might feel?

Aboriginal identities

We mentioned at the beginning of this chapter that legal issues of definition of Indigeneity have emerged over time. Thus far in this chapter, we having been calling people 'Aboriginal' or 'Indigenous' as though that were a natural, uncontentious and self-evident category. But the reality is more complex. We take up the current Commonwealth government definition of Aboriginality—in some respects a strange definition, although it works so well in practice. A person is Aboriginal if they meet all of three criteria: that they are of Aboriginal descent; that they identify as Aboriginal; and that their community recognises them as Aboriginal.

This definition works well precisely because it is fuzzy, not stating how much Aboriginal descent is enough. Instead of tightening the definitional screw, as was done in the past, the definition adds two other criteria, which act together to provide a workable definition. This fuzziness has been criticised by people who claim it allows anyone to be Aboriginal just by saying so, but the definition clearly rules that out. This definition has allowed the number of Indigenous Australians to expand greatly over the past decades, often by reclassification, not reproduction. But this is a merit of the definition: that it is dynamic and open. Many 'new Aborigines' are stolen generation children, rediscovering the identity that was 'stolen' from them, able to correct some of the effects of this now discredited policy.

This definition emerged after 200 years of struggle, mediated through the crisp, binary categories of a schismogenic, delusional monoculture. The delusion began by dividing the population into two races, each supposed to be pure, homogenous and unchanging. All Indigenous people were seen as the same, culturally, socially, racially and finally legally. But this simplistic view had to grapple with a far more complex reality which quickly emerged, one that included Aboriginal difference *and* Indigenous people's competence (if given a chance). It also included a variety of relationships, including sexual relationships. The binary view, of course, knew that sexual relations would happen. It knew how to disapprove and punish, but not control, them, and conceptually it could not cope with impurity on such a scale. The anxiety generated such complexity that Aboriginal academic Marcia Langton claims there were at least 67 definitions of Aboriginal people. This reflected:

> not only Anglo-Australian legal and administrative obsession, even fixation, with Aboriginal people, but also the uncertainty, confusion and constant search for the appropriate characterisation: 'full-blood', 'half-caste', 'quadroon', 'octaroon', such and such an 'admixture of blood', 'a native of Australia', 'a native of an admixture of blood not less than half Aboriginal', and so on . . .
>
> This fixation on classification reflects the extraordinary intensification of colonial administration of Aboriginal affairs since 1788 to the present. Elaborate systems of control aimed, until recently, at exterminating one kind of 'Aboriginality' and replacing it with a sanitised version acceptable to the Anglo invaders and immigrants. Perhaps Aboriginal affairs is the longest 'race experiment' in history? (Langton 1993, pp. 28–29)

This is the taxonomy that the current Commonwealth definition abandons. This new dispensation at least leaves 'Aboriginality' a space, not a set of boxes. We can see some of the tensions and complexities of this space from some comments by Aboriginal staff of the Centre for Aboriginal Studies at Curtin University in Perth. Darlene Oxenham reports her early experience:

> As I got older I also realized that there was a difference between traditional people and urban people or between 'full bloods' and 'half

castes'. From the gaze of non-Indigenous people, the assumption was that the traditional ('full blood') people were the 'real' Aboriginal people, and the rest of us weren't . . . Urban ('half caste') people like me were seen as being both acceptable and unacceptable. Acceptable, because we were closer (in lifestyle) to 'whites'. But this only lasted so long as we were 'good'. As soon as 'half caste' people got into trouble or were in conflict with someone they were once again a 'boong'—as this explained your 'badness'. (Oxenham et al. 1999, p. 30)

She reports here how identity is constructed from outside, and the bewildering, schismatic shifts in its use by these hostile, powerful white others. Young Darlene at one moment was not 'really' Aboriginal, and so not valued, and at another she was not valued, so she was 'Aboriginal'. We notice her use of quotation marks around the labels that surrounded her, part of her consciousness of herself which she has internalised yet which still feels alien to her. This split consciousness is not something that makes her powerless, but a complex level of awareness that she has achieved—one many whites never reach.

Pat Dudgeon, in the same book, argues for a richer, more diverse (in our terms, multicultural) space that Indigenous people also need:

I think there needs to be in-depth discussion about what identity means for all of us (blackfellas, that is). I believe that we should *not* try to come to some accord or consensus about our different conclusions: I think we should relish and honour our different opinions, as we should appreciate our rich and broad differences as individuals and groups who make up Indigenous Australia. (Oxenham et al. 1999, p. 39, her emphasis)

Multiculture empowers contemporary Indigenous people like Pat Dudgeon, because she can explore issues of identity in ways that were once unimaginable. This is the multiculture that supports and is supported by Indigenous Australia. To be sure, there remains a complex relation with the dominant culture, as Pat Dudgeon insists: 'I also believe that this needs to be a dialogue led exclusively by Aboriginal people, because non-Aboriginals do not help our confusion.' (1999, p. 42) This contradiction, like the contradictions in Oodgeroo's text, expresses a multicultural wisdom. Its different parts do not cancel each other out.

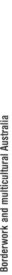

White blackfellas?

In 2004, Germaine Greer, an overseas Australian and celebrated feminist from former times, published *Whitefella Jump Up: The Shortest Way to Nationhood*. Her 'shortest way' is for whites to respect and value Aboriginal life and culture, and place Aboriginal identity at the centre of Australian identity, like Indigenous people themselves.

The book was controversial and provoked much discussion. The response from Aboriginal people was sometimes positive (Lillian Holt wrote: 'I wanted to clap every word she uttered') but mostly not: Tony Birch saw her as just another white person appropriating Aboriginality. Aboriginal writer Anita Heiss (2004, p. 10) was in between:

> Greer's work made me smile at times because it was so absurd, but it also haunted me. Why? Because my life as an articulate, educated, grass-roots urban blackfella, like that of many of my contemporaries, is already a daily exercise in helping my 'other' (whitefellas) to understand the diversity of the Aboriginal experience, and that's chore enough. I can't imagine what life would be like if I have to start teaching them what it means to be a whitefella being a blackfella!

Is Greer out of touch? Or did she need to be outside to see and say something important?

Living Aboriginal culture

Since 1967, Indigenous Australians have *officially* been allowed to contribute to Australian culture *as Australians*, and they have done it spectacularly well. Already, in 1990, Bob pointed to 'an Aboriginal cultural renaissance, a flowering of achievement that has already made its mark in Australian cultural life' (Hodge & Mishra 1990). We now look at three instances where that success story has continued, in ways that contribute directly to the co-construction of a new Australian identity.

First, and in pride of place, is Aboriginal art. In 1971, only four years after the referendum vote, a young white art teacher, Geoffrey Bardon, began working closely with Aboriginal people in Papunya, a community in the Northern Territory. His role was as catalyst, not teacher. He offered modern art materials, canvases and acrylic paints

Borderwork and multicultural Australia

to community elders, who proceeded to adapt the language and themes of their traditional art to create a new form of art, traditional in its themes, postmodern in the surfaces it created: Aboriginal multiculture.

From this small beginning, this form of art is recognised around the world to a degree not achieved by any earlier Australian artist. In the 1960s, Australians who could not paint could still take pride in the art of Sidney Nolan, and its minor but significant place in world art. Now Australians who are not Aboriginal can take a similar pride in the achievements of Aboriginal art, a major contribution to world art.

One of the strengths of this art form is its capacity to represent relations between people and land, and to construct complex identities from local to national and beyond. In a 1999 popular competition for a new flag for Australia as republic, Aboriginal motifs dominated. We expect that when Australia becomes a republic and adopts a new flag to signify its identity, the flag design will be based on the Aboriginal visual language.

Already in the 1980s, when architects and politicians gathered to design the new Parliament House, consciousness of Aboriginal origins was built in. 'Capitol Hill' was recognised as being historically important to Aboriginal people, as well as a natural site, and the pathway to the building included an Aboriginal design by Michael Tjakamarra Nelson, a Western Desert artist.

The image is a mosaic, formed of some 100 000 granite pieces: not an Aboriginal art form but corresponding to the dot form that has become its signature. The giant image is set in a pool, representing the ocean around Australia, with the mosaic an image of Australia itself, the continent and nation constructed through the lenses of Aboriginal forms.

The mosaic itself has a red centre surrounded by four circles of dots, surrounded by a further five non-geometric circles: the Aboriginal signifier of a very important sacred place, fire–water–cave–home. This is the Aboriginal translation of 'parliament', a meeting place of different groups, which also conceives that meeting place as sacred, a concept that the present Australian parliament sorely needs. Twelve paths converge on this centre—different groups of kangaroo, wallaby and goanna ancestors—signifying that this is a multicultural meeting place. Again, this is a modern meaning which can easily and richly be signified in Aboriginal art. At the same time, details are coded into

Before Parliament House. Photgraph by John O'Carroll

the image whose meaning is not public, as is the way of Aboriginal culture. One such meaning, we guess, may be the identity of the red dot at the centre, surely an Aboriginal sacred place—perhaps Uluru, the great red monolith at the geographical heart of Australia, close to Tjakamarra Nelson's Warlpiri homelands.

Uluru is our second instance of Aboriginal success. Uluru now symbolises Australia to the world. Its history also has its messages. Robert Langton's history of Uluru states: 'The survival of Aboriginal owners of Uluru was discovered by government agencies in November 1971.' (1989, p. 93) 'Discovered'? Such government ignorance was typical then, but ignorance and indifference did not continue for long. Elders emerged with a voice which was heard, heralding a period of struggle which led, in 1983, to the handover of the rock to its Aboriginal custodians, an experiment in joint management. Many territorians predicted it would be a financial disaster, destroying the tourism industry in the process. In 2004, Anangu Tours, the Aboriginal-owned tourist company running Uluru, was inducted into the Australian Tourism Hall of Fame. In the same year, it was the only Australian winner in the International Legacy Tourism awards. Some disaster!

Our third instance concerns the Indigenous 'circle of justice' approach to habitual offenders, pioneered in Nowra. Aboriginal people are hugely over-represented in the justice system, so this approach—which mixes traditions, notably Indigenous Christian traditions of dialogism and restoration—is highly relevant for them. Pearlman (2004) describes one illustrative case, a persistent offender with 40 convictions by the age of 23. Instead of another entry into the old vicious cycle of punishment and reoffence, this man faced a 'justice circle'. The circle contained three local elders of his community, plus two victims and white officers of the law.

The circle is dialogic. Victims and offender hear each other and are heard. Aboriginal elders speak on behalf of the community, and their judgments are respected by the magistrate who is present. The offender sums up his response:

> Just the fact you're looking into their eyes and they care and you know they care and you don't want to hurt them or let them down.
>
> I would have preferred a [circle] court any day. If I would have gone to a normal court, I would have wanted to go to jail. To escape my problems and then get out scot-free. It's not as much pressure. But this is what I need: help and pressure at the same time. (Pearlman 2004, p. 17)

The circle is practical multiculture. Its rulings mix white and Aboriginal law, suspending some sentences, adding other requirements, including the oversight of the Aboriginal elders. Justice circles are no instant fix for deep-seated problems. But they show the relevance of a multiculture built on Aboriginal co-creation and participation.

This is the originality of multiculture. The fact that it took so long to be allowed to happen should not stop us applauding its emergence.

7. Imagining Islam

We mention Islam many times in this book, because since 2001 Islam has been at the forefront of discussions about racism and multicultural Australia. Studies of racism by HREOC now focus on two groups especially exposed to racism. Aboriginal Australians are the single group most discriminated against, now as they have been since settlement. As we said in the last chapter, they have a special role in Australian multiculture: constructive, intrinsic, complex. Other groups have followed another pattern. In Australia since 1900, successive groups have been caught in the spotlight as the problem, symbol of the dangers posed by a new culture, by cultural diversity itself. As a sign of how quickly things change, Stephen Castles and his collaborators subtitled their important mid-1990s book, *The Persistence of Racism in Multicultural Australia*, but gave 'Islam' and 'Arab' only one entry each in the index. Using this index as guide, the 'crisis' of Australian multiculturalism then concerned 'Asians' and 'Aboriginals'. Now the spotlight is on Muslim Australians, who feel the heat of Australian multiculture in the making. In this chapter we look specifically at them, as the complex culture that Australians today most need to know about.

In practice, Islamic Australia is old, diverse and a crucial element of the multiculture. Yet, for many, Islamic Australia arrived late to multicultural Australia—and multicultural Australia only started in the 1970s, didn't it? We have already challenged this mythic history, which here as elsewhere has been damaging, as well as poor history. Australia has always been a multiculture. Similarly, the Islam depicted in the media is a much reduced version of the extraordinary realities that lie beyond these commentators' front doors, in Australia as in the rest of the world.

In dealing with Islamic Australia, we confront the inadequacy of 'race' to understand the situation now and in the past. In the first place, 'Islam' is a religion, not a culture or a race, though it does have connections with cultures and races: it is in practice multicultural and multi-ethnic. The complex connections between categories make nonsense of common reductive stereotypes, as in the dominant media image of Muslims as Middle Eastern. This collapse of categories of race, culture and religion comes up against important differences between 'Arab', 'Indonesian' and many other peoples and cultures of the Muslim world. All complexity and diversity is reduced to a stereotype of stereotypes of a Muslim who now, of course, is also a terrorist.

All this gives a special value to looking at Islamic Australia to see schismogenesis at work. Islam is a major world religion represented in all nations, which is treated as though it were a race and subjected to racist attacks. As we saw in Chapter 3, religious persecution proved so disastrous to emerging European nations that tolerance had to be invented to allow civilised social life. Then and now, Christianity is divided between different groups, defined by differences of doctrine which seem barely comprehensible to outsiders, yet are matters of life and death to believers. The same is true of Islam, which has different sects, whose differences are usually invisible to outsiders. Islam is not a single race or culture: it is in some respects not even the same religion.

This is the complexity that is so badly managed by the kind of borderwork we described in Chapters 1 and 2. The crisp categories and linear thinking unleashed by such traumatic events as September 11 are the underlying cause of what has been truly disastrous in the 'post-September world'. Islam's huge footprint in the world today brings with it connections that Australia cannot ignore: the benefits or necessities of being a multiculture in order to thrive in a global world.

A tale of two jihadis

In the course of the war in Afghanistan in 2001, the *Daily Telegraph* ran a succession of headline stories on one young *jihadi* captured by

US soldiers. David Hicks, an Anglo-Australian, had joined the fight in Afghanistan. This justified a *Telegraph* headline, 'Traitor's Poem':

> His dream for at least three years was to wage war with his Muslim "brothers" in the Middle East. Australian traitor David Hicks bragged proudly to his family and friends about becoming a warrior for Islam in a war of terror against the West. He shared his twisted vision in poems to his family, bragging about the supremacy of Islam and itching to travel to the Middle East. (Heggen et al. 2001, p. 1)

We note a number of things from this passage. First, it is clearly biased against Hicks. It makes use of the same sorts of tricks of discourse that we looked at in Chapter 3. A key word that indicates discourse-position is 'traitor'. It is *emotive*, not legal; Hicks was not fighting for a country at war with Australia, so he was *not* a 'traitor'. Note too this paradox, a sign of a far from equilibrium situation: 'Australian' as linked to 'traitor' makes him *worse*, not better. It cancels and inverts the positive value of his nationality. His vision is 'twisted', and the war he fought in has another loaded word attached, 'terror', in case we did not know what to think about him.

This much is fairly obvious. Less obvious is the way that the passage creates a positive value for Australians purely by negating the enemy. The philosopher Charles Taylor (1992) points out that the West struggles to name the positive moral values on which it is based. In their absence, a 'whole class of modern positions descends from the radical Enlightenment. Because their moral sources are unavowable, they are mainly invoked in polemic. Their principal words of power are denunciatory.' (1992, p. 339)

This is a profound insight. It tells us that, in our modern societies, we struggle to value affirming cosmogenic views. Denunciation is far easier. It offers the crisp, binary logic of schismogenesis we have seen before. In a society that struggles to say what it stands for, 'our' position can be expressed purely by negatives. 'We' are not Islamic extremists, not warriors, not braggarts, not twisted, etc., so we must be good.

Hicks went on to languish on the American base at Guantanamo Bay in Cuba. His crime, 'terrorism', was created retrospectively by the events of September 11. For many months, the Australian government made no effort to assist him, despite the fact he was being held without charge in the legal limbo-land created by the White House between the US civil system and the Geneva Convention. Yet his very existence does us all this service: he reminds us that Islam is a faith and its doors are open to all. It is a faith, not a race or geography or culture.

He also reminds us that the causes that attract our youth are many and varied, and sometimes, every now and then, one of us makes a mistake. 'I'm fed up with Westerners,' declared Ishar ul-Haque. Ul-Haque, who had 'just failed his second year of medicine at the University of NSW', went overseas to fight in Kashmir (Connolly & Kennedy, 2004, p. 1). Returning disillusioned with this struggle, he took up his studies again and gained 'the respect of teachers and students' (Connolly & Kennedy, 2004, p. 1). Despite the fact that he assisted police in their inquiries, that even 'the Crown conceded that . . . ul-Haque was not planning any terrorist act on Australian soil', he faced up to 25 years' gaol 'under the new terrorism laws of training with a banned organisation' (Connolly & Kennedy, 2004, p. 1). While the trial proceeded, ul-Haque was refused bail, and 'housed in solitary confinement at the maximum security Goulburn Gaol' (Connolly & Kennedy 2004, p. 4).

These two stories show schismogenesis at work in far from equilibrium situations, marked by a strange logic. Time is warped, so that a lawful action in the past becomes a serious crime in the present. Space folds on itself, so that what 'terrorists' do in America turns Hicks from a freedom fighter in Bosnia (on the US side) and Afghanistan (a former US ally) into a criminal, and ul-Haque's minor adventure becomes a major crime. It is not 'racism', because Hicks' race is effortlessly erased. 'Racism' like this is not only a problem for its victims; it is also the signal of a situation far from equilibrium, in which normal causality breaks down, with consequences for all of us.

September 11: The day the world changed?

It is only a time, only a date. Yet 'September 11' (or *9/11* as Americans call it, echoing their police emergency number) is a powerful signi-fier—so powerful that one only has to name it for a range of other meanings to come into play: the war on terror; the United States and the Middle East; the War in Iraq; the United Nations; Al Qaeda; *the day the world changed*. The last of these associations is the most charged. We know it to be so because we were repeatedly told that this was what had happened. In the week the events took place, two major Australian newspapers, the *Australian* ('The Day the World Changed') (2004, p. 1) and the *Sydney Morning Herald* ('8.45 a.m. September 11, 2001, the Moment the World Changed') (Summers 2004, p. 23) both ran special stories on the same theme.

The idea that life changed utterly because of an event like this is, of course, preposterous. The tsunami of December 2004 caused over 200 000 deaths—far more significant in terms of loss of life and anguish, as a human catastrophe. Yet there is a difference in the way we perceive natural disasters and the way we perceived an event like September 11. Given its location, in a major centre of the planet's sole superpower, the events of September 11, 2001 seem to have changed much.

At first, it didn't *feel* like that. Life went on. But the sense that something had changed pervaded the media-sphere, everyday conversation about the world, and particular communities victimised by a backlash against Islam. Under the grim shadow, people went back to work, changed jobs, and carried on much as usual. We only slowly came to appreciate the gap between the ordinariness of our everyday life and this new crisis, involving large amounts of national and international taxpayer funding, meetings of world leaders and heated debates. Far from the media reflecting our world back to us, they gave us a distorted kaleidoscope of caricatures and malevolence that had no relevance to our everyday lives.

Yet something *had* changed. This event took place in a super-charged, far from equilibrium *semiosphere*, an interconnected web of meanings that affects meaning-making at every level. Because this web is global, it had massive effects everywhere. In the United States it rescued the ailing presidency of George W. Bush, and gave him a second term. In Australia it had complex effects. Initially it seemed just to boost schismogenesis, but the resilience of Australia's multi-culture seems to have withstood this assault to some degree. But that is a part of the story that we will defer till later.

At the global level, the story seemed to fit a primal European narrative, drawn from the medieval European history of the 'Crusades', constructed as a war of Christianity against pagan Islam, Good versus Evil (though the reality of the 'Crusades' was of course very different). In modern times, this became the 'clash of civilisations' thesis of the political scientist Samuel Huntington, who declared that the world now faced an ultimate struggle of cultures, the West versus Islam. In this scenario, Islam is set up as the ultimate enemy faced by a West which needs above all to be one. This narrative affected Australian political thought, even though Islam in Australia has never posed any realistic threat. As geopolitical analysis, it is not much better, since the 'War on Terror' had to bring Islamic nations on side.

Yet in many parts of the world, including Australia, this narrative gives rise to the classic binary structures of schismogenesis we looked at in Chapter 5, which mark a group as homogenous and different, and then treat it in a particular way. When Islam became important as difference, a self-evident division of non-Muslims ('us') and Muslims ('them') occurred. Then 'they' were divided into 'good' Muslims (whether client states in the Middle East, or Western-ised, respectful, secular individuals within Australia) and 'bad' ('rogue states'; or, inside Australia, fundamentalists, fanatics, etc.). But crisp logic can't cope easily with such complexity in far from equilibrium conditions, and this second difference was unstable, often collapsing back into a belief that 'they' are all the same, or impossible to tell apart.

We discussed René Girard's exploration of symmetrical schismogenesis in Chapter 5. He applied this analysis directly to the September 11 case. Asking 'by the knowledge that they had of the United States, by their training, were not the authors of the attack at least somewhat American?', he argued (2001, 2002) that those who attacked the US World Trade Center should be seen as part of a crisis of *sameness*, which he called 'mimetic contagion'. By **mimetic**, Girard means the terrorists were uncomfortably *like* what they claimed to despise. Perhaps, too, Bush's strong support from the 'Christian Right' in the war and in the 2004 presidential elections had a fundamentalist quality that is symmetrical with aspects of the supposedly different foe.

Girard does not make another point, but we make it on his behalf. Of the world's great religions, none are so similar as Islam and Christianity, with their common origins in Judaism. In terms of shared stories and values, these two great monotheistic religions were neighbours at birth. Our students (like most Australians) are regularly surprised to find that Jesus has a major role in the Koran. Few are so ferocious in battle as those who see each other as rivals.

Yet this commonality can also be a basis for deeper understanding and common purpose, between Christian and Islamic multicultures in a multicultural Australia. 'September 11' is a challenge to multiculture, but it does not have to be destructive. It could equally remind Australians of their collective achievements (even those not on the official record), on who we are becoming and would like to become. Multiculture does not prevent racism; nor does it inoculate against cultural amnesia. 'Australia', an imagined community among others, can be rethought, refocused and re-dreamed. It is up to all Australians to reimagine who we could and should be after September 11.

Life after death

There was, of course, an impact on Australian Muslims arising from September 11, and the bombings in Bali of October 2002 brought the issues closer to home. HREOC (2004) commissioned a study which found that the majority of Muslim participants in it had experienced prejudice because of their race or religion, made worse by these high-profile media events. The provocations ranged from 'offensive remarks about race or religion to physical violence' (2004, p. 2).

But this review was only part of the HREOC brief. HREOC also set up national consultations, group discussions with 1423 Arab and Muslim Australians, not only to find experiences of discrimination but also to tap the ways people were already trying to do something about it, and what other actions they recommended. As well, HREOC carried out an audit of 100 local and state government groups and community organisations to get an overview of existing strategies, and to identify gaps. This was a proactive, coordinated response, not just listing the wrongs suffered by helpless victims. It relied on and activated an existing multiculture, underpinning an effective network organisation. This aspect of the inquiry is new. It did not happen in 1991, and it would have been unthinkable in earlier periods. Something has changed, a structure that can turn negatives into positives.

In Chapter 2, we saw how 'liberal' Australians were mobilised by the asylum issue, which put multiculture back on the agenda. 'Treat Asylum Seekers with Compassion—Not Cynicism' headlined an opinion piece by Claudia Karvan, a well-known actress who revealed in the article that she was of Greek descent:

What I want is a country I can be proud of. I want to open up the newspaper in the morning and not be faced with articles that describe the locking up of people who have fled their homeland in fear for their lives. (Karvan 2002, p. 15)

After the *Tampa* refugees had survived the pains of incarceration, many were accepted as genuine refugees, and became good-news stories. A report on Mohammed Asif, for instance, a member of the minority Hazara ethnic group who fled the Taliban in Afghanistan, pictured him smiling and employed, but still grieving for his wife and child (Berry & Walker 2004, p. 37). Another story contrasted New Zealand's treatment of *Tampa* refugees pointedly, under the headline 'Life after *Tampa*: Australia's Castaways are Happier to Call New Zealand Home'. New Zealand gave its intake of 350 refugees full permanent residency rights, unlike Australia. Carol White, principal of a school which took 45 refugee children, is quoted talking about their prospects:

Today the *Tampa* boys are passionate about their education. 'Many of them are extremely astute,' says Ms White. 'They have a political sense, they take a big interest in world news. I hope a lot of them will stay here because they've had opportunities which will make them good leaders ... in due time the community is going to reap a very rich reward.' (Banham 2003a, p. 1)

In 2004, a film was made about the asylum issue. *Letters to Ali* follows a middle-class family who travel 6000 kilometres from Victoria to Port Hedland to visit 'Ali', a refugee incarcerated there. This shows the response of 'tolerant', middle-class Australia, which we see as an emerging force brought into the light by the controversy. Their long, gruelling journey was not just 'patronising tolerance', it was hard work.

But the angle of the film had its own message. The filmmakers, Clara Law and Eddie Fong, were Chinese now living in Australia, 'Chinese Australians':

It was clear to her [Law] that Ali's story should be told from an immigrant's perspective. 'One of the reasons why I felt so strongly about this was that I could project myself into Ali's situation and realise what it might have felt like,' she says. Law moved to Australia from Hong Kong in 1996.

'I understand what it is like not to have your family here, or friends, or to be unable to speak the language.' (Zion 2004, p. 17)

For Karvan and Law, living a multiculture has given them a vision of what Australia could and should be like, but did not seem to be in the aftermath of September 11 and the *Tampa* crisis. Neither ignores the problem of paranoia and racism, and neither speaks as a confident member of a mainstream majority. However, what they are is also significant: multicultural citizens who are not swayed by the post-September 11 rhetoric, who know that that rhetoric is more dangerous than terrorist bombs, or occasional boatloads of desperate refugees.

Globalisation: Problem or solution?

We have seen repeatedly in this book that the word 'globalisation' has many negative connotations, like cultural homogenisation, outsourcing and the weakening of local communities. Yet one aspect of it is the new capacity Australian audiences have to receive international media, and it is important to remember such things when considering the nature of a 'globalised' world.

In 2003, under the heading of 'Salamat', Morris (2003, p. 25) reported that Sydney audiences could now tune in to the 'sultry voice' of Lebanon's Rima Njeim. Njeim is estimated to have been reaching 'nearly 50,000' listeners a day with her specially formatted drive-time program (2003, p. 25).

Callers could ring from Australia. Morris (2003, p. 25) cites Njeim herself in order to make the point about interconnection: 'I get children calling from Sydney to speak to their grandparents, or family members wishing their mothers a Happy Mother's Day.'

Is this so bad?

Sex in the suburbs: A problem for multiculturalists

In 2002, the New South Wales media were dominated by the 'Lebanese rape case', as were our class discussions. This case received massive publicity because it involved a 'Lebanese gang' who brutally raped a 'white' girl. The judge in the case (an Anglo male) set new standards of severity in the sentence he awarded: 53 years for the leader of the gang, the sentences to be served consecutively. (The sentence was reduced on appeal in mid 2005.) The severity was widely applauded in the community, encouraged by media who were unanimous in how they covered the case.

The case raised many important issues. One is the problem of 'reverse' or 'minority racism', which is embedded here in a more common structure of community racism. This, as we saw in Chapter 3, is a *tolerance paradox*, in which the issue of 'tolerating the intolerable' comes to the fore. Advocates of multiculturalism often focus on the way the media 'construct' these gangs, so that the media beat-up is somehow the only problem. Beat-ups happen, in this case as in many others. But our students rightly would not let us get away with this as the only response. They showed us how contentious were the issues, how polarising, how real were their feelings.

Our classes divided into three groups. For one group, comprising mainly women, gender issues overwhelmed issues of ethnicity. They felt that 53 years was about right for a rapist, whatever his ethnicity (preferably with castration added). A smaller group, men, mainly of Arab (but not necessarily Islamic) background, felt that the sentence was a judgment by an Anglo-Saxon judge on the entire Lebanese community. Another group of men and women felt so confused by the case and its coverage that they did not know what to think. At once repelled by the crime, suspicious of the police, and sceptical of the coverage, they felt justice should somehow be done, but they could see no way of assuring that.

We offer no formula for resolving these issues, or deciding what the penalty should have been. Instead, we use a three-body analysis to help to make the irreducible complexity more thinkable. Multiculturalism is normally seen as distinct from issues of gender and class, which are either ignored or *added on* as further complications. We see a multiculture as irreducibly formed by ethnicity, gender and class, each interacting with and formed by the others, none comprehensible on its own.

We began with social class, though it was not considered in media discussions of the case. One factor mentioned by the judge was that the group had mobile phones. He cited this as evidence of how calculating they were. They were also markers of class in this context, showing their middle-class status, whose actions betrayed a class they did not truly belong to, just as David Hicks' Australianness made his 'betrayal' worse. As Girard noted, greater fury is aroused against someone who is almost but not quite the same.

What of racism? Did it play a role? The judge explicitly ruled it out. But we thought it likely that 'race' did play a role (and maybe in more ways than one). The judge would naturally deny racial prejudice, because it could form grounds of appeal. He also denied he was influenced by media discussions. Again, we doubt him. The popularity of the judgment showed that he was indeed in tune with the collective mind of the populace, expressed through and shaped by the media.

And gender? Did it play a role? Again, we thought so. The extremely punitive sentences show a symbolic severity. As our feminist women students said, this severity appears to express value for women, taking hate crimes against a woman seriously. But the same judge did not hand out such penalties in rape cases where ethnicity was not involved. The actions of the gang were driven by a mix of race, gender and sexuality within a class framework. This structure collided with a mix of the same qualities in the outside community, and the justice system responded in these terms to what was perceived as a crisis in the community. The judge filled a role in a mythic narrative, as the heroic rescuer of a maiden violated by monsters. This myth and this role are built into his Anglo-Celtic culture. In this, as in many other instances, gender is part of culture.

These factors are not constant or predictable. If the roles are reversed, we sometimes find double standards. Witness this account of an attack in the early 1990s:

> My daughter was marrying and we were celebrating and preparing to go to the reception hall. In the neighbourhood there are a few 15–17 year olds—Anglo Saxons—who are violent and create problems for us all the time. That night they came close to the house and started throwing eggs on the bridegroom and bride . . . We could not bear this which was in addition to shouting 'Wogs', 'Bloody Lebanese' and 'Go Home' and damaging the car. We called the police which know all the kids but nothing was done. (HREOC 1991, p. 423)

This incident was reported as an instance of race hatred, but sexuality and gender were clearly issues as well. The victims celebrated an event with the regulation of sexuality at its centre. The youths are so obviously boys ('being boys') that their gender is not even given. This time the authority figures do not overreact—in fact, they hardly react at all. The complainants suspect complicity between police and perpetrators, in contrast to the relation between the judge and the Lebanese gang.

The veil worn by many Muslim women has become a hot topic of debate, which illustrates for us the inseparability of issues of gender and culture. Hage (1998) quotes an interview with a white woman who tore the veil from a Muslim woman. He saw this incident in terms of power, the violation of the Muslim woman's space, as it surely is. Yet it is also a core gender issue, for the women of both cultures. This is symmetrical schismogenesis, woman against woman, but no less fierce for that fact. The veil is a visible symbol of religion and culture, in Australia and in the world (witness the controversy sparked off by the French government decision to ban the veil in French public schools). It is very easy to see it in purely religious terms, as a singular issue. But, as is often the case, reality proves to be more complicated.

Gender, religion and culture are so closely fused as to seem almost one, but they interact in distinct ways to produce a wide range of effects. Zuleyha Keskin, director of the Affinity Intercultural Foundation, wrote on the tensions involved in her wearing a veil: 'Because I am a Muslim woman who wears the veil, I am very visible in public. So basically everyone knows I am a Muslim. Does this worry me? No.' (Keskin 2004, p. 74)

But the sign means one thing to her, and other things to others: 'People think that I am oppressed, suppressed and depressed, while I really am not. Many times people think that I have been forced to wear the veil, even though it was my choice to wear it. They think that my husband does not allow me to work, but I work as a pharmacist.' (Keskin 2004, p. 74)

This set of meanings, we note, may be patronising but they are not simply hostile. On the contrary, Keskin's friends express a desire to 'save' her, like the rape case judge: these are different kinds of would-be saviour, each with a different take on a different situation, united by a common gendered assumption in which woman-as-victim is at the centre. This is not to say that some Muslim women do not need help. In a schismogenic context in which the veil itself is politicised, there can be pressures applied to young women to wear the veil from *within* the community itself. These pressures can come into conflict with the rules of tolerance or—at worst—the laws ensuring women's rights in the nation as a whole. In such contexts, action is sometimes called for, but even here discourses of salvation are best avoided.

The veil now clearly signifies not just Islam, but specifically Muslim *femininity*. It carries assumptions about women's place in a gendered culture, and projects what that place must feel like to a *woman*, not just a Muslim. Minoo Moallem, a Muslim woman scholar, reflects on the meaning of the black chador, a garment that marks orthodoxy more strongly: 'The black chador carried symbolic local and global meaning. Locally, it transcended all differences of class, religion and ethnonational origin among women; globally it created a transnational Muslim femininity.' (1999, p. 332) Moallem's comment applies to Keskin's veil. Moallem notes a reversal of meaning as the context passes from 'local' to 'global'. At what she calls the local level, the chador eliminates class and ethnic difference, creating not a multiculture but a monoculture which assimilates all difference, in which the categories of gender and religion are so taken for granted that they are invisible. But on the wider stage she calls global, which is the stage Keskin and Australian Muslim women walk in public life, the taken-for-granted categories are what is most visible; gender and religion, producing meanings from the surrounding society and culture.

Haideh Moghissi (2001) asked how Islam and feminism would best be situated in relation to each other: Islam in the framework of feminism, or feminism in the framework of Islam? We ask a related question of the various dilemmas we dealt with in this section. Is gender more important than ethnicity and religion, or social class? Or is one of the others the primary issue? Our response is to insist that the three are inseparable, acting together in a culture made up of all of them.

When the multiculture separates out into distinct and opposing cultures, as has happened to some degree with the relation between Muslims and others in the highly charged post-September 11 atmosphere, even points they share in common create a more explosive sense of difference: symmetrical schismogenesis. An Anglo-Celtic judge condemned aberrant youths from a patriarchal culture different from his own. A traditional white woman was as disturbed by the decorum of a Muslim woman as some in the past might have been by a naked prostitute. Ann Summers (1975) used a famous phrase,

'Damned whores and God's police', to capture a deep split in early colonial attitudes to women. In this modern incident, 'God's police' attacked the Muslim woman precisely because she *wasn't* a 'damned whore'. It is a strange inversion. But strangeness, we have seen, is the signature of schismogenesis in far from equilibrium situations.

Multiculture: Breakdown or success?

After one cross-cultural marriage ended, the matter of the son's schooling was referred to the courts:

> A Sydney court has ordered that the child of a Muslim–Christian marriage be sent to a secular school . . . The case arose after the marriage ended and the mother, a Muslim, sought orders that the boy live with her and that the father, of Lebanese Catholic Maronite background, be prevented from taking him to church on contact visits. The mother . . . later withdrew her church objection, but the father pressed on with his wish that his son be educated at a Maronite Christian school. (Lamont 2004, p. 1)

The court ruled that, because he would be likely to be victimised in a 'predominantly Muslim' school and because attendance at the Maronite Christian school would lead to faith different from the parent with whom he lived, it would be best for him to attend a secular school (2004, p 1).

Did this judge get it more or less right in this case? Is the secular state a useful 'third body' in such cases? Or should gender (the mother's wishes) or culture (the father's rights) have prevailed?

Language in multicultural Australia

The authors of this book come from different parts of provincial Australia. When John came back to teach in Sydney after some years abroad, one of the first things he taught was our subject, 'Multicultural Australia'. While convening this subject for the first time, he received a practical demonstration of a principle both of us have taught elsewhere, which linguists call 'phonemic salience' (sounds that stand out) and 'minimal pairs' (pairs of items with a minimum difference between them). According to this linguistic idea, minds trained in a particular language 'hear' only salient oppositions, deleting sounds that do not fit the set of oppositions that make up the given language.

The incident was this. In class, in Richmond in northwest Sydney, a discussion took place about how people felt about difference. One student—mistakenly, as it turned out—assumed the class was a 'white community', and spoke about going to the city:

> *Student*: It was OK. 'Cept for all the legs.
> *John*: Legs? (thinking fast—some new code that has not yet surfaced, a lot of people maybe, crowded perhaps?)
> *Student*: Yeah, legs.
> *John*: Oh (didn't help much) . . . Um . . . could you say why that bothered you?
> *Student*: Well, they don't like us either.

Legs don't like you? The word, as everyone else in the room knew, was the insult, 'Lebs'. For someone from another part of Australia, the term was simply nothing, not a word at all. John's ear automatically corrected the speaker's 'leb' (non-word) to 'leg'.

This small, trivial incident carries a larger truth about how meaning works. Just as, under the pressure of the occasion, John's alphabet collapsed, 'b' fusing with 'g', so other minimal pairs can collapse under pressure, such as distinctions between Christian and Muslim Lebanese, or Lebanese and other Muslims. In the case of 'legs', the error was minor, ridiculous and easy to correct. When minimal pairs of social categories collapse, as happens in highly charged, schismogenic environments, the error can be major, dangerous and hard to correct.

But of course, what actually happened was a common case of racist abuse, which HREOC reports are full of. We can see the process in a clear form with this student. The world is divided into 'them' and 'us', each reduced to a homogeneous entity, which thinks and feels as one. 'Lebs' reduces 'them' to a single word, stripped of extra syllables, packed with different meanings, wrapped in a single powerful negative value judgment: 'we' don't 'like' them, and 'they' don't like us either.

Joseph Wakim, Lebanese Australian and founder of the Australian Arabic Council, objected to one trend he saw in the wake of the terrorist attacks: name changes by Muslims to conceal their identity. He noted that the recent HREOC report, *Isma* (2004), recorded 'employer aversion to people with Arabic or Islamic names'. So he understood when a friend asked him to call him 'Michael' not 'Mohammed' at work. He remembered his own experience 'during the (un)civil war in Lebanon in the 1980s. If my Lebanese surname was identified, I was bombarded with the same questions: why are you people always fighting? Why can't you live in peace?' (Wakim 2004, p. 17) He understands Mohammed's decision, but regrets he had to make it.

These two linguistic moves are complementary. In the case of 'Lebs', the richness of Lebanese identity is reduced to one syllable, and attached aggressively to all members of the group. In the case of 'Mohammed', the set of Islamic names, which often connect with heroes of Islamic culture, is reduced by ignorance and racism to a single meaning, 'Muslim', which then acts like 'Leb' as a reductive identifier in a structure of discrimination. So 'Mohammed' hides behind 'Michael' to break the cycle of reduction, as many immigrants to Australia have done in the past. Perhaps it will work, though it would need him to control other 'marks' which act in tandem—his physical appearance, perhaps his speech. But why should he? And what is the cost?

In the same space and time, linguist Vera Rieschild studied a counter-tendency: the emergence of 'Lebspeak' in Sydney, a new 'language' or 'ethnolect' which is emerging amongst Lebanese Australian teenagers (Cameron 2003, p. 5). She gives as example *habiib*, Arabic for 'darling', which she finds used by young men with a sense similar to the Aussie 'mate', to indicate strong solidarity and friendship. As such, it simultaneously transforms both Lebanese and Australian traditions, finding a point of contact yet departing from both. It marks an identity which is double and neither. It is unobtrusive but creative, a form that apparently has not yet entered the mainstream and may never do so, but which illustrates the relevant richness of what cultural and linguistic diversity can add, if it is allowed and valued.

The linguistic diversity that seems a problem for a monocultural community is an asset for Australia in the global world, as Linda Doherty noted in a report on language exams in Sydney (2004, p. 8). The growth in language numbers since 1955 has been spectacular. A peak of 8400 students was reached in 1994, but this fell away.

Languages are booming again, she says, with one in eight students now taking a language. The number of students of Arabic is impressive, from a small base, but still far short of what Australia needs to compete globally.

English may be the dominant language in the world, but it is far from the only one, and a rich variety of important meanings and perspectives are still coded in other languages, including Arabic. Elissar Mukhtar (2004, p. 6) points out another potential 'use' of Australia's linguistic and cultural diversity: the capacity of speakers of languages other than English to tap in directly to other perspectives on world news, via pay TV and satellite. A study by Ang (2002, p. 57) showed that 54 per cent of Lebanese in the sample group had pay TV, and 86 per cent of these watched programs in a language other than English. Only 25.5 per cent of the national sample had pay TV, and less than half of these watched programs in a language other than English.

So what do these Lebanese viewers know? asks Mukhtar. Her answer is controversial: it may be information from Al Jazeera, the Arab-language broadcaster that regularly screens messages from Osama bin Laden, condemned as dangerous propaganda by the US propaganda machine. There is little doubt that the Western media, the mainstream media we get in Australia, are biased on these topics, if only from a cultural point of view. Some messages (like those of bin Laden) are censored. Programs like those of Al Jazeera will have few of these Western biases. They claim to be free of bias themselves, but equally surely have biases of their own. In a multiculture, these messages should be shared and discussed. In the far from equilibrium conditions that arose after 2001, however, the dialogue of communities was weakened by the different information streams, not strengthened, if only because an entire audience's perceptions of what was going on differed markedly from that of the mainstream representations.

In a famous speech after September 11, President Bush asked: 'Why do they hate us?' But it was only a rhetorical question, which he answered without asking 'them': they hate our freedoms. It remains a good question, and Australians need to hear a range of answers. Some should be in Arabic, one of the many languages of Australia. Arab Australians should be valued more, not less, in the climate of the 'War on Terror' for their priceless role as sources, translators and mediators.

Afghans are symbols of new arrivals in the contemporary Australian mind, Muslim refugees from war-torn Afghanistan, the latest wave of boat people, survivors of the *Tampa*, distressed and distressing inmates of Woomera. Yet they were also Australia's first major Islamic community, part of a forgotten history of the making of Australia. This is a story that needs to be told because it challenges one of the foundational myths of monocultural Australia: the myth of the bush.

This myth tells a story of an identity forged in the frontier, men putting up with hardships and adversities, always without complaint. Even though that moment and that figure have long passed (if they ever existed), versions of the story, from the time of Henry Lawson onwards, continue to define identities and practices in very different terrains. This borderland produced the Australian identity, and continues to do so if current advertisements for four-wheel drives are anything to go by. Whatever the travails of the wrinkly faced hero, be it Banjo Paterson's Clancy of the Overflow on his horse, the actor Paul Hogan on the bridge, or zookeeper and public figure Steve 'Crikey' Irwin in his theme park north of Brisbane, there is always a story of Anglo-Celtic identity.

In Chapter 4, we saw the role history has to play in constructing national identity, in rethinking a more inclusive Australia. The history behind the myth of the bushman was often incomplete. The British empire was always a plural formation. The cities and the bush were inhabited by people from all over the world. Feminist historians like Kay Schaffer (1987, p. 58) have played a crucial part in revisiting the monocultural (all-white, macho) image of the bushman. We have seen the movement among historians that has restored Aborigines as key protagonists in the drama of Australia's multiculture. In this section, it is the turn of Islam, and the tale of the Afghan bushman.

The story of the Afghan immigrant community is one of the harshest in Australian history. Imported from the 1860s with their camels from northwest 'Pakistan' (as it would one day be) and 'Afghanistan', these men were not allowed to bring their wives with them, and only with difficulty made any kind of life in Australia. Their story has been told by Christine Stevens (2002), who records the circumstances under which they were brought in to assist with exploration and travel, the hardship and discrimination they endured in the early years of their settlement, and the harrowing tale of their retreat, before the technology of the train, to outposts like Cloncurry, Marree and Meekatharra.

Immigration brought hardship to some migrants, but many of their descendants went on to become prosperous. Not so the 'Ghans' (as they were derisively known). Exclusion and utter destitution broke their spirits for many. When their skills as cameleers were no longer needed, their camels were dispersed and shot (Stevens 2002, p. 274), their livelihoods ruined, and the Ghantowns eventually abandoned (2002, p. 278). But, in the midst of the hardships, a plural space developed, the site perhaps for a new bush mythology. After the early years:

> many stayed beyond their initial contract periods and began to establish more permanent bases, to become a more familiar sight at outback settlements. Gradually fears and suspicions about them began to relax in some sections of Aboriginal and European society. The earliest marriages were mostly to Aboriginal women or half-castes. By the latter part of the 1800s Aboriginal tribal society was fragmented in areas settled by Europeans. (2002, p. 218)

From these difficult beginnings, small inter-communal links began to form. As we look through the images in this book, we feel the power of this largely uncelebrated story. The images show utter poverty, defiance, courage and survival—the bush myth itself, in short. From it, there remains a legacy to this day. Stevens traces some of these descendants in a fragmentary chapter at the end of her book. Some major Indigenous artists (like Jack Davis and Ian Abdulla) have Afghan as well as Indigenous heritage.

But perhaps the most important legacy these thousands of Afghan men and their descendants leave us today is the reminder of what a plural society it was that made up this mythic bush frontier. Few have imagined the face of the Australian bushman as an Afghan. Few think of the bush skyline as silhouetting a 'tin mosque'. Instead, Australian Islam is constructed as an urban, latter day problem. That is not only inadequate history: the Afghan story could be woven in to become part of a richer, more inclusive myth. Australia has an Afghan—and Muslim—history. And as harsh and as unfair as it was, it is something the country should be proud of, something to

The Ahmadi Mosque. Photograph by John O'Carroll

celebrate. It was a story of survival against extraordinary odds, a true bush myth.

The Ahmadiya

We taught 'Multicultural Australia' on two University of Western Sydney campuses, Richmond and Blacktown in northwestern Sydney. The two campuses were linked by Richmond Road, and we often drove between them. About halfway, in the suburb of Marsden Park, a dazzling white mosque rises like a palace from the bush: a mark of Islam in Australia, we thought. We later found that it is indeed a mark of Australian Islam, but not as we'd supposed. Maqs Masood put us in touch with the Imam of the mosque, and we were delighted to accept his invitation to bring our class for a visit.

Our students were treated to the hospitality of the mosque. They removed their shoes as a mark of respect. Some women wore scarves, but there was no issue with those who didn't. Then we listened to an address that proved surprising. Dr Riaz Akber is a physicist from Queensland University, not a cleric, and his Powerpoint lecture began by explaining Australian multiculture, drawing on government documents our students ought to have known. The surprise was not the content, but that this Muslim found it so valuable.

He also made a strong case about Islamic multiculturalism. He quoted from the *Koran*, and from the Prophet Muhammad's last sermon:

> O men, your God is one and your ancestor is one. An Arab possesses no superiority over a non-Arab, nor does a non-Arab over an Arab. A white man is in no way superior to a black nor that matter is a black man better than a white, but only to the extent to which he discharges his duty to God and man.

Our students knew that Dr Akber was presenting a case for Islam—not a full picture, but even so his sincerity, intelligence and goodwill were plain to see. For most it was their first visit to a mosque, and their first contact with a Muslim given space to explain his culture and beliefs in his own terms. They were moved and impressed. It should have happened before, they agreed, but better late than never.

But the Ahmadiya are not 'typical Muslims'. The Ahmadiya community were only founded in 1889, in the Punjab district between what is now India and Pakistan. Its founder, Hazrat Mirza Ghulam Ahmad, was a reformer whose reforms were and still are heretical in Pakistan. Some of the 1000 Ahmadiya in Australia came as refugees from persecution in their own country (Masood & Sultana 2002).

We could see why Dr Akber valued multiculturalism. Pakistan, their place of origin, is a multiculture denied, where the diversity of Islamic and non-Islamic communities is suppressed in the name of a unitary Islam. In Australia, this fragment of a fragment is able to manage its differences more easily, making contacts with other faiths and (less easily, Masood indicated) with other Muslims. Dr Akber's multicultural vision was born out of a deep reflection on extremes of racism.

Yet diasporic Ahmadiyas are dynamic. We saw their well-equipped communications centre, able to send and receive materials by satellite from across the world, from Africa, Europe and America as well as Asia. Education ranks high for Ahmadiya, which helps them to be 'good migrants' in Australia and elsewhere.

Dr Akber also told us with pride of one distinguished Ahmadiya scientist. In 1979, Abdus Salam, a devout Ahmadiya all his life, won the Nobel Prize in Physics for his work on 'weak interaction' in nuclear particles. We asked Dr Akber if he thought that Salam's discoveries reflected in any way his Islamic or Ahmadiya beliefs. Not directly, he said, though the Ahmadiya commitment to education was crucial in taking this poor son of a Punjabi community to Cambridge and the Nobel Prize.

Later, after reading more about Salam, we could see some other connections, tenuous but suggestive. Weak interaction is one of three kinds of forces, with 'strong' and 'electromagnetic', its importance explained in a press release by the Nobel Committee:

> The actual strength of the weak interaction is also of significance. The energy of the sun, all-important for life on earth, is produced when hydrogen fuses or burns into helium in a chain of nuclear reactions occurring in the interior of the sun. The first reaction in this chain, the transformation of hydrogen into heavy hydrogen (deuterium) is caused by the weak force. Without this force solar energy production would not be possible. Again, had the weak force been much stronger, the life span of the sun would have been too short for life to have had time to evolve on any planet. (Royal Swedish Academy of Science, 15 October 1979)

Whether or not this theory came to Salam in some way from his origins, it works as a fine allegory for the Ahmadiya. Like 'weak interaction', the Ahmadiya in their doctrines as in their position in Pakistan were catalysts for change: weak and easy to ignore but invaluable, as they can be in Australia. Paradoxically, if they were stronger the transformation might go out of control—their weakness is part of their strength. They are like the moon in Poincaré's three-body problem: easy to ignore, but part of the architecture of the solar system.

And, without allegory, Salam's achievement illustrates the contribution that Islamic migrants like Dr Akber can make to Australian life. Islamic civilisations were 'superior' to Christian-based civilisation for many centuries. Their commitment to learning is just as Islamic as the distrust of learning expressed by fundamentalist Islamists. Australian multiculture is a site in which these tendencies can be expressed and developed more freely, to the benefit of Australia, Islam and the world.

3. Austral/Asia

There is a tendency to see multiculture as a domestic issue, affected by global forces no doubt, but something whose dynamics remain enclosed by national boundaries. This is a misleading way to view multiculture, which is always a relationship across boundaries on different scales. In this chapter, we will use the case of Asia to develop this crucial theme. Like Islam, Asia is very, very big. As with Islam, Australia has a number of alternative futures, two of which bear thinking about. One is to follow the line it took for much of the twentieth century, as an isolated, defensive Anglo-Celtic enclave preserving its purity in its region. The other is to view itself and its contexts as a complex multiculture, and welcome the cosmogenic possibilities of its complex and ever-changing environment.

Problematising 'Asia'

Asia is a multiculture, so multicultural that the term 'Asia' is problematic. The term comes from a schismogenic European history of disregard for other peoples, places, cultures and histories. Yet it is never possible to cleanse a language of its difficult words, and nor do we need to. Purity, here as elsewhere in multicultural studies, is not only impossible to achieve, it is unhelpful. We will instead give histories, contexts and possibilities that allow us to use the word flexibly, not be used by it.

In Chapter 5, we looked at the HREOC inquiry *Racist Violence* (1991). In the body of that report, the Commissioners use the term 'Asian' to organise their analysis. They comment:

> There generally seems to be little distinction made by those holding prejudice or perpetuating violence between different Asian groups. There appeared to be an assumption on the part of the perpetrators that Asians are Asians, and ethnic distinctions amongst them do not matter. When specific groups of Asians are the focus of hostile attention, there is an assumption that all Asians belong to that group. (1991, p. 141)

Is there not a contradiction here with HREOC when the authors use the term 'Asian' to organise their text, while warning us not to lump all Asians together? When they write headings such as 'Violence Against Asian Australians' (1991, p. 140), are they not doing exactly this themselves? Could they be inadvertently contributing in this way to the perpetrators' belief that 'Asians are Asians' and that 'ethnic distinctions amongst them do not matter' (1991, p. 140)?

This is a real issue. But we don't want to exaggerate it or present it as insoluble. Words like 'Asia' (and 'Australia', for that matter) can be created for one purpose and used for another by different people in different times and places. A multicultural context creates a new, at times chaotic, semantic field in which words can acquire new, contradictory forces and uses. 'Asian' can express a dismissive will to power over a large number of very different peoples, as used by racists or colonial powers. It can also recognise problems shared by many otherwise different people, as used by an anti-discrimination body like HREOC. Finally, it can project alliances and create common interests when used by 'Asian' people themselves, who do not have to be slaves to any word forever, even if they first heard it from European colonial administrators.

We begin to reposition the word with some etymologies, which take the word back to a formative past which has been forgotten, but which still lives on in the present. 'Asia' was originally a Greek word which referred to lands to the immediate east of Greece, the present 'Middle East'. Its origins are shrouded in mystery. Perhaps it came from a word that meant 'slimy' or 'muddy', or perhaps it had a more positive sense, referring to the rich alluvial plains of Mesopotamia, scene of the first great urban civilisation in 6000 BC. As Greek understanding of geography grew, Asia came to name the whole land mass to the east, one of the three great continents recognised in the ancient world. But ignorance was built into the term. The Greeks knew little of the rich, diverse cultures they lumped under the single term. 'Asia' as a term began in ignorance, from a point of view outside all the peoples living there. This history weighs on the word, even today.

Before the Greeks and the Greco-Roman culture from which modern Europe traces its origins, there were earlier great civilisations. When European powers conquered the heirs of these great civilisations in the nineteenth century, they tried to rewrite history to make them seem always inferior peoples, destined to be ruled by their new masters. They developed a discourse which the Palestinian-American scholar Edward Said named 'Orientalist', 'the idea of European identity as a superior one in comparison with all the non-European ones' (Said 1978, p. 7). This discourse created a European monopoly of ways of representing the other, telling them what they were really like. A term like 'Asia', with its vagueness and vast simplifications, was ideal within Orientalism to superimpose on the world map of European imperialism.

Because of this history, 'Asia' does not usually signify diversity, but rather the contrary. Historically, when deployed as a race discourse, it had the characteristics that Appiah (1990) calls 'extrinsic': it was a way of talking *about* people, rather than a way used *by* people to band together (Appiah's 'intrinsic' variety) (1990, pp. 10–11). Recent decades have complicated this picture. Within a nation like Australia, communities have banded together as 'Asians' to deal with issues of common concern, or to affirm a common cause. Paradoxically, this use of a term that was born out of racism and schismoculture comes to signify an 'Asian' multiculture within an Australian multiculture, where the groups combining are all fully aware of the differences of language, culture and history that continue within the term. At a global level, nations from Indonesia to Japan, from the Philippines to India, have formed 'Asian' associations to hammer out trade and political arrangements around common interests. The name has acquired a strategic value based on the kinds of solidarity that Appiah describes.

Ambivalence is the starting point of this chapter. 'Asia' names a vast multiculture, far more diverse than 'Australia', more diverse even than 'Europe'. 'Australia' is a definable place, and 'Europe' has relatively definable traditions and boundaries, however vast. 'Asia', by contrast, has a strikingly uncertain shape and boundary, depending on when, why and by whom the name is being used. Groups who proclaim themselves 'anti-Asian' are utterly wrong in what they are most certain about: that there is a single group and culture corresponding to the word 'Asian'.

Here we note an irony built into a term Australians use of themselves: 'Australasia'. Australians use it of two Anglo-Celtic nations huddled together at the bottom of the Pacific, who almost joined forces at the time of Federation and who now have increasingly close economic ties. But etymologically it contains a secret: 'Austral' means 'south', and 'Asia' is Asia. Australians, part of 'Australasia', are literally South Asians. This repeats from a different angle Labor Prime Minister Paul Keating's claim that Australia is 'part of Asia'. In a new map, we are part of a single emerging multiculture on a massive scale, including a diversity of people, whose name we blindly took to ourselves without noticing what it meant: 'Australasia'.

Australia in Asia, Asia in Australia

In *The Teeth are Smiling* (Vasta & Castles 1994)—that excellent, thought-provoking book of essays to which we hope the present work is a worthy successor—the final essay by educationalist Fazal Rizvi poses some well-framed questions about the motivations of 'Australians' *vis-à-vis* 'Asia':

> It is no longer possible to separate the issues of regional politics involved in our attempts to forge new relationships within the region—in trade, in education, and in the arts and cultural exchange—from the issues concerning the way Asian-Australians are treated within Australia, that is, from the issues of the racisms that reside *within* the country. (Rizvi, in Vasta & Castles 1994, p. 174)

Written in the early 1990s, against the backdrop of an Asia-oriented Keating government, this is perceptive analysis. The move towards Asia is bipartisan, and Rizvi's words are still a challenge. There are intrinsic links between external politics and internal issues of racism and treatment of Asian Australians within Australia.

At a summit of ASEAN nations in Vientiane, Laos, in December 2004, some of the implications of the broader move surfaced in a dispute that flared before the summit began. The name Association of South-East Asian Nations (ASEAN) includes the vexed term 'Asia', but all its members are aware that this term covers a wide diversity of nations and cultures. The project of the summit was a form of three-body thinking. These nations felt that their association needed to look in two directions: towards the Asian superpowers, China and Japan; and to the two 'non-Asian' regional powers, Australia and New Zealand.

Australia had never previously been invited to an ASEAN summit, in spite of the best efforts of the then ALP prime minister, Paul Keating, waving the banner of Australian multiculturalism as a credential. Australia's presence at this summit, and the possibility that it would join a Free Trade Treaty, was seen as a coup for the Australian government, redeeming it from its image of not being 'friends of Asia'. But ASEAN ministers also wanted a Treaty of Amity and Cooperation to be co-signed by the assembled nations, which Prime Minister Howard announced he would not do, insisting that 'the issue isn't important to ASEAN nations' (Allard 2004, p. 2).

However, ASEAN diplomats disagreed. They were reported as seeing this issue as very important: 'It would greatly help Australia's bid to attend future summits if it showed signs it would accede to the treaty.' (2004, p. 2) Howard used the old tactic of speaking on behalf of the other, but nowadays these others have the power to speak very well for themselves. Howard's perspective also put crisp boundaries between issues of trade and regional security. But the ASEAN countries acted as a complex multiculture, managing differences between members sufficiently to come to cohesive action on both trade and security, seeing the intrinsic connection between trade and social and cultural issues.

The example is minor, but—given the example of Keating's failures before them—it does seem part of a long-running pattern. What is going on? In our view, Australian governments would do well to continue to heed the warnings of Hoffman from 1984: 'we cannot afford to fuel accusations that we are regional fringe-dwellers in several senses, and that we are far from understanding the fears and aspirations of our neighbours' (1984, p. 59). Hoffman quotes Sir Arthur Tange, former head of the Department of Defence, accusing

Australia of a dangerous 'egocentricity', advising us to 'look at the problem with Asian eyes *and see the great influx of Europeans into the region over the past two centuries as a cause of concern*' (Tange, quoted in Hoffman 1984, p. 59). Tange here envisaged a kind of multiculture at the global level, in which Australia recognises and respects difference, coming to a more complex, practical understanding of 'Asia' as a single region inhabited by many nations and peoples.

Hoffman connects these developments explicitly to multiculturalism, but not in a simple way. Asian nations, he claims, are likely to see Australia's efforts on multiculturalism as 'an "in-house" issue amongst white Australians' (1984, p. 64). He adds:

> Unless our awakened concern for multiculturalism can expand (instead of compacting) into regional identification and awareness, we shall have wasted much of our new appetite for other cultures. Our present stress on ethnicity in multiculturalism may thus have to broaden into more emphasis on understanding of the region. (1984, p. 64)

Hoffman seems to accept the triumphs of multiculturalism, as far as they went in the 1980s. His point is that the scale of such triumphs is too small to have any impact outside the nation. His vision of the scope of multiculture is a quantum leap in scale.

To be sure, this new understanding of multiculture starts from recognising that Australia's credibility on the world stage requires multiculturalism at home. But this important first step does not go nearly far enough. It remains limited and instrumentalist, and in the often chaotic global world of today, when far from equilibrium situations arise, it probably will not work as intended. The new conception of multiculture, as we have argued throughout this book, cannot just be a policy about, or for, 'ethnics'—especially not just for recent immigrants. It *minimally* has to include a new conception of Australia's diversity *and* the diversity of the region that *includes* Australia. Australia is *in* that region, already part of it, framed by it— not part of a mostly Anglo-Celtic Australasia looking at Asia, but a complex multiculture interacting with other groups in 'Australasia', within 'Asia'.

There is no doubt that much of Australia's current prosperity arises from our interchanges with our region. The two decades since Hoffman wrote have witnessed a transformation of Australia's place in this world, transforming in turn ideas of what Australia could be. Externally, we can indeed talk of Austral-Asia. This is an open society, crossed by dialogues, formal and informal, throughout the entire region. Formal dialogues are enriched by the interactions of people who have moved here and remain in touch with their families. As a middle-order power with a comparatively small population, Australia has much to offer. Yet it also has much to learn and to gain.

Internally, too, we can speak of Austral-Asia. This transformation has been quieter (despite the Hanson years), and yet profound. Migration patterns already evident in the late 1970s continued after Hoffman's essay appeared. By the end of the 1990s, migrants born in non-English speaking countries outnumbered migrants from English-speaking countries (14 per cent to 9 per cent of the total population), and 32 per cent of overseas-born people in Australia came from an 'Asian' region (Southeast Asia 12 per cent, Northeast Asia 7 per cent, South Asia 4 per cent) (DIMA 2000, p. 4). In the period 1999–2000, it remained true that New Zealand and the United Kingdom supplied the largest groups of permanent arrivals, but the next most significant source country for permanent arrivals was mainland China (2000, p. 6).

Hoffman's dream of a knowledge-led 'integration of the fringe-dwellers' to the 'Asia mainstream' is yet to be realised (1984, pp. 64–65). Williams (2004, p. 4) points out:

> The Asian Studies Association of Australia says Indonesian language courses at most universities are 'endangered' because of plummeting enrolments, suggesting that Australia's advanced linguistic skills base could be lost entirely within 5 to 10 years.

For pragmatic reasons, Australia must continue to engage with the region. For economic reasons, the benefits are obvious. But the main reason for engagement lies in the mutual benefit that comes from sharing what we have, from learning from others, and occasionally from allowing them to learn from us—in other words, from being good citizens of an 'Australasian' multiculture.

The new Chinese revolution

Most texts on multiculturalism note Australian histories of paranoia towards Asia, with good reason. Epidemics in the nineteenth century led to riots against 'Asiatic races', where the medical image of a 'yellow plague' was taken with deadly literal-mindedness. The goldfields during the 1850s saw the largest influx of Chinese until the present, and also witnessed many atrocities. From 1901, the 'White Australia' policy systematically excluded and deported Asian Australians from the new nation. These are important histories. Australians of Asian background who survived them here did so under great duress.

Yet how do we include in that history an episode like former ALP Prime Minister Bob Hawke's response in 1989 to the position of Chinese students in Australia, in the wake of the massacre of pro-democracy demonstrators by the Chinese government in Tiananmen Square? The prime minister publicly wept, and promised that all Chinese students then in Australia would not be forced to return to face the wrath of the despotic Chinese regime. It was a grand gesture, with consequences. According to Cynthia Banham (2003b), in a fine newspaper article, 42 000 were ultimately allowed to stay under this dispensation, 100 000 including family reunions (2003b, p. 19). Given that the total number of Chinese immigrants in Australia after this influx was only 143 000, Tiananmen Square people were 70 per cent of the total.

Unprecedentedly large numbers of Chinese migrants were admitted—bodies and lives, a 'problem' for the system. According to Banham, immigration officials today say that the program was 'poorly managed' (2003, p. 22)—'a debacle', according to one critic, Dr Birrell. It was also, thirteen years later, a success story by many criteria. One recurring fear with big influxes of a single stream of migrants is that they will form ghettos, hostile encampments within the dominant society. But this did not happen with these migrants. Banham gives statistics which show eleven suburbs with more than 3000 Chinese people, the highest proportion in any one being 8.1 per cent. These are significant concentrations, but this is certainly not ghettoisation.

These migrants were all students, of above-average education, 'refugees' by one standard, but well-qualified applicants by another. Dr Peter Wong, a former student, now member of the New South Wales Upper House, makes a strong claim: 'The Chinese migrants—with their Mandarin, connections in China and understanding of Chinese culture—have become "the conduit of business in China", playing a pivotal role in trade between it and Australia.' (Banham 2004b, p. 22) Hawke's ideological inversion, which turned 'them' (Chinese students) into 'us' (Western citizens) is complicated by the fact that 'they' continue to be Chinese, bearers of a rich, complex culture and civilisation as well as citizens of Australia. This is not a problem, but rather the contrary.

Signs of conflict

Amanda Wise has been researching tensions in multicultural sites in Sydney which do not feel so multicultural to all who live there. For instance, in Ashfield she reports a seemingly minor dispute over Chinese language signs in some Chinese shops, to which some Anglo-Celtic ratepayers objected (Wise 2004). Wise quotes some intriguing figures from the latest census: of Ashfield's population of 39 500, 48 per cent are Australian born, and 36 per cent come from NESB (non-English speaking backgrounds), mostly from 'Asia'. Anglo-Celts are by far the largest group, but they are not quite a majority in Ashfield.

Wise quotes two more interesting figures. There are 10 per cent Chinese speakers, and 10 per cent 'Anglo-Celt seniors'. Probably neither group is aware of this symmetry. It is easy to lump the Anglo-Celts with the 48 per cent Australian-born near-majority, but that is the same logic as sees 'all Asians the same', which would lump Chinese speakers together with all other NESBs. But from another point of view the figures mean what they say: these two groups are equally in the minority, each able to react in similar ways to this fact. Each group, in this situation, becomes schismogenic, forming barriers and boundaries which in practice separate them from many others whom outsiders would see as 'the same'.

Wise quotes some comments of the 'Anglo Celtic seniors'. 'Marjorie' says: 'Chinese signs, they say to me, "don't enter". It's saying to me, "Don't come in". "You can't read these signs, so you're not welcome."' Marjorie's analysis is acute. Paradoxically it shows that communication is indeed happening across the language barrier. But the signs probably also say: 'I can't speak your language, but please look and explore.' Schismogenic and cosmogenic tendencies coexist, and could go either way. Gender probably also plays a role in her response. Wise calls her 'working class':

Borderwork and multicultural Australia

another dimension that always needs to be taken into account in multicultural analysis.

Wise asks the practical question: what should be done? Should Chinese businesses be required to have English language signs? Should English language shops be required to have Chinese language signs? Or does this translation problem, which is a real one, have other more cosmogenic solutions?

What is a 'successful' immigration program?

'Being Choosy Works When it Comes to Immigration' headlines a *Sydney Morning Herald* story by Adele Horin (2004) on a study by Sue Richardson and Laurence Lester. The article and report celebrate the economic success of Australia's migration programs compared with Canada's otherwise comparable patterns. It is a reward, Horin says, for Australia's 'emphasis on skilled migrants, proficient English speakers, and on vetting the professional credentials of would-be migrants' (2004, p. 1).

This system is designed to make sure that all the claims that migration and multiculture contribute to the wealth and prosperity of the country will be proven true. But there is perhaps a cost. Richardson describes it as selfish 'because it drew the most talented away from poorer countries, but it was in Australia's interest' (2004, p. 2). There seems no compassion factor here—and indeed, one of the reasons for the 'success' is identified as a greatly reduced number of refugees, and fewer family reunions.

Ghassan Hage criticises the mentality behind these criteria for 'success'. He quotes a 1993 article by David Jenkins, which reflects on the ten years since a famous intervention by Professor Geoffrey Blainey raised the issue of Asian immigration, and suggests that it had gone too far:

> What has happened on the Asian front in the past decade? Have we become more or less tolerant towards Asians? Do people worry about the 'Asianisation' of Australia? A look at the demographics suggests we have 'Asianised' faster and more thoroughly than anyone—including Professor Blainey—could have anticipated in 1984 . . . Can we carry it off? Can we rearrange the demographic mix without recreating the tensions one finds in much of Western Europe and North America? (Jenkins, quoted in Hage 1998, p. 125)

Once again, Hage's acute ear for language allows him to make some strong points about this seemingly positive, fair-minded text. For instance, the 'we' is unconsciously an Anglo-Celtic collective self, not 'Asian', however much 'we' claim we have been Asianised. (If 'we' include Asians, the question 'have we become more or less tolerant towards Asians?' does not make sense.) This 'we' then takes on the task of government, to 'rearrange' the mix as though this is an obligation shared by all (non-Asian) citizens. Jenkins' 'we' invites his readers to join him and the government in wielding power. It is indeed, as Hage calls it, a 'fantasy'.

Perhaps this is just the turn of phrase of a media pundit, but the kind of governmental control signalled as necessary by Jenkins in 1993 underpins the success Richardson saw in 2004. Numbers now are more strictly controlled, reduced in many 'undesirable' (economically unproductive) categories, boosted in a few 'beneficial' categories. The terror of inassimilable numbers or kinds of immigrant has been allayed.

Yet we have another take on Jenkins' article. In 1993, just before Pauline Hanson raised the issue of immigration and attacked the level of Asian immigration in particular, this article did what good journalism should do, identifying a groundswell of opinion as it was forming. Jenkins also looked back at the previous wave of media hysteria, provoked by a few chance remarks by a professor, and found that hysteria wave one (in 1983) was not justified. Ten years after Jenkins wrote this piece, we (the two authors) see the same thing: wave two of hysteria (in 1993) was not justified either. Crucially, Jenkins' 'we' not only did not include Asians, it did not include the mass of Australians already living their multiculture. But the restrictions implemented by the government maintain some (reduced) level of ethnic diversity, though not diversity of class. The success Horin (2004) reports should be applauded, but it is only part of the full story of Australian multiculture, even in the past decade.

Crime and Fortress Australia: A cautionary tale

Multicultural Australia is overall a cosmogenic society, but that does not mean it is free of tensions or conflicts. Schismogenesis arises within communities as well as between them. We illustrate with one case reported in the media headlined 'Bashed and Drowned in Bath at Fortress Home' (Kennedy 2001, p. 2). Forty-seven-year-old Cam Van Chau, divorced mother of three, moved into a home in Strathfield, in South Sydney, in September 2000. She immediately installed an elaborate security system around the house, but in spite of it she was found six months later, bashed and drowned in her bath. Her sense of insecurity was justified, yet it was still not enough. She made her house into 'a fortress', but still needed more barriers, greater protection. Whatever the nature of the problem—we presume that the fact that she was a woman played some part in the drama that unfolded—her situation illustrates the problematic nature of borders.

There is a general lesson here: schismogenesis produces boundaries, not security. The fear and threat they are a response to are real, yet borders on their own may not be enough. While the story might make us focus on the shocking irony of the border she created being implicated in her demise, there is also this sobering contextual fact for us to recall: part of her vulnerability had to do with her isolation, a failure not just of her immediate community, but of an entire society.

A study of attitudes to crime amongst 'ethnic' communities in Western Sydney (including Strathfield, where Mrs Chau lived) found that 88 per cent of adults felt 'concerned' or 'very concerned' about crimes, but only 62 per cent of young people from those areas felt this way (Collins et al. 2002). These rates are comparable to the level of concern from older established groupings. Yet these groups, who lived in districts seen by outsiders as centres of risk, mostly perceived their own district as relatively safe (two-thirds of adults, 80 per cent of youths).

One author of this report, Professor Jock Collins, wrote of the immediate context of this study:

> The politicisation of the ethnic crime issue by both parties and the media's obsession with the issue in the lead-up to the 2003 state [NSW] election not only intensifies the fear of crime but undermines the feelings of community safety and threatens to undermine social cohesion in the city. (2002, p. 11)

The casualties in the process, says Collins, include everyone. This accords with our approach to borderwork in general, as well as to particular borderwork sites. A more fearful community feels less safe, its members divided against each other. The image of Cam Van Chau bashed inside her fortress can apply to all Australians, migrants and non-migrants alike, in a paranoiac, over-defended community. A vibrant, trusting multiculture is a way to restore care and safety. It is not the problem it seems to be to those who anxiously patrol the ethnic borders.

Eating Asia

No one doubts that there has been a revolution in Australian eating habits since the 1950s. Before 1960, most Australians ate mainly at home. Now they eat out in great numbers. Outside eating places now include US fast food outlets like McDonald's, but they also include a rich array of ethnic cuisines, amongst which Asian foods have a major place. Ang's study (2002, p. 31) found that 72 per cent of her national sample enjoyed eating food from other cultures. These figures confirm what is evident from everyday experience: eating ethnic is now part of mainstream Australian culture.

This 'revolution' has taken place over the same period as the multi-culture revolution entered the mainstream. Was this just a coincidence? Is this just a fad, a superficial trend that serves to mask the continuing structural dominance of the dominant, as Hage (1998) for instance argues, seeing this practice as merely a marker of 'cosmopolitan status' for the middle classes? But 72 per cent surely goes beyond the middle classes. Are there deeper connections between the two?

David Parker (2000), looking at 'Chinese takeaways' in England, is sceptical of what he calls 'celebratory multiculturalism' there (2000, p. 77). His concern is with what he calls 'power geometries': the re-lations of power at these contact points between Chinese workers vulnerable in isolated sites, providing their commodity to non-Asian clients: 'multiculturalism is held within the confines of service indus-tries at the disposal of the dominant' (2000, p. 79). Interviewing workers in these outlets, he finds a pattern of abuse, sometimes even violence, in these sites of tension.

In Australia, HREOC's 1991 study found a small number of cases of racist violence against ethnic restaurants. We mentioned Jack Van Tongeren's imprisonment for just such an offence. We also argue that racism like this is now a minority form, which is likely to coexist with Australia's multiculture for a very long time. As fuzzy logic tells us, it is wrong to deny that Australia is a multiculture just because there is racism, just as it is dangerous to deny continuing racism in claiming that Australia is now multicultural. Australian multiculture, we claim, is more vigorous and diverse than is the case in England, and this crucial difference affects what may seem like the same site. The Chinese diaspora in Australia is not so confined in terms of class and employment as Parker says is the case with England. The 'power geometry' is as important in Australia as in England, but that geometry includes power networks surrounding any specific site, not just the relationship of provider and client within the contact space.

Ang's 2002 study found differences in a multicultural sample between 'long-term Australians' and migrants, both English-speaking (ESBs) and non-English speaking. This adds a little to the complexity of the issue. Long-term Australians have a high approval of 'ethnic cooking', as do second-generation non-English speaking people, but first-generation non-English speaking migrants are much less approving, with just 38 per cent of them claiming to enjoy food from other cultures. Conversely, most (around 90 per cent) enjoy food from their own background (Ang 2002, p. 31). These figures are consistent with a version of multiculture in which diversity does not have to be renounced. They also show something which is lost sight of in many sociological studies of food: that food is a rich and powerful signifier of culture and group membership.

Food taboos are important in many of the world's religions, enshrining an age when food carried major cultural meanings. This was also true of Australian Anglo-Celtic cuisine before the 1950s. Nowadays, Anglo-Celtic cuisine is supplemented—even at times supplanted by—the wide range of cuisines of the world. The shift should not be seen as simple, superficial or without meaning: it is a *social* instance of multiculture that nevertheless reflects *individual* acts of choice all around the country.

We illustrate further with an example from Jean Duruz's (2000) fine study of what she calls 'ethnic grazing': different practices of eating performed across the range of multicultural Australia. She quotes an interview with 'Dot Ryan', an older Anglo-Celtic Australian:

> *Dot*: I have tried about every other country's food . . . but I still prefer home cooking [laughter]. A nice baked dinner . . .
> *Jean*: Are you a good cook?

Dot: Oh, I wouldn't say good . . . You know. I just follow what my mother did . . . grills . . . casseroles . . . My husband, he likes a lot of fish so he goes to the fish markets and he does his own [cooking] . . . He went to Tech and did a Thai [cooking] course . . . so he's learnt to make sauces . . . so he does that with his fish. Then another night I'll do it in my old-fashioned egg batter which is the only way I'll eat it . . .
(Duruz 2000, p. 292)

Duruz sympathises with this older woman, renegotiating her gendered role (as wife and cook for the family) while refusing to renounce the signifiers of 'old-fashioned' cuisine. Duruz does not comment on the complex dynamics implied by this brief fragment of a discourse and of a life, but there are enough traces to allow us to do so. The husband's interest in Thai cooking is clearly not superficial. Nor is it a mere relationship between an exploitative client and a humble service provider. Different tastes in food now reflect tensions within this multiculturalised couple. Duruz is discreet about this aspect. Dot is quoted as saying: 'Anyway, that works out all right.' (2004, p. 292) But she also jokes: 'I'm really pleased he's learnt to cook . . . 'cos he won't mind now when I go away and leave him.' (2000, p. 294)

Tensions within this couple mirror tensions between generations for both 'long-term' Australians like Dot and communities of more recent provenance. The figures we cited earlier on the differences in eating habits between communities reflect the transformations of generational change that are part of multiculture. In Dot's case, the marital relation is still holding, but perhaps only just. She expressed acceptance of other cuisines in Australia to this interviewer, but it is clearly a volatile situation, no doubt with some pain. While we agree that the widespread Australian practice of 'ethnic grazing' is not a simple affirming signifier of multiculture, we also contend that we should not dismiss it (as tokenism or as snobbery). For many of our students, eating is one of the first positive signifiers of multiculturalism they mention. We believe they are not superficial, and not wrong.

Modern traditionalists get wed on the web

It sounds like a deeply traditional Indian marriage, between a bride and groom with complementary astrological charts who only saw each other once before the wedding.

Borderwork and multicultural Australia

Only this alliance between Deepti Chandel, a Wollongong audiologist, and Navneet Mittal, a New Delhi travel agent, was forged in an internet chat room and kept alive by email, text messaging and a webcam, which the groom's boss let him install in his office . . . Matrimonial classifieds have long appeared in newspapers such as *The Times of India*, but the internet is allowing the Indian diaspora to arrange trans-continental marriages with both traditional and modern elements. (Pryor 2004, p. 11)

This article plays with contradictions—tradition and modernity, astrology and computers, love and calculation, global and local matters—as though this is just a joke. Yet these contradictions complicate and enrich Australia's multiculture. It is happening on a large scale (following on from the newspaper advertisements in the past). But nowadays, the Indian diaspora is also on the net, since Indians are well represented in the worldwide computer industry.

The power of the net to connect across space creates a symmetrical union—very like with very like, two people who share the same contradictions. This allows Chandel to exclude non-Indian Australians from his most intimate life: schismogenesis in the personal sphere. The version of Indian culture the couple weaves into the Australian mix is surprising but enriching. Australia gains a good audiologist and competent user of the net, and a competent professional woman, along with Indian traditions reinterpreted and transformed for modern contexts.

Memorials to Asia

Squire Park, Cowra, New South Wales, 5 August 2004. John is driving to Cowra, in central-western New South Wales, to visit the well-known tourist site there. Close to the town, he tunes into the local radio:

This is the *Morning Show* on ABC in the Central West and Western plains . . . it's Jen Lacey with you . . . we've set up our little machine in Squire Park in Cowra, right in the middle of town across from the post office to bring you all of the wonderful commemorations of the sixtieth anniversary of the Cowra Breakout which occurred on this day 60 years ago. Coming up before ten this morning we're going to take a tour of the war cemetery where all of the Japanese POWs and also the four Australian guards who died during the breakout are buried.

We have said that memorials can fade into oblivion, but they exist because some people, living people, care about certain histories and certain visions of the way the world should be. A memorial like Cowra is fascinating because it shows us how potent and un-predictable a role is played not only by the 'facts' that are being recorded—however accurately—but also by the angle on those facts. In this case, the main meaning of the memorial is the scale of the change of angle: from schismoculture to multiculture, from a device to separate out two warring groups to an experience designed to create commonality, communication and understanding.

During World War II, Cowra's remoteness from the coast made it seem ideal for an internment camp for prisoners of war. The camp was located just outside the town. Like refugee internment camps today, it was divided internally to reflect the identities of its prisoners, an image of the strongly schismogenic society it was. In this case, there were four sites: one for Italians, one for ordinary Japanese prisoners, one which housed Japanese and Taiwanese (then called Formosan) and one for Korean prisoners. The camp has a number of memorials. Near the camp is a large Italian monument. But the Cowra camp lives on in the cultural memory of Australia because of the inmates of section B, the non-commissioned prisoners of war from Japan. We remember them for:

> the uprising that occurred ... in the frosty early hours of 5 August 1944, and resulted in the deaths of 231 Japanese and four Australians, the wounding of 107 Japanese and four Australians, and the escape for periods of up to nine days of 334 prisoners (Gordon 1994, p. 3).

The motives for the uprising had less to do with camp brutality than the cultural shame of being a captive. This multicultural aspect of the events is now well understood, but is worth bearing in mind as a general principle: things that are harmless or insignificant in one culture can mean a lot in another.

The sheer weight of numbers led to a form of 'success', if breaching the camp lines in two places is the index, but the price of the breakout was awful:

Borderwork and multicultural Australia

They had talked outside the hut briefly, but there really wasn't much to say. The lame Fujita could be a burden in the attack. They both knew it. Kakimoto looked around the hut, noted the still-swaying body of Yamashita, and nodded to Fujita . . . 'It's time, Mr Fujita. Do it now.' Fujita was heard to repeat several times, 'I'm sorry to go ahead.' Then he tossed a piece of rope across a rafter, fastened it around his neck, stood on a bed, bowed to his superior, threw himself forward and died very slowly on his birthday. (Gordon 1994, p. 136)

Those who did break out were not accorded the regular rules of combat engagement. Whether through fear or hatred or both, some escapees were summarily gunned down. Gordon puts it this way:

Some did not get the chance to surrender. Roy Treasure [and his brother] . . . guided its members to a vantage point where they could see the five prisoners crouched among bushes near a huge box tree. The Australians did not bother with warnings. They simply opened fire, and shot all five prisoners dead. (1994, p. 185)

There is something shocking in reading these accounts today. Not least of the horror is what happened when the fugitives chose to abandon the struggle:

The environs were nightmarish. Atkinson was suddenly alerted by the sight of an upright Japanese, apparently watching. Torches flashed in his direction to reveal: 'He was hanging from a tree, with a loop around his neck, facing towards us, and appeared to be very much alive . . . but he turned out to be dead.' . . . 'Continuing towards the crest of the hill with the back-drop of the full moonbeams coming through the trees we observed six Japs who had hanged themselves from boughs of trees . . . A more eerie sight you could not imagine'. (1994, p. 201)

The dead were buried in mass graves. After the war, the Japanese government resolved to retrieve the bodies for interment in Japan. But the people of Cowra—part of that rural Australia which is supposedly so irredeemably rednecked that they will never accept so unnatural an idea as multiculturalism—had already moved to dignify the terrible history with a memorial. Long negotiations followed with

The Japanese Tea Garden in Cowra (Photograph by John O'Carroll)

the Japanese government, leading to a jointly sponsored memorial to the Japanese dead and to Australian–Japanese understanding.

The Cowra cemetery honouring the Japanese war dead is now a shrine to this event. Nearby, the Japanese tea garden continues the theme, with gardens and an information centre, a fine example of the Japanese art of gardens. Some eucalypts have been left on a round hill, Australian trees inserted into a Japanese art form. Australian rocks also are part of this quintessentially Japanese art, which celebrates nature, including Australian nature, in a way that Australians could identify with and learn from. A small pond fed by artful streams contains a small island, signifying the world—a world which includes Australia and Japan.

Sixty years ago, these two nations were at war. Japan already had this rich spiritual tradition and its landscape art. It was also a ruthless foe, committing atrocities against Australians and others in the war, as Australians themselves did in the Breakout. The memorial reminds us of the contradictions, then and now. Australia's multiculture is strengthened by including the contradictions, just as it is strengthened by the presence of the many 'Asian' peoples, some of whom (like the Japanese and Chinese) fought each other bitterly not so long ago.

Global Austral/Asia

There are now over one million 'Asians in Australia' (ABS 2001b). If we look at the Australian Bureau of Statistics' attempts to define 'Asia', we can see that it includes around a quarter of the world's landmass, and an even greater proportion of its peoples. Asia, the multiculture, has taken its place *inside Australia*, and 'we' are the better for it.

We have described many of the changes that have taken place in Australia as a result of its place in the Asian multiculture—and its place in Australia. The word 'Asia' is at once impossible and yet enabling (making connection possible between apparently disparate peoples). In reflecting on historical events such as the Cowra experience now, a 'touristic moment', as it can be called dismissively, at the same time records a genuine multicultural achievement. Sixty years ago, a small fragment of Asia was in Australia, separated out, feared, misunderstood and destroyed. Since then, much has changed.

It is true that some have questioned the changes. Now Japanese tourists come to Australia, visiting tourist resorts that may be owned by Japanese interests, buying mementos of dinky-di Australia whose labels report the embarrassing fact that they were made in China. Advocates of a pure Australian identity see this as a disaster. But the story is much more complex than this.

We take, as a typical and representative example of these complexities, a story about that famous 'Aussie' icon, Streets ice-creams: 'When Australian mums and dads buy their kids a Paddle Pop or Calippo Frost at the beach this summer, few will bother to read the fine print on the wrapper. If they do, they will see ... the words "Made in China"' (McDonald 2003, p. 29). The process of taking factories offshore is called outsourcing. It means local people lose their jobs, but it also means the ice-creams are cheaper for consumers. As in most such cases, there is more yet to this story:

> But for the 200 workers making Streets ice-cream at the Unilever plant in Minto, on Sydney's southwest, and another 60 workers at the Norco factory in Lismore making Streets brands under contract, China is the threat constantly being waved by management to get them to sign individual contracts and sign away conditions. (2003, p. 29)

Note the global context to this story: Streets is no longer an Australian company. It is owned by Unilever, an Anglo-Dutch multinational company whose concerns are with costs and returns, not with Australian workers.

In Chapter 1, in our discussion of the relationship between the left and multiculturalism, we defined the term 'globalisation'. The word is an abstraction, but is useful so long as we remember it always happens *somewhere*. Its borderwork effects are ambivalent; some benefit while others suffer (and most people experience both suffering *and* benefits). The tendency is always to praise it for job creation or to blame it for the ills of society—in short, to seek to reduce its complexity. Yet, like the global and local borderwork processes it seeks to explain, globalisation cannot be grasped reductively.

Globalisation's advocates are quick to point to cheap products, new jobs. Yet, to repeat, jobs have also been lost, and for those affected the suffering and frustration are very real. To take the above example, in the Streets story the company is not an Australian one, so the decision may not even have been made here. This process has transformed our choices—and our workplaces. Jobs *have* been exported, but new ones have been created. It seems, indeed, that this balance currently runs in Australia's favour, as the unemployment rate is quite low. Historically, things made here that used to be sold to the United Kingdom, other European countries or the United States (almost 70 per cent of our exports in 1950) are now more likely to be sold to 'Asia' (Fagan & Webber 1994, p. 50). The story of interlinkage with Asia is as surprising as it is deep and strong.

There is, in the case of workforce change, a tendency to focus on *our* sufferings (job losses, wage levels) and to weigh them up against the benefits (prices, new opportunities). This is important. But we should also remember, as we consider the changes in Australia, that there have been corresponding changes for the peoples of Asia themselves. In this respect, there has been a tendency to focus on 'success' stories like Japan and China.

There are harder realities too. Many people in parts of Indonesia and the ASEAN region still struggle to put food on the table. And then, many people imagine that those who come to Australia from 'Asia' do so largely as unskilled workers. But even this is not a particularly accurate picture. Of the skilled migrant intake in the year to 2000, only 16 per cent came from the United Kingdom, while 41 per cent came from the Asian region (DIMA 2000, p. 17).

The point that no statistic can reflect is the sheer breadth and diversity of the region—a region in whose diversity we profoundly share. This is the sense in which we are 'part of Asia', not just geographical coincidence, but shared potential and promise; not just as a country that is 'in the Asian region', but a country which has Asia within. This is the meaning we attach to multiculture and, in this case, to Austral/Asia. In the next chapter, we extend this geocultural consideration to the Pacific. Just as the 'boundary' in Austral/Asia needs reimagining, so too can we imagine a more complex three-body system built up out of the sets of pairs the Asia/Pacific and a Pacific Australia.

# 9. Rethinking the Pacific

In this chapter, we focus on the Pacific region. It's not usually a theme in books on multicultural Australia; in fact, it isn't a part of the world that Australians generally think much about. That is precisely why we write on it, at this stage in our book: as a rich way to make the important point that Australia's multiculture does not stop at its borders. We want to challenge the idea that 'multicultural Australia' is a private, national affair, essentially unrelated to what is happening in the global context, which friends and enemies of multiculturalism alike agree is too important to ignore.

In the previous chapter, we saw Australia as part of a complex, dynamic multicultural region we called 'Austral/Asia'. In this chapter, we argue the value of seeing Australia as a Pacific nation, as part of a Pacific multiculture that has been invisible to most Australians. This framework allows us to see what we can learn about ourselves from our multicultural others from Pacific nations, some now Australian citizens, all living in a single, interconnected world in which Australia looms much larger than most Australians know.

This chapter is about vision, ways of seeing the world, and the different worlds we know about when we can see them. Australians need to learn how to see some things better, because they have a long, dishonourable tradition of not seeing, starting from a notion of *terra nullius*—the idea that the land was empty when the invaders arrived, in spite of its many Aboriginal inhabitants who were already so obviously there. For many generations after the first invasion, settlements grew along the coast, a string of overgrown beads strung around a huge, frighteningly empty space. Australians need new ways of thinking about the landmass that gives them their identity. Those ways, we argue, can come from a multicultural perspective that looks with new eyes at Australia's history and context, and listens with new ears to other cultures which are part of our multicultural context.

The large island, the far sea: Donut vision

Epeli Hau'ofa did not have Australia particularly in mind when he rose in early 1993 to address a conference in Hawaii. A Tongan resident in Fiji, who had spent time in Papua New Guinea and earned his doctorate from Australia, Hau'ofa was then head of the School of Social and Economic Development at the University of the South Pacific in Fiji. What he had to say stunned many of those present. Five decades of Western economics, political and cultural modelling of the Pacific were wrong, he said. They were wrong in how they construed the Pacific, wrong in their diagnoses and predictions. A new approach was needed.

Hau'ofa's target was what he called a 'donut vision' that impoverishes every aspect of our lives. Donut vision? The donut he had in mind was the Pacific rim, whose antithesis he reimagined as 'Oceania', a region based on an ocean which linked various islands and landmasses, large and small. Donut thinking is another dimension of the process we described in Chapter 8, by which Australians view themselves as always marginalised victims of big-world systems of defence, economics and culture. Donut thinking sees Australia as the large island in a vast, empty, distant sea, when the reality is this: we are interlinked in our cultures and destinies, in defence and economics, by a vast sea, the Pacific. That sea is not empty, it is full. And it is not just full of fish and coral. It is the site of a thriving human multiculture, *and we are a part of it*.

Hau'ofa reinvented 'Oceania', the colonial name for the region, as a way of rethinking, from the ocean up, the meaning of human beings in this part of the world. From the geographical vision follows a deeper insight into the unique Pacific multiculture:

The idea that the countries of Polynesia and Micronesia are too small, too poor and too isolated to develop any meaningful degree of

autonomy, is an economistic and geographic deterministic view of a very narrow kind, that overlooks culture history, and the contemporary process of what may be called 'world enlargement' carried out by tens of thousands of ordinary Pacific islanders right across the ocean from east to west and north to south . . . making nonsense of all national and economic boundaries, borders that have been defined only recently, crisscrossing an ocean that had been boundless for ages before Captain Cook's apotheosis. (Hau'ofa 1993, p. 6)

There is, writes Hau'ofa, a 'gulf of difference between viewing the Pacific as "islands in a far sea" and as a "sea of islands"' (1993, p. 7). The former view 'emphasises dry surfaces in a vast ocean far from the centre of power' (1993, p. 7), while the latter 'connotes a sea of islands with their inhabitants [part of] . . . a large world in which peoples and cultures moved and mingled' (1993, p. 8). Or as we would put it, a profound, extensive multiculture.

Australia is a part of this extraordinary world. Sharing in Oceania's legacy and destiny, Australia occupies an important mediating role. This is so for the Pacific islanders who live in Australia, for the Pacific peoples themselves, and for Australia's own potential as a relay point for this multiculture's connections with the rest of the world. If embraced, Australia's own political and economic role in the region could lose its often opportunistic and naively pragmatist focus, and transform how Australia imagines itself. The idea that the Pacific might have more to offer Australia than the other way around seems not to have occurred to Australian thinkers of nation, or to writers on multiculturalism.

But this is a real promise and possibility, even in the areas of arts and culture. As the president of the Pacific Wave Association (which has hosted four festivals of Pacific culture in Australia) points out: 'Sydney's Pacific Islander population numbers 70 000, but many Australians "don't understand the culture".' (Lobley 2004, p. 28) In some respects, Pacific islands culture also has links of its own with Australian Indigenous conceptions of land and sea. These links are valuable in and of themselves, for they promote new ways of seeing Australia itself. In the 2004 festival, there was a play by Percy Bishop who calls himself a 'Mozzie' (Maori Australian), and whose play had a message: 'The message he wants to get across is, simply, "Why can't we just be cool with each other?" He set his play beside the Murray

[river] "because it's the life source of Australia—just ask blackfellas".
(Lobley 2004, p. 28) The transformative promise of multiculture,
paradoxically, is that it allows the potential for reconfiguring the story
of settler-society (an issue we will consider in greater detail in the
next chapter).

Hau'ofa's essay was expressed as a vision, but it contained a stark
challenge. Scrutinising the history of terms for Pacific nations
('Australasia', 'Australia and the Islands of the South West Pacific',
'South Pacific', 'Pacific'), he shows a correlation between metropolitan
ideologies and naming practices. He remarks grimly that:

> Two other terms for our region are significant indicators of our pro-
> gressive marginalisation. The first is Asia-Pacific as used by certain
> international agencies . . . to lump us together with hundreds of millions
> of Asians . . . The other term is Asia Pacific Economic Cooperation
> (APEC), which covers the entire Pacific Rim, but excludes the whole of
> the Pacific Islands region except Papua New Guinea. Thus . . . we are an
> appendage (or perhaps an appendix) of Asia, and in the APEC we do not
> exist. It should now be evident why our region is characterised as the
> 'hole in the doughnut', an empty space. (Hau'ofa 1997, p. 130)

'Donut thinking' describes approaches that treat complex systems
reductively or, more radically as in this case, seek to blank them out
altogether. The map between the east coast of Australia and the west
coast of the United States is not empty. It is full—full of cultures and
issues of vital concern to us. Indeed, our very existence is determined
by it. It is not just a matter of us being an island in the ocean, but
rather—as Hau'ofa's essay suggests—*of recognising the ocean in us.*

Aotearoa/New Zealand

New Zealand also is an island in Hau'ofa's 'sea of islands'. It is more
conscious than Australia of its status as a Pacific islands nation, and
of the Pacific context within and without. There is much we can learn
from this country which is, in so many other ways, akin to Australia.

Maori navigators named it 'Aotearoa', the land of the great white
cloud, because of the signature cloud that hung over this great
landmass in the ocean. Hau'ofa's sea of islands model makes an
obvious kind of sense in New Zealand that can perhaps be instructive

for us too. The four main islands take their place among many islands in the sea of islands, with New Zealand strikingly more comfortable with this role in the region, and the world.

The reasons for New Zealand's role in the Pacific lie in the peoples and their histories. Long before the rise of official multicultural policy in Australia in 1972, there was a chain of multicultures from pre-European contact times to the present. We have repeatedly seen how there was plurality wherever we turned: from Anglo-Celtic Australia to Afghan-Islamic Australia, to Chinese Australia—and all of this in the nineteenth century.

In Australia, these populations were dealt with in different ways at different times, reaching a low point in the 'White Australia' policy years at the time of Federation. In New Zealand, a different reality emerged: like Indigenous Australians, the Maori did not prevail in war against the European colonisers but, for a range of reasons, the British concluded a treaty in 1840 known as the Treaty of Waitangi. Thus, as in Australia, schismogenic tendencies were present in New Zealand from the beginning, but cosmogenesis also has played its role in different forms to make the present situation in New Zealand something that Australia can learn from.

The treaty formed the basis of a 'bicultural' polity. Biculturalism was eventually enshrined as a policy, and affects the way official multiculturalism is viewed in that country. In a useful essay on varieties of official multiculturalism policies as well as the different forms of exclusion of Indigenous peoples they entailed, the postcolonial critic Sneja Gunew remarks that

> Further difficulties encountered by indigenous groups are highlighted in Australia where the Aborigines refuse to be included in multicultural discourses on the grounds that these refer only to cultures of migration, whereas in New Zealand 'biculturalism' is the preferred official term because multiculturalism is seen as a diversion from the Maori sovereignty movement. In Canada First Nations are occasionally trapped in multicultural discourses and practices and are also consistently trapped between the French-English divide. (Gunew n.d.)

The different grounds of objection show how the same word, 'multiculturalism', can mean different things in different places. More important still, the 'bicultural' policy reflects the different power relations between Indigenous and non-Indigenous peoples in Australia and New Zealand respectively. At around 15 per cent of the population, Maori are numerically more significant than Australian Indigenous peoples, and they can look to the treaty document which cannot be swept aside. Indeed, as David Williams points out, its force has been augmented by the passage of law in New Zealand:

> It was [Matiu] Rata who as Minister of Maori affairs in the Third Labour Government had introduced the Treaty of Waitangi Bill to the House of Representatives in 1974 and he had overseen that Bill's enactment as the Treaty of Waitangi Act 1975. The 1975 Act established the Waitangi Tribunal and statutorily recognised the original Maori language text of the Treaty, along with an English language text, as part of New Zealand law ... This was the first time that Parliament had responded positively to calls by Maori groups and movements for 'ratification' of the Treaty. (Williams 2004)

Williams uses a lot of Maori words in his text, noting that this is 'reflective' of the impact of bicultural developments in New Zealand. In New Zealand, the two communities are known as 'Maori' and 'Pakeha', with the latter word referring to non-Maori New Zealanders. This has led to a different sense of interconnection from the situation in Australia.

Now our point is *not* that New Zealand's models of society and politics are 'better' than Australia's; indeed, they are interestingly and powerfully different. Alan Ward (2000), for instance, points out that:

> Even the Native Rights Act of 1865, which gave statutory authority to the third article of the treaty [of Waitangi]—according the Maori the rights and privileges of British subjects—proved a double-edged weapon. It enabled Maori to bring actions in the Supreme Court in defense of their legal rights and led, in 1867, to their representation in Parliament; it also enabled the government to treat those who took up arms against them as rebels rather than foreign belligerents—and to hang them. (2000, pp. 401–02)

This difference gives deeper meaning and effect to the flow of New Zealand bodies to Australia. Many of them have Maori or Pacific Islander backgrounds, adding to those who come to Australia by a more direct route. With all this in mind, we can now dwell on the way this dynamic works today.

Across the Tasman

When Australia negotiated to become a nation in 1901, the way was left open for New Zealand to be part of the federation. Even though that did not happen, the two nations have moved closer together, cooperating politically, economically and culturally. Money, goods, bodies and ideas flow easily between the two, even though New Zealanders are often more conscious than Australians of the tensions involved. But these differences are no greater than is normal in a multiculture, and that is what we say the two nations have become.

New Zealanders migrate to Australia in large numbers, though this is a two-way flow. Although it is not usually put this way, New Zealanders are a significant part of Australia's multiculture, its second most influential migrant group. This is a long-standing tendency: in terms of birthplace, New Zealand (8.1 per cent) ranks second only to the United Kingdom (26.2 per cent) as a source of overseas-born Australians (DIMA 2000, p. 4). But British migration is in long-term decline, whereas the New Zealand percentage is increasing (up 20.1 per cent in the five years to 1999). Permanent arrivals from New Zealand rose 28.1 per cent in the year to 2000 (DIMA 2000, p. 5).

The point is simple: New Zealanders are coming here in substantial numbers, such that in 2000 they represented 24 per cent of all settler arrivals (ABS 2002b). They are also younger than the national average (62 per cent are between 20 and 49 years old), and this implies a powerful and ongoing contribution to Australian multiculture. They have been formed within a significantly different multiculture, and their ways of seeing enhance Australia's own society and institutions.

Australia's major cities are regarded by many New Zealanders as multicultural powerhouses. But others cast a critical eye on Australia, its relations with Indigenous peoples, its apparent indifference to its true Pacific regional heritage. New Zealand ways of seeing are complex. We believe that their addition will enrich Australia's currently developing multiculture. It also points us more strongly towards the Hau'ofa model for the Pacific region. And that model in turn helps us to understand alternative possibilities in the relations that Australia might have with this region, by learning from New Zealand and respecting the rich connections New Zealand has achieved with other islands in that ocean.

What is our 'backyard'?

Another common metaphor for Australia's relations with its region is the 'backyard'. From one point of view, this metaphor illustrates what has been called the 'space-time compression' of modern globalisation (Harvey 1989), bringing together regions that were once separated by the 'tyranny of distance'. The increasing intensity of relations between Australia and various parts of Asia is, we have argued, creating an Austral-asian multiculture. As always with multicultures, there is no need to choose between multicultures. They weave together in a richer, multifunctional fabric. But when the 'backyard' metaphor is viewed through the lenses of a donut vision, the result is an impoverished map of the world.

We illustrate the 'donut' mentality in the highest levels of planning with some words of Professor Paul Dibb, probably the country's most distinguished strategic planner. Discussing his new phrase, the 'arc of instability', he commented informally on radio on our relations to our north that this was not 'our backyard' but was in fact 'our front yard'. In keeping with this concern, in a formal paper he argued for an increase in defence spending, from 'the current budget level of 1.9 per cent of GDP' to a level much greater (he was looking at a figure of 'at least 2.5 per cent') (2003, p. 9). The paper, delivered at the Northern Territory University, reflected his ongoing thesis in its title, 'The Arc of Instability and the North of Australia'. In an earlier website posting, he argued that:

> we face an arc of instability to our north, a weakened South-East Asia and an uncertain balance of power with the rise of China. Indonesia— the fourth largest country—has an unpredictable future. Prudent Australian defence planners must consider that Indonesia has the attributes of a friend and a potential adversary. (Dibb 2001)

Consider this so-called arc: Papua New Guinea, Indonesia and East Timor lie to our north, so it makes sense to see them as part of a 'northern neighbourhood'. There is plenty going on there that should be of direct interest to us. What happens here is of direct interest to them, making us equally 'neighbours' to them, though Dibb doesn't look at it from this point of view.

Instead, he sees a threat. But it is a very abstract one. Dibb's metaphors are still immersed in and determined by his 'donut vision'. The 'arc' is just another curved line, the edge of a different donut whose centre is still empty. He fails to register the richness and relevance of the intervening cultures, and their connections in all directions. Dibb's idea of 'neighbours' and 'backyards' sounds homely, concrete and positive, but if we look at it more closely we can see how reductive it is, eliminating distances to construct something that feels more manageable, rather than trying to represent the living complexity of the region as a network—not just a ring around a hole.

The reasoning of a strategic analyst like Dibb shows a reductionism similar to the Orientalism we described in Chapter 8. That a quarter of the planetary surface (and a similar proportion of its peoples) could be reduced to a single threatening structure collapses all these many diverse cultures into a single line, an *arc*. It arches above us, like some kind of evil rainbow stretched above the unwitting sunbakers of Bondi and City Beach.

In this world, we find a combination of warm, soft metaphors (neighbours, homes, backyards) and cold hard abstractions (the geometry of the arc). In some versions, as in this posting to *Defence Systems Daily*, which advocated 'consolidation of the defence industries', we are told: 'Closer to home, New Zealand's new government has taken a number of decisions . . . And in our own backyard, the non-military question for dealing with the early detection and apprehending of boat people remains controversial.' (Salteri 2000) Our problem with such metaphors ('home', 'Australia's backyard', our 'northern neighbourhood'), so beloved of economists and defence analysts and the politicians who quote them, is that they lack any sense of what a home or a backyard or a neighbourhood is like (unless they have in mind a home or backyard which is just a hole in the ground, which we doubt).

If we use Hau'ofa's model of a 'sea of islands', a richly interconnected space, rather than donut thinking, the 'backyard' metaphor can become a good one, enriched by a sense of the reality of how backyards can work in a multicultural neighbourhood.

For instance, southwest Sydney, which is regularly represented in the media in terms of (race) crime and the problems of housing commission estates, presents a different picture if we stroll down its suburban streets. Richly sprinkled amongst the houses we find innumerable examples of real Pacific homes and backyards. We find them in parts of Brisbane too. These places look much the same as other neighbourhoods: kids, clotheslines, the lush green plants thriving because they live on the right side of the rain shadow that stops rain falling on the plains in lower Western New South Wales.

Decorative plants? They certainly are attractive. But one has to have an eye trained to recognise them. In the towns of the Pacific islands, especially where rich volcanic soil can support them, we find similar 'backyards'. Some plants—kumara, taro, yams —grow discreetly. Others—cassava, breadfruit and mango—are rather more obvious. The land supplies a crop—and often, if necessary, gardens are tended in common, or on common land used for the purpose.

In South Pacific shops, this produce converges in mini-marketplaces, along with spices, Hindi films, tinned fish, Chinese bric-a-brac, Ayurvedic remedies, and people of all backgrounds drinking 'grog' (kava) out the back. Despite the casual attire, some of these chatting are business managers, entrepreneurs, small business owners and IT professionals. Family networks spread out across the city, making a parallel sense of the nation and the landscape, and building a bridge across to Pacific homelands from Tuvalu to Rotuma on the one hand, from Vancouver to Auckland on the other, including Sydney and Brisbane.

From outside, 'they' look like a single category: islanders. But 'they' are, in reality, already a multiculture in multicultural Australia. Their homelands are many, as are their faiths. There are many languages, mediated sometimes by English as a common language.

After sharing a bowl of grog, families play cricket and Rugby, have barbecues, and so on. On Sundays, suburban churches resound with the singing of Samoan, Tongan or Fijian choirs. From month to month, seasons are marked out by familiar milestones of faith, be it Eid or Diwali or, as in most of the islands nations themselves, Methodism or Catholicism. The idea of a 'Pacific backyard' is indeed a powerful way to think of our context. That backyard is not far away either. In fact, it *is* right next door.

The Pacific superpower

If people in Australia see the Pacific as the hole in the donut, that is not the case when the telescope is turned around. Australia is solid dough, a very big island amongst the islands, and Pacific peoples and governments cannot afford to ignore Australia or 'get Australia wrong'. Nor do they. Australia's status as a superpower in the region rests on a number of factors: its wealth and power; its aid and trade behaviours; and its history. We cannot cover all this, but offer instead a sketch of the 'big brother' island from a Pacific perspective, from the centre of the donut. From there the picture is unfamiliar to Australians used to seeing Australia as small and defenceless.

Australia looms large as a regional power, and its decisions on trade, aid, education, tourism, immigration, mining and development, and the environment resonate powerfully in the vast Pacific region. Under protective trade deals, Pacific industries ranging from garment production to fisheries have developed. Australian aid produces roads and bridges, and in the case of Papua New Guinea a substantial percentage of the government's operating budget. Australia and New Zealand help fund the University of the South Pacific, as well as teacher training colleges and training institutes. There are scholarships for Pacific students to study in Australia.

In commerce, Australian tourists visit Samoa, Vanuatu, Fiji and even Hawaii. Australia's immigration policies—visitor and resident—are studied closely, and understood widely. They affect the lives of hundreds of thousands of Pacific Islanders whose families are already divided by migration. Australian companies mine Pacific mines, and transport Pacific timbers. Australian pronouncements on business practices affect the business environments of these small nations. Australia's stance on the environment is perhaps the best known aspect of Australian conduct: the huge ecological footprint of Australia is well understood and resented. Australia is seen as contributing to the greenhouse effect, which according to current science would lead to entire Pacific nations and cultures disappearing forever. Tuvalu and Kiribati are in special danger because their atoll structures are not far above the waterline.

Australians seem, in this respect, to move like tourists in their own region: unaware, looking at a far horizon and ignoring what is near to hand. Pacific peoples, on the other hand, study both tourists and the unconscious giant closely. The disregard for Pacific sensibilities is sensed, and resented. In Australian discussions of such issues, the views of Pacific peoples are rarely considered.

Australia also has a history as a colonial administrator—something of which many young Australians are unaware. Like other colonisers, Australian behaviour has been a mixture of good and ill, a combination of disinterested governance and generosity and big dashes of capitalist exploitation. The fruits of the latter are visible in territories even if they were not colonised. The devastated landscapes of Nauru and Ocean Island are one legacy of Australian 'buccaneers' (to use the phrase Tupeni Baba—one-time academic colleague, then deputy prime minister in Fiji in 1999—turned on a group of visiting Australian academics). Entire national histories have been distorted by this history. This history is also Australia's responsibility.

The most important legacy of Australian activities lies in Papua New Guinea. This story begins before Australia was even federated. The colony of Queensland sought control of parts of Papua New Guinea in 1883; in 1884, Britain seized the southeast part which became known as British New Guinea: 'Britain offered British New Guinea to the newly federated Australia, which accepted the territory in November 1901. Transfer was formally made in March 1902.' (Evans 1997, p. 224) The motives for the acquisition were expediency rather than affection, with Australia's most formidable early politician, Alfred Deakin, seeing only commercial advantage in the arrangements (Evans, p. 227). Yet World War II made Papua New Guinea a battleground in which many Australians fought and died alongside Indigenous peoples. After that war, Australia's colonial relationship continued until independence was conferred in 1975. Now Papua New Guinea and its neighbour the Solomon Islands are both seen as being in danger of becoming 'failed states', and Australia remains an ambivalent but often constructive ally.

In Papua New Guinea too, Australia was involved in a shameful episode, endorsing the transfer of the western half of the landmass (a territory that had been Dutch) to Indonesia in spite of the clear opposition of the people concerned. Australia was also involved in a crisis at Bougainville, triggering a civil war around arguments about mining. Yet if Australia had a role in creating problems in Papua New Guinea (and mining has led to a highly unstable, inequitable economic structure), it also has a role in fixing them. These links of reciprocity, in the present as in the past, are significant features of our environment, as they are for Pacific peoples. They provide the material underpinning for a Pacific multiculture that is already a fact, however invisible it is to the 'donut' gaze.

Difficult histories

Connections with the Pacific region are easier to see in northern Australia. John grew up in Far North Queensland, and well remembers when the family Holden was packed up for a drive to Charters Towers or Ravenswood. These old gold-mining towns were full of stories of British and Irish history. Yet there were other histories too: Indigenous and Chinese, and also Pacific Islander.

Pacific Islanders have a long association with the North Queensland mainland, not just through colonisation, but also because of centuries of trade and mobility. With colonialism, many Pacific Islanders were imported into Australia in conditions close to slavery to work on sugar plantations, as well as in other jobs in North Queensland. Their descendants, and those of the Torres Strait Islanders who moved to the mainland, are part of the North Queensland landscape.

Or at least they *should* have been. The profile of Pacific peoples is smaller than it might have been had it not been for the effects of Australian Federation in 1901. It is difficult to imagine, now that 'Australia' is an accomplished fact, that the pre-Federation colonies came close at times to forming a nation that excluded both Queensland and Western Australia (the home states of the authors of this book), and yet nearly included New Zealand. The colony of Queensland was deemed problematic because, like the southern states of the United States, it had a significant population of non-white inhabitants. Unlike in the United States, these were not (quite) slaves, but paid indentured workers often living in harsh conditions.

In one sketch of the scenes leading up to Federation, Evans et al. (1997) introduce some original materials with this remark:

> Between 1863 and 1904 Pacific Islanders were the principal labour force in Queensland's sugar industry . . . [the] total number of individuals involved was closer to 50,000. Until about 1880 islanders also worked in the pastoral and maritime industries . . . In its quest for a 'White

Australia' in 1901 the new federal government ordered that recruiting cease from 1904 and that as many as possible of the Islanders be deported by 1907. A total of 7,068 Islanders were repatriated between 1904 and 1908 and a further 194 departed up to 1914. (1997, pp. 217–18)

Each of these deportees had a story. The stories and the people deported are, for the most part, lost. But the authors included a story from Louie, an Islander deportee, published in the *Ravenswood Miner* in 1906. The story is an example of official implementation of guidelines that are oddly similar to more recent official acts that we looked at in Chapter 2. In such behaviour, we see that a 'crisp' sense of borders comes from an exaggerated fear driving a sometimes distorted sense of duty. On the part of the officials who implement it and the society that supports this 'tough line', such policies lead to people steeling themselves against their own sense of being human. This is true not just in the story we are about to relate, but also in the stories of removal of Aboriginal children, and later in the rise of detention camps in Australia.

Let us simply listen to Louie's words from across the years. Louie writes to his wife, Rosie, a white Australia-born woman he is being forced to leave behind and never see again:

Dear Rosie,

I got your letter alright. I glad you got money. I sorry that I can't come see you before I go home. Government he hurry along we fellow. We go away along Monday—no matter you stop. Might I come back to see you. I take money to go home £29. Tell Herbert [his son] that I can't see him no more. Suppose I go home if I alright I come back. Suppose I no see you any more along this ground we will meet in heaven . . . Suppose I go home I no married any more. Suppose I write letter from Home you answer back. Tell Mable good bye . . . You tell Mr Rae to let you go down to Cluden and you take Herbert with you, and you take all my things. Boxes, clothes, everything belong you . . . We no stop along Townsville, but we go all the way along Boat . . . Tell Mr Rea good bye. I sorry I no see my missus any more. Mable Rae, good bye, now I no say any more. Good by Rosie and plenty of kisses . . . This last letter. You no more send letter to Burdekin. Your loving Louie. (cited in Evans et al., 1997, pp. 222–24)

We as teachers have read this letter repeatedly in class, but it is still hard to read it aloud and not come close to breaking down because of the terrible things done in this case, and the things that were to follow in the twentieth century, and now again with detention camps in the twenty-first century. The letter, written from Ayr (south of Townsville), a sugar centre, was published at the time in the *Ravenswood Miner* paper (Ravenswood is southwest of Townsville).

Yet, without diminishing the grief at this kind of senseless, dehumanising act, we also note that this letter was written in English, which Louie had obviously learnt, to a white wife whom he clearly loved, published in a local newspaper whose editor must have known what he was publishing, read by readers who surely were not so dehumanised as to react to it any differently from us or all our students. There is a danger, in looking at pieces of evidence like this, of reacting so strongly to the story that we don't take account of the complex context it also carries with it.

The circulating spirit of multiculture

Along with many other cultural forms, goods and ideas, philosophies and ways of doing things, the idea of 'multiculture' has circulated around the 'sea of islands', taking new forms as it returns to Australia. For instance, we set our students an article on multiculturalism written by Subramani, a Fiji Indian writer who resides partly in Fiji, partly in India and partly in southwest Sydney. The article comes from a speech delivered in Fiji, where the context gives resonance to what otherwise might seem, to Australian eyes, a fairly standard view. The point of the context is that Fiji, since its independence in 1970, has been a divided society, its schismogenic tendencies erupting into no less than three coups, all apparently provoked by tensions between Fijian islanders and the nearly equal numbers of Indians. Fiji is not a glowing example of multiculture, but it is one where it is possible to see more clearly than in Australia how desirable it is, what form it must take. 'Most people in Fiji are in favour of multiculturalism,' writes Subramani (1995, p. 251), but it is not yet a transforming vision. Subramani looks beyond the coups and struggles to what it should be:

> Here in these multicultural political communities we should actively face the challenge of living with each other, and discover the value of

Borderwork and multicultural Australia

not just co-existence, for co-existence isn't enough, but also the significance of others in our own self-advancement or self-enrichment. (1995, pp. 253–54)

Subramani makes no reference or comparison to Australia here, but he is the complex meeting point of ideas from three cultures—Fijian, Indian and Australian—and his multicultural vision can legitimately be called a part of Australia's multiculture as well as (more significantly) a part of Fiji-Indian multiculture. He has also enjoyed a late career renaissance as a creative writer. His *Dauka Puraan* (2001) was a comic epic, uncompromisingly written in Fiji Hindi, an interlanguage rarely used for literary works, and distinct from standard Hindi though the book was successfully published in India itself. He also has an English language novel planned. One excerpt from it, 'Exiles in a Park', tells the story of Baaj who, seeking to migrate to Canada, ends up in Sydney, almost by mistake. Baaj is a very creative individual, hard-working and successful. He is creative in love too: having left Durga (his wife) behind in Fiji, he marries again, this time to a *firangi* (foreigner), a white woman, who nevertheless, in true Romantic style, insists on all the finery of a traditional Hindu wedding. Bedlam ensues when his first wife turns up, but Baaj settles everything by working 'double shift' to pay for both (1997 p. 58). The story reflects Subramani's view that the Pacific has *widened* rather than diminished in scope as a result of transmigration.

The point Subramani makes is not so very different from Hau'ofa's: we live in an interconnected world, and we need new ways to think about it if we are to thrive—ideas like multiculturalism travel. This is an age when families are on the phone to each other. They do it whether from the Brisbane suburb of Inala to a place just across the road in Oxley, or to Apia in Western Samoa across the ocean. And modern technologies overlay older sea routes. When reliable news from Fiji broke down in the context of the Speight coup attempts in 2000, websites like 'Fijilive' kept Fijian Australians in touch with what was happening.

 Ambivalence

Refugees are usually casualties of the schismogenesis they have left, which should make them better able to appreciate what Australia has

to offer. But even when it is relatively benign, without razor wire and detention centres, the initial encounter can also be a schismogenic experience, with people recoiling from the differences at the same time as they are welcomed. Here, for instance, is a story by Asha Chand, written in 1998—a year after she and her Fiji-Indian family had made their forced move to Australia:

> Moving to Australia was the hardest decision we ever had to make. Many friends and family had told me that Australia was a land of opportunity . . . However, like the stories of hundreds of other Fiji Indians who left the island Paradise after the military coups of 1987, in search of a better life, my experiences have been a mixture of good and bad.
>
> In Australia's melting pot of cultures, I am still proud to be Indian, proud of my past and I want to cling to my culture, religion and, of course, my past. Nevertheless, I feel all these identities are being threatened with the expectations and challenges of the new environment.
>
> I do not speak as much Hindi as I did in Fiji. We do not munch as much curry. I want to do that. I sometimes crave to don a *sari*. I am always dashing around and feel that a *sari* would inhibit my movements.
>
> I feel so trapped within myself. This feeling of ambivalence is torturing . . . I am so headstrong in many ways but in situations like this I am searching for an identity. (quoted in Duarte 2001, pp. 30–31)

Translocation can trigger schismogenesis within, at the same time as cosmogenesis is happening, making the ambivalence more intense, a 'torture', as Chand says. Multiculture contains tensions; it does not cancel them. It is not always simple or comfortable, and 'gratitude' is not the only or most appropriate response to the new situation.

Donut con salsa: Invisible Mexico

John became more aware of the importance of the Pacific Islands—and Australia's ambivalent links to them—by living and teaching in Fiji for three years, forming deep relationships in the process. Bob became aware of another part of our region that is normally invisible to most Australians: Mexico. He visited it often, developing a network of friends

Borderwork and multicultural Australia

and ultimately marrying a Mexican, Gabriela Coronado. Mexico is a major nation of 110 million people just across the Pacific to our east, just as close as the United States, not much further than much of Asia, on the other side of the Pacific Rim. However, the Mexican presence in Australia is microscopic, around 1200 by the 2001 census. Even if there were many 'illegals', the total numbers would not be large enough to cause much of a blip in the normal picture of 'multicultural Australia'.

This illustrates a complex geometry of holes in donuts which is part of a general pattern. There is one hole in this donut, this time not in its centre but on the Australian side, matching another larger hole along a whole opposite side. By a bizarre causality, the small hole in our side of the donut creates a much larger hole on the other side. Latin America is a continent that Australians cannot see, a huge, populous region that is part of our multicultural global world. There is a causal link between the two holes. Why can Australian governments so clearly see Anglo-America, especially the United States, yet not Spanish- or Portuguese-speaking America?

A limited view has also limited the multiculture that could have reversed this trend. Australia has only a few Mexicans, and a sprinkling of other Latin Americans—many of them former refugees. Why are there so few? A major reason is the restrictions that operate. Not only do Mexicans have to fight quotas to gain entry visas, but even tourist visas can be difficult to obtain. In 2000, Gabriela's daughter with her boyfriend were initially refused a tourist visa for a three-month stay. They only managed to make the trip by buying a ticket from an LA travel agent, who easily arranged for a visa on the spot.

It seems that Australian immigration services operate from an internalised map borrowed from the US unconscious, in which Mexicans are all potential illegal immigrants whose highest aim is to settle in the promised land. But US immigration officials see no problems in allowing Mexicans to go to Australia, which for them is just another tourist destination. This is hardly an appropriate sort of map to be adopted uncritically by Australians.

Paradoxically, the government seems aware of the need to improve Australia's links with Latin America. In May 2002, it set up the Council on Australian and Latin American Relations (COALAR) to address the barriers of attitudes on both sides that are currently blocking a major economic development that would benefit both. In a joint press release by Alexander Downer, Minister for Foreign

Affairs, and Mark Vaile, Minister for Trade, on 5 October 2002, the ministers—who had both visited the region—said that the council would enhance Australia's economic, political and social relations with Latin America: 'As a result of our respective visits, we are convinced that this is a region which has much to offer Australia. In particular, Latin America is a place where Australians can and should do business. As such, we will look to the Council to assist in breaking down outdated stereotypes to help facilitate greater commercial exchanges.'

Trade, here as elsewhere, acts as a cosmogenic force, creating the contacts, flows and energies out of which new cultural forms will emerge. Ministers Downer and Vaile do not use the word 'multiculture', and they do not link their proposal to any aspect of Australian multi-culture, yet we do so on their behalf. A richer Anglo-Latin multiculture linking sites in Australia and North and South America across the Pacific would be a new kind of order, which in turn would give value and impetus to Australia's own potential Anglo-Latin multiculture. In this case, as in so many others, a comprehensive multicultural perspective allows us to see how valuable a role multiculture can play in supporting Australia's vital interests. More Mexicans (and Brazilians, Chileans, Argentinians, etc.) would make Australia a better, more prosperous country. Likewise, a (multicultural) Australian presence in an emerging trans-Pacific multiculture would benefit all participants. At the moment it is happening almost accidentally, without much conscious government planning. Governments could do more to remove current blocks, and encourage fruitful contacts, but there are signs that cosmogenesis is already coming from below.

A new materialism

We will finish this chapter by addressing what some may feel is a contradiction or confusion in our argument. In the case of Latin America and Asia, we seem to be saying that trade and policy imperatives have been driving a multiculture which will then have an economic payoff. In the case of the Pacific, we seem to be putting things the other way around, arguing for cultural values in spite of the fact that they seem associated with nations too weak to ever be of any economic or political importance.

This seeming contradiction arises from our sense of the connections between culture, politics and trade as three-body systems. While many works on multiculturalism criticise talk of cultural value for reflecting terms of a hidden agenda of economic value, productive diversity and other such utilitarianisms, we have been talking about utilitarian issues in terms of culture. The material basis Hau'ofa (1993) signals in his model of interconnectedness makes nonsense of any attempt to hold these apart. This does not mean that multiculture cannot be described on its own terms. Quite the contrary: its foundation in human cultural practices precedes both economic and military strategy. The 'sea of islands' approach reminds us that we should attend to the real criss-crossings of communications, migration and culture, and beware of mere geometries of power.

It is not as if Hau'ofa, a former professor of sociology and head of a school of 'economic development', did not know about economics and politics. He was merely concerned with an imbalance, in which one aspect of political economy excluded consideration of everything else. A year or two before the 'Sea of Islands' essay was published, he remarked in conversation with John that he was 'fed up' with the sociological and economic approach in general, and wished he could return to an anthropological way of looking at things. Now we can understand what he meant. Hau'ofa's materialism is anthropological, which includes economics and politics. From this point of view, economics is just one of a number of human systems of organisation of exchange relationships—important of course, but part of a wider field of human interaction. By actively retrieving earlier constructions of the Pacific world, Hau'ofa argues that we can see a truer, fuller reality than that afforded by GDP-based modelling.

His view makes remissions of money from countries like the United States and Australia to the Pacific homelands part of an anthropological familial relationship, a concept of widening of influence rather than a relation of economic dependency. His view makes us rethink what counts as 'production'. The many non-formal (in the economic sense) trading relationships that characterise Pacific societies are not counted in their GDP, because they are part of economies of reciprocity, of exchange, or of local markets outside the formal economy.

To say this does not mean we have to demonise conventional trade as against cultural factors: commercial *or* cultural values, profit *or* principles. This logic of *either–or* is widespread in popular and academic thinking. We believe it often distorts a more complex reality. For instance, in a history according to binarism, after World War II, Australia engaged Japan in a series of important trade deals. Trade offered economic benefits and prosperity, yet it was to be conducted with a former adversary. *Either* trade, *or* principle. Expediency seemed to win out, and trade triumphed over principle. When the Whitlam government recognised mainland China as China in its first year of office, trade flourished. For many, though, the deal with 'red' China was anathema. *Either* trade, *or* principle.

We hope that the falseness of these oppositions is clear by now. Trade genuinely warmed relations with Japan; cross-cultural understanding followed. Japanese society became more outward looking because nations like Australia engaged it in trade, and Japanese culture became part of Australian culture—Mitsubishis and Walkmans as well as sushi, Astroboy and *manga*. An outward-looking China offers more hope, both to its own people and to us, than the closed system it could have been. It is not a matter of endorsing the values of the 'People's Republic' or its present undemocratic regime. A country is far more than its political system, or its current political leadership. Hau'ofa's warnings against donut thinking encourage us to be inclusive, to value holes and donuts, donuts and holes. It is at the heart of the multicultural perspective that we have been arguing for in this book.

Borderwork and multicultural Australia

10. Imagining multicultural Australia

In this book we have traced the many forms and histories that make up multicultural Australia, yet there is still a task we need to carry out. With all the talk of cultural diversity, there is a danger that there can seem to be nothing left in common, holding the weave together. We suggest that one such principle is the complex fact of Australia itself, as it is experienced and imagined. The landmass and its features are part of physical geography, not directly of the 'culture' as such, but those features are always understood by people through various histories, experiences and categories. Australian geography is one key thing common to all Australians, whatever their backgrounds. As a three-body system, interactions between people, histories and places constitute any culture, including Australia's multiculture.

We believe that all peoples of Australia relate to 'Australia' as such, including its physical environment, the heat and the cold, the distinctive plants and animals, a sense of it as a significant place, made significant by stories they hear and stories they bring. The multicultural weaving together of stories began early in Australia's history, with the German explorer Leichhardt adding a different vision from the Scotsman Stuart and the Englishman Grey. Yet we also feel the presence of many powerful barriers, concepts and maps, in the way of seeing Australia differently, in space and time, as the emerging multiculture it is, set in the kind of world it is part of.

In this chapter we will try to identify these limiting concepts, to show how limiting they are, and to suggest—in a tentative, speculative way—some alternative maps and histories to make better sense of a multicultural Australia. We will sketch a broader framework in time and space, deep history and global space as the minimal context in which to set the strange story of 'Australia'. In this spirit, then, we seek to 'discover Australia' yet again, reimagining it as the same place, yet now different. We offer this chapter as a multicultural guide to a multicultural Australia, for citizens and visitors alike.

Weird geographies

'Australia' is mainly seen today through the strange geography used by the Europeans who came to this southern continent 200 years ago. These visitors, however, did not simply transpose terms and mindsets that made easy sense of where they came from. Instead they viewed the new continent through a template from their deep past. This process created a weird geography, multicultural and multitemporal, which has undergone many transformations on the way to the present. For a concept taken for granted by most Australians, it is full of quirks and irrationalities, many of which are hard to fit into a coherent picture of the country and the world. Yet we want to understand it, not to sweep it away—even if that were possible. It turns out to be far less merely 'Anglo-Celtic' than Australians think, more open to a rich range of reflections and uses by all Australians today.

There are four main compass points in Western geography. In the course of this chapter we will consider these, focusing especially on the two points south and east. In order to 'get our bearings', we will begin with the south. *Australasia*, as we saw in Chapter 8, is south and east. The name 'Australia' itself comes from Latin *australis*, south. 'Australia' is a feminine noun in Latin, a language which gives land itself a gender. Grammatical gender is not the same as gender in society, but the fact that it is feminine resonates with ideologies of land as woman, mother.

Nor is *australis* as south a neutral geographical description. All cardinal points—north, south, east and west—had profound and complex *meanings* for successive cultures that make up what is often wrongly treated as a single, homogeneous 'Western' culture. What does our first compass point, *south*, mean? It means different things in different parts of the world. In the Roman empire that stretched from Britain in the West to the 'Middle East', from France to the north to North Africa to the south, Rome was naturally the central reference point. *Australis* is related to *auster*, a dry, hot wind from the south: and heat and drought was part of its meaning. For Romans, 'south' meant the hotter parts of Italy, and the deserts of North Africa. 'North' meant the wild, unconquerable tribes of Germanic peoples. North and south, in their different ways, were extremes outside the known centre, Rome.

When *auster* came south to Australia, it had undergone at least three acts of translocation. Translocation (movement in space) is a key term in understanding the dynamic history of the globe, in which things have always moved from place to place and changed in the process. The Roman *auster* became the North European 'south' before it came to Australia. Each time, the term gained new meaning from a different marker-point: Rome, England, Australia. With each shift, what was once a periphery became a centre.

North and south look unproblematic on a small, flat, two-dimensional map, but the world is a three-dimensional space, which scholars speculated more than 2000 years ago was a sphere, a globe. It is common today to suppose that everyone believed the world was flat until the heroic Columbus showed it was round, but this is a libel on ancient thought and intellect. By 200 BC, the Greek Eratosthenes not only knew that the world was round; he had calculated its circumference to a high degree of accuracy.

The idea of a three-dimensional globe lay behind another common name for Australia: 'the Antipodes'. *Antipodes* in Greek means feet-upside-down. The image seemed to some to defy common sense. St Augustine, a major figure in the early Christian church, remarked around 400 AD that if there could be antipodeans—that is, 'men who have their feet facing ours when they walk—that is utterly incredible' (1958, p. 367). For Augustine, theory and experience clashed, producing disbelief or absurdity. From his point of view in time and space, as a citizen of the late Roman Empire, 'the Antipodes' signified something strange, unnatural, an inversion of the known, 'natural' order.

If Augustine's geography now sounds strange, his views on multiculture are modern enough:

What is true for a Christian beyond the shadow of a doubt is that every real man, that is, every mortal animal that is rational, however unusual to us may be the shape of his body, or the color of his skin, or the way he walks, or the sound of his voice, and whatever the strength, portion or quality of his natural endowments, is descended from the single first-created man. (1958, p. 365)

These views are not inexplicable or anachronistic. Augustine lived in a multiculture: he was a black bishop in Northern Africa, in the *southern* lands of the empire—and thus, in a literal sense, 'Australian'. His Rome was in decline, threatened by barbarian hordes from the north who would ultimately finish the Roman empire. During his lifetime, Roman legions were withdrawing from Britain in order to better protect Rome, just at the moment he was imagining a universal Christian church. 'Empire' then, as now, was highly complex, always to some degree a multiculture.

So Australia, the 'land down-under' (antipodes), in the words of the contributor to one excellent set of accounts of our prehistory, 'was invented before it was discovered' (van den Boogaart 1988, p. 43). This imagined geography produces self-images of Australia as an antipodean anti-world, a frightening, hot, dry, southern land. One legacy has been hostility to nature and the fragile ecosystems of this small continent. It also underpins a deep idea of Australia as a difference machine, challenging all who come here, from whatever background. Australia still has the meaning of an anti-world, where normal (European *and* Asian) reality is inverted. In this world, surely, *anything* is possible.

Australia: East/West

Anglo-Celtic Australia normally sees itself as part of 'the West', as opposed to 'the East'. The geography here is far removed from any physical basis, influenced by ideological meanings that have clustered around this particular axis. These meanings are more complex than many people suppose, with a long, strange history. World history since the sixteenth century has been seen as an era in which 'the West' (European powers) have colonised much of the world, forming what Immanuel Wallerstein (1974) called a 'world system'. This system formed the template for globalisation today.

This process was political and economic from the outset, moving goods and bodies around the globe, establishing systems of control—direct and indirect—which have become part of the contemporary landscape, producing effects over time which show traces of the non-linear environment in which they formed and acted. It also had an ideological dimension, equally influential, which Norbert Elias (1982) called a 'civilising process'. These European nations gave themselves a mission: to 'civilise' the barbarians they wanted to exploit.

The 'civilising process' was both cosmogenic (pulling together peoples and ways of seeing) and schismogenic, since it was in practice based on a difference between rulers and ruled. This process of legitimation was managed through a set of discourses which, as we saw in Chapter 8, Edward Said (1995) analysed as 'Orientalism'.

Let us think about this compass point again. 'Orientalism' comes from *oriens* (the rising of the sun, the east), so it connects with basic cardinal points in a map, with all the problems we saw with 'south'. East has a more constant meaning across the globe than south, because the east is always where the sun rises: life, origin, the beginning. West is where the sun sets: death, the end (hence perhaps the strange fetish for theses about the 'decline of the West'). In the history of 'Western' culture, this primary sense reflects an aspect of the agreed history of civilisation, which arose around 8000 BC in what is now called the 'Middle East', but which then was the centre.

Again, a history of translocations from centres to peripheries plays havoc with meanings derived from this system. 'Civilisation' went both east and west from its first centre. To the east were great civilisations of India and China; to the west was Egypt, followed by Greece, followed by Rome. The shifting centre created confusion around the primary meaning of 'east'. Greece learnt from Egypt and the 'Middle Eastern' civilisations, and Rome in turn learned from Greece, so that 'east' signified the origin of their civilisations. With the collapse of the Roman empire and the rise of powerful kingdoms to its north and west, from 1100 there came to be a new, diffuse centre in the *north*, Northern Europe, which (despite its own compass) still saw itself as the 'West', as the old empire had seen it.

When European powers came to dominate those earlier centres to their east, the 'civilising mission' was imposed on an earlier map, in terms of which these had been the sites where everything valuable in the 'Western' tradition began. The ideology of the 'civilising mission' faced the contradictory task of creating a sense of inherent 'Western' superiority out of a term which carried with it a long history of 'Western' *inferiority*. According to Said, Orientalism refers to a way the 'West' constructs the 'Orient', 'the place of Europe's greatest and richest and oldest colonies, the source of its civilizations and languages, its cultural contestant, and one of its deepest and most recurring images of the Other' (1978, p. 1).

For Said, Orientalism arose out of the period, after 1800, when European nations had subjugated the former empires of the 'East', just as England was taking possession of Australia. It is an imperial gaze and an instrument of imperialism, a strategy for understanding and representing subject peoples. It is schismogenic because the otherness of the East could not be put in doubt, yet it had a contradiction at its heart because these peoples, constructed by Orientalism as inherently inferior and incapable of rule, had themselves invented Western civilisation, when peoples of the 'west' and 'north' were barbarians.

Said stresses how the West used the 'east' to define itself negatively ('*we* are what *they* aren't'). As he puts it, Orientalism created, out of real people and places, a 'theatre' on which to stage itself:

On this stage will appear figures whose role it is to represent the larger whole from which they emanate. The Orient then seems to be, not an unlimited extension beyond the familiar European world, but rather, a closed field, a theatrical stage affixed to Europe. (1995, p. 63)

Yet, as Said's narrative makes clear, Orientalism was woven out of a series of real if unequal contacts between agents of the 'West' and peoples of the 'East'. Orientalism circulated in popular culture as well as in the language of government, enshrined in stories by travellers, tourists, academics and other visitors from the 'centre' who were affected and changed by their experiences. 'Orientalism', in its way, was a kind of multiculture—albeit one that had both cosmogenic and schismogenic tendencies.

So to call Australia a part of the 'West' is geographical nonsense, and to see it as nonsense is a step towards dismantling the ideology that is carried through the term. It carries with it the crisp logic of Empire, as expressed definitively in Rudyard Kipling's famous lines: 'East is east, and west is west/ And never the twain shall meet'. In the fuzzy logic of a dynamic globe, this is completely wrong. East is

Borderwork and multicultural Australia

always blurring with West, becoming West (or vice versa) whenever there is movement around the globe. With Australia, for instance, if it is West, what is its East? New Zealand? The United States? Does that mean that one or both of them are decadent and inherently inferior, destined to be ruled by Australia? Somehow we don't think so.

New terms for a global world

Instead of fixed categories on static maps becoming nonsensical as applied to a dynamic world, we need dynamic terms designed to cope with a world of multiple flows and fuzzy boundaries, commonly described as **postmodern**. There is an extensive literature on this theme, so we limit ourselves here to a small number of concepts relevant to our present task: to find new kinds of map to help us better imagine a multicultural Australia in a multicultural world.

David Harvey (1989) has talked influentially of 'space time compression' as a new characteristic of the postmodern condition. By this he refers to the effects of modern systems of communication and transport, now capable of moving bodies, goods and meanings on a scale and speed that is a quantum leap from anything that has gone before. In this context, Benedict Anderson (1992) notes that increased mobility challenges notions of fixed identities, suggesting that we now might be 'faced here with a new type of nationalist: the "long-distance nationalist"' (1992, p. 13). What he is talking about here has since been called **transnationalism**.

Transnationalism is a sign and product of the breakup of large-scale liberal-democratic social orders, in which new global entities form across the former fixed national boundaries (Fonte 2002). Kastoryano (2004) sees a pattern that reminds us of Anderson's (1991) idea of the nation itself as an imagined community, but on a grander scale: 'For Islam, the rhetoric of "Umma", that is, a worldwide unified Muslim community, is reinterpreted in such a way that reframes all national diversity as one imagined "political" community, getting away from its religious definition. Therefore, transnationalism appears as a new type of nationalism.' (Kastoryano 2004)

In this view, the 'rhetoric of mobilization recentralizes' (Kastoryano 2004), and threatens the nation state itself. From this point of view, Australia can be seen as a site that has been penetrated by multiple transnationalisms, full of transnational citizens who owe their allegiance to a new kind of state. Yet, as we have seen with Islam and Asia in Australia, a strong form of transnationalism (including political as well as cultural allegiances) has not happened. In theory, the greatest threat to the integrity of Australia comes from the British Empire as a shadowy transnational body, whose head of state, the Queen of Australia, still requires allegiance from her 'Australian subjects', according to the current Australian Constitution.

Linked to the phenomenon of 'transnationalism' is **diaspora**, an older idea that has been adapted to describe some features of our postmodern global conditions. 'Diaspora' comes from a Greek word, meaning 'spreading a seed'. It was used in the first place to describe the scattering of Jewish people from their homeland into new places where they maintained their links and their identity with the place they had left. The Jewish diaspora held together for 2000 years with incredible tenacity, maintaining a sense of identity across time and distance. Diaspora now refers to any community, dispersed through one or more places, whose unity and identity derive from a claimed connection to an originary place, real or imagined, from which its members have been scattered or displaced.

We find the term diaspora very suggestive, as it gestures towards the kinds of affinities groups actually experience in their lives. It is not that everyone in a group feels the same way. But diaspora is an important aspect of multiculture, and thinking about it is as important as understanding processes of schismogenesis and cosmogenesis. The diasporic community of Jews interacted with many different cultures to produce a diasporic Jewish multiculture. The schismogenic pressure of their official identity still allowed in many elements from their surrounding cultures. At the same time, they enriched the many places they went to, in spite of occasionally deadly outbursts of prejudice against them. The value of the term for us is that it captures the dual identity of all arrivals to Australia, products of and connected to many places, histories and cultures, as well as forming an accidental multiculture in the new context.

All component cultures in the Australian multiculture are also diasporic cultures, even many Aboriginal peoples, dispossessed from their home territories and way of life. This point has been made in one of the most important essays considering the complexities and contradictions of diaspora (Clifford, in Vertovec & Cohen 1999, p. 222). This essay, written by James Clifford, is republished in a collection that itself deserves mention because it includes works by other leading theorists of diaspora and transnationalism.

More locally, the Australian-Fiji-Indian scholar Vijay Mishra (1996) has written usefully of the term, focusing especially on the different kinds of Indian diasporas around the world (including Australia). Mishra's account is especially rich because it includes successive migrations. In this framework he proposes two kinds of diaspora: a modernist kind marked by a 'schismatic break' (1996, p. 434), where a homeland is left; and a more postmodern kind where 'the idea of a homeland . . . is always present visibly and aurally (through video cassettes, films, tapes and CDs)' (1996, p. 434).

Many, like Fiji-Indian playwright, critic and poet Sudesh Mishra (2002), criticise the tendency of 'diaspora' to hide the class and gender workings of a society behind a unilinear screen of ethnicity. Vijay Mishra, too, is wary. He argues that the 'diaspora is a particular condition of displacement and disaggregation'. Far from supplanting the nation, 'diasporas confirm that postmodern ethnicities are here to stay' (2002, p. 442). This means precisely what we affirmed at the outset of this book—namely, that multiculture implies not just a sheered-off plane of culture, but also interlinkage with job, wealth, status, gender and so on.

What we most like about the term is its ability to capture a distinctive sense of multiple allegiances and contradictions. In this respect, Sudesh Mishra also sees the need for it: 'What is peculiar about the diasporic consciousness is its ability to make connections based on an underground logic of colours, tropes, sounds, texture, moods and secrets.' (2002, p. 3) In agreeing that it is a difficult and contradictory term, one that can obscure as much as it reveals, we say that if it is used aptly it can describe both structurally contextualised relationships on a cultural plane and also, as in Sudesh Mishra's words above, the sharp sense of cross-connection and inter-cut significance that is the lot of those who live *between* worlds. A heightened version of multiculture, perhaps, diaspora accents the affective links to imagined homelands and languages, while yet participating in another, quite different cultural framework—in this case, 'Australia'.

The thinkers of diaspora are right to say that these connections are sometimes contradictory, sometimes problematic. Yet their creative appropriation of this term has made powerful sense of what was once a very local idea. Those who write of the Indian diaspora have made such powerful sense of this term that we believe it has ongoing relevance to all the communities that make up Australia's multiculture.

Australia as a 'settler-society'

Of all the 'diasporas' that have reached Australia, the most important has been one that is not usually recognised as such: the core group of British settler-invaders who arrived in 1788 and thereafter. Their legendary longing for 'home' and their alienation are not usually seen as diasporic precisely because *they* formed the 'host' culture that others struggled to fit into. This is more than a definitional quirk. There is a diasporic aspect to the British experience since they fulfil, as a community far from an imagined homeland, many of the other agreed features of the diaspora.

The ensemble of problems we are about to treat is usually dealt with under the heading 'Australia, the settler-society'. In this section we want to look at the reality and the myths surrounding the structures of this event, while bearing in mind the diasporic qualities that it too bears. To help us in our double task—to set up a narrative of 1788 and counter-narrative of the richer reality for Australia as a 'settler-society'—we draw on the work of a United States historian, Louis Hartz (1964).

Hartz, who wrote in the 1960s, looked especially at the founding moment of settler-colonies like Australia. We draw on him not to bring him back to life, but because we want to provoke discussion on a neglected question: are settler-societies characteristically different from other societies and, if so, which tendencies do they exhibit? We pose the question in the light of the cautionary account offered by Michael Mann (discussed in Chapter 3) that settler-societies have distinct forms of schismogenesis. But we also pose it to ask about the prospects of multiculture itself. It may be that there is something about settler-culture that tends towards multicultural self-articulation.

Hartz was attacking the attractive 'frontier thesis' of Frederick Jackson Turner, the idea that the challenge of the hostile, open spaces of the American frontier produced a peculiarly American culture. Australians liked this theory as applied to themselves—two pioneer cultures forging similar dynamic, egalitarian societies. Hartz proposed a new model that discarded the image of the frontier in favour of the

Borderwork and multicultural Australia

logic of the *founding cultural moment*. New colonies, he argued, are always 'fragments' of the culture and politics of their home country. Their debates will be framed by cultural forms and values that came with them at the point of settlement or invasion.

Hartz claims that it is the fragment culture's destiny to be profoundly unself-aware. The reason he gives is that the founding fragment is partial, cut off from the contexts that formed the dialectical basis of its debates. Instead, a value that previously was merely one of a number at that point in time is reified into a national self-consciousness, becoming the way the fragment defines its identity as a nation.

In place of the notion that the New World teaches the Old, that the New World is full of new ideas, that the New World is radical, Hartz proposes that, after its initial rush of foundational excitement, the culture is profoundly conservative—even ossified. In place of the idea that the New World teaches us about the Old, Hartz insists that debates in settler-societies are antiquarian relics of bygone ages, linked to the moment of foundation and not any contemporary realities. Thus, in the arts, Hartz says there seems to be a kind of 'discovery' of the nation, but this is illusory. It *seems* that 'Whitman discovered American democracy or Furphy Australian mateship. In terms of "honesty" it makes no difference that what is discovered is really something very old and European, in this case bits of Puritan and Victorian England.' (1964, p. 12)

One problem with Hartz is that he uses two-body analysis, working always in twos: the two components of the fragment and then, separately, the metropolitan centre and the fragment society. While he did consider the Indigenous inhabitants, he does not grant them any significant role in creating the new society and its cultural forms. But these binary terms are all limited, excluding too much that was also important. The Pilgrim Fathers were *not* the only fragment to arrive in America and, as we have said, the first settlers to Australia were a profoundly multiple body: settlers, convicts and warders, English, Celts and others.

Settler-societies do not have a static structure fixed for all time by the moment of foundation. Nor is any fragment forced to be alone. In the past, as in the present—if now at a greater rate—diasporas of different kinds have extended across the globe, separating from yet maintaining contact with their points of origin, enriching the culture of the centre at the same time as they produce new forms, new multi-cultures in their new homes.

Yet two things are of enduring interest in Hartz's attention to origins. The first is the issue of (multi)cultural memory, of how old structures linger. His is a useful corrective to the amnesia that makes us see apparently new debates as if they are happening for the first time, when sometimes they are problematic re-runs of old enmities and desires. The second is that there might be something distinctive about settler-societies as such. On the one hand, they have patholo-gies of origin that made them blind to people there before their year zero (in Australia's case, 1788) and yet, on the other, they might have the potential to be creative with their rereadings of their scenes of origin, seeing how it is not just pathological, but also transformative, enabling, powerful—and not forever closed off. With this in mind, we now take up the crucial question of stories of origin themselves.

Scenes and origins

Hartz's story is both history and myth, living in the rich, fuzzy terri-tory where the two interact. Celebrations of Australian identity focus around a foundational moment of this kind, commemorated on 26 January, the anniversary of proclamation. As throughout this book, we do not wish to replace the myth of this culture with a different 'multicultural' one, because Australia's multiculture has to include this one. Instead we will reframe it in a more inclusive, multicultural story which we believe is based on better history. In augmenting and challenging Hartz's claim that the seeds of future developments for these societies began on board the first ships of the first settlers, we offer an alternative hypothesis that builds on what he began.

Eric Gans (1997) has tried to capture the role of foundational moments in his concept of the 'originary hypothesis' about an 'originary event', which can be adapted to support the idea that settler-societies have a clear shape or morphology, distinguishable from other societies. He argues that there is always not just an event, but a context for that event. He calls this context a 'scene', because it describes a very particular place and time.

So what is the scene of origin of Australian settler-society? A ship approaches; it lies at anchor. A long boat puts ashore. What are the minimal dimensions of the resulting encounter? As Hartz says, there

is a fragment of a world on those ships, and we agree with him that
the polarity between governors and governed can be read in terms of
pre-Victorian England, the metropolitan centre from which these
settlers came.

Governor Phillip disembarks, and plants his flag. But he is not
alone. What of the women, too few at this moment for a sustainable
society? Gender relations also exist at this originary moment, and
they are schismogenic, which the feminist historian Ann Summers
(1975) claimed laid down a continuing pattern of gender relations in
Australian culture, in which women were seen as 'Damned whores and
God's police'. Summers takes the phrase 'Damned whores' from an
early colonial officer, Lt Ralph Clark, who was denouncing a boatload
of women sent to correct the desperate gender imbalance of the First
Fleet. Already the fragment was reacting against its limits, in terms of
what was at first a simplistic idea of a minimal social whole (men *plus*
women). The nature of the fragment, in this aspect as in others, is a
contradiction between a specific lack *and* the desire to fill it.

Apart from Phillip's own retinue, there are others present,
namely Indigenous Australians. Integral to the foundation of the
settler-culture of the Australian kind is the scene of a three-body
system, the polarity between rulers and ruled, and the relationship of
these two points to the people who greeted them. Whatever was to
follow, the terms of this meeting—between the white invaders and
the Aboriginal people they encountered—became intrinsic parts of
this foundational moment. Despite their self-conception as settlers in
a 'new land', the first settlers were *very* aware of the first inhabitants
of the land. Nor did this presence merely shadow the main actions of
the colonisers. These were active engagements, full of meanings that
would reverberate for generations.

Hartz (1964) considers, but does not incorporate, the Indigenous
encounter into his approach. Nor to his credit does he ignore it:

> The logic of the fragment unfolds, in this case ambivalently . . . But
> since its impact is to exclude all possibilities other than those the
> fragment contains, it also has the effect of giving to the citizens of the
> fragment the notion that there can be no conceivable ways of dealing
> with the non-Western impact, the challenge of alien Indian and African
> cultures, save the ways they instinctively elicit from the ideological code
> they have made universal. (1964, p. 19)

And then:

> To be sure, there is one method for implementing the Western ideolo-
> gies, especially in connection with the unco-operative aborigine, which
> is simpler: extermination . . . [But] the elimination of the recalcitrant
> aborigine is never complete . . . (1964, p. 50)

Hartz's grim, self-confronting honesty is a powerful forerunner to
other more recent writers, such as Michael Mann, whose essay
we looked at in Chapter 3, who also saw a link between liberal
democracy and genocidal impulses in settler-societies.

Here, as elsewhere, we note the schismogenic frame through
which this originary scene is presented, and this is a recurring
problem. A series of questions can be posed at this point to indicate
the unfolding nature of the process. Does the 'originary moment'
forever enshrine schismogenic relations that existed strongly at that
time, as though this will remain a defining truth for the nation, in
spite of the cosmogenesis that must happen if it is to become
a cohesive nation? Does it rather (or also) give the initial terms of a
dynamic which is open and productive, not condemned to reproduce
forever the initial conditions? Or, better again, does it not supply the
resources for a multiculture that will eventually and inclusively grasp
its terms of foundation in an increasingly replete way, to the extent
that it might not just understand these contexts, but eventually
exceed them?

The originary scene is not closed and frozen in time; it is
reanimated by our restaging, our revisions. The unfolding logic of the
three-body system afterwards is not one of convergence, but prolifer-
ation. In the case of the United States, the creativity that Hartz denies
surely came from the waves of immigrants that have come to the
United States since the mid-nineteenth century (including, we
presume, his own ancestors). Likewise, Australia had many other
nodal moments in the burgeoning logic that produced its multiculture. There were to follow Chinese, Indian, African and Pacific
Islander migrants.

Gans' account offered a single, never-to-be repeated originary
scene that we have adapted to our account of settler-society. It
includes not just the 'facing up to history' we described in
earlier chapters of this book, but also the surprising openness of

settler-society morphology that allowed the ideal of multiculture itself to flourish as policy and way of life. The foundational moment is inexhaustibly significant, as it is revisited and replayed from different points in a multicultural history. It makes new kinds of sense as the society moves forward, as it mines its past for the meanings of the present. But between that moment and whichever present is at stake, there is a world of meaning and history.

The stories of subsequent migrancy themselves have originary qualities. How should we conceive of these? They too are foundational of things to follow. For instance, a young Afghan girl reported her first contact experience in Australia, in a detention centre:

> It felt like we were in a cage. We could not go anywhere with all the fences and that stuff . . . We were at war in Afghanistan because of the Taliban and we thought we have come to another war here. In the detention centre, always soldiers all around us. Oh my God, can the Taliban get us again? (Teenage girl, reported in NSW Commission for Children and Young People)

This girl, a fragment of a schismoculture, is horrified by the differences treated as sameness in this strange place, enclosed by fences. We remember that the first 'settlers' (including the convicts) also were in a kind of cage, an open prison. She sees the guards as 'soldiers', interpreting her new environment through the old, as diasporic cultures tend to do. At the same time she is here because she wants things to be different.

This text does not count as history, yet it gives us insight into how originary scenes really work, then as now. It is a moment of chaos and unpredictability, and no one present has any idea how things will turn out. It would not have seemed likely (if anyone had thought to ask) that the descendants of the First Fleet would ultimately build a multiculture, yet that is what has happened.

Writing the land

A country is not only made sense of and incorporated into a culture through maps. The crucial, culture-building intersection of histories, places and cultures is created in everyday life, through our daily steps, our lives, our work. It is also managed through *memorials*, monuments, markers set in a landscape to tell a story to those who care to read it. A book project Bob was involved in during the 1980s, *Myths of Oz* (Fiske et al. 1987), looked at the importance of monuments in Australian society. The authors remarked that:

> Monuments exist to give lessons from the past to the present. Normally these are oppressive, threatening messages, death speaking to life. They tend to be heavy, impressive rather than beautiful. The word 'monster' comes from the same Latin root . . . If it's difficult to ignore them, it's equally inappropriate to like them. (1987, p. 137)

They saw monuments as highly problematic in the lessons they transmit (they tend to celebrate dominant official interpretations of Australian societies). As records of a complex, often contradictory history, monuments are often as significant for what they fail to say as for what they actually do tell us:

> White Australia's problematic basis of right is handled not by [epic verse] but by silence. Australia was founded by an act of conquest, and the right of white Australians to their land derives ultimately from this. In a series of invasions the original inhabitants were driven from their lands, shot and poisoned, raped and plundered, in a war that was never declared and therefore cannot be officially ended. (1987, p. 138)

From the fact that war was never ended officially came the effort to develop the Reconciliation process we discussed in Chapter 6. But monuments to this alternative history are scarce.

So how do we think about all this? Back in 1987, Bob and his fellow authors noted the messages built into the *absence* of monuments and memorials. Writing seventeen years later, we still feel it is an important and valid point to make about Australian culture. In a sense, Aboriginal cultures had already created their own kind of monument, which only needed new eyes to see, new ears to hear the stories. Uluru is a monument in this sense—one of the two most significant monuments in Australia. So is Kakadu National Park, and the 'Three Sisters' in Sydney's Blue Mountains, and many more, restored to some degree to their traditional custodians. This process was already underway in 1987, and has continued to develop since then.

But what of monuments to other cultures of multicultural Australia? We have looked at monuments to Irish Ned Kelly, and the Japanese prisoners of Cowra, but surely there is more to be done. So, instead of just noting absences, let us imagine some grand monuments *that are not there*. They need not be heavy harbingers, death speaking to life; they can be kitsch, yet respectful, depending on how those who remain wish things to be recalled.

Here is our preliminary list of imaginary (absent) monuments. We find *The Golden Cameleer* just outside Meekatharra or maybe Quilpie, sandstone against a desertscape on which a corrugated-iron mosque stands. (There is no memorial to the Afghans who linked the nation in the nineteenth century, whose only powerful memorial is the half-remembered, insulting name for a train, the 'Ghan', that still travels one of the routes they opened up.) Then, in Ballarat or Darwin or Broome, there is *The Temple*: a secular reminder of Chinese sacred space, where these hard-working pioneers retreated to replenish their spirits. Or we have *The Giant Pearl*, a dome-shaped glassy sphere to recall all those who dived off the northwest coast. Or there is *The Cane Fire*, a sculptured field of blackened cane, men standing by with cane knives idle as orange flames rise above the whole.

These proposals may seem ridiculous, and we do not intend to gather subscriptions to make them a physical reality. Yet they are no more bizarre than many of the memorials that do dot the Australian landscape. The proposals come out of a strong sense that multicultural Australia needs a more richly inhabited landscape, a storied landscape, for all its peoples.

Aboriginal maps

There are many ways of mapping, many ways of inscribing the land. There are many geographies and many histories which all inflect us, whether we can put them into words or not. We are well used to the stories of the great mapping feats of the European past, of Greek Eratosthenes, of Mercator's brilliant projection that still serves as the basis of maps today. But all cultures know their lands in particular and complex ways. In this respect, shouldn't we consider the contribution of those who have lived here longest, those great cultural cartographers of Australian space, the Aboriginal peoples who have made different kinds of sense of this space for so long? At risk of

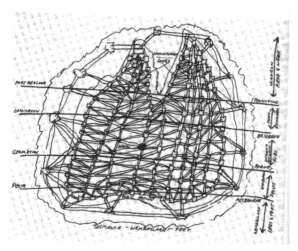

David Mowaljarlai's map of Australia

romanticisation, we can surely say theirs is an art of integrating *place and meaning* into Australian multiculture.

Much Aboriginal art is a form of mapping, representing landscapes, myths and histories so seamlessly that they seem like a single order of reality. We have mentioned the international success of 'Western Desert art' in world art and as a major component in the current dominant image of Australian identity. Here, as an appropriate conclusion to this book, we try to bring out the power and value of Aboriginal representations of space for multicultural Australia.

David Mowarljarli is an Aboriginal elder from northwest Australia who drew on Aboriginal traditions to construct a map of Australia, reprinted below. This modern work of art challenges non-Aborigines in a number of ways, not least of which is the patterns we instantly recognise within it.

As a map, this text has learnt from European navigators like Tasman, Cook and Flinders, so it is a multicultural form, producing an object, 'Australia', which did not exist as such for pre-invasion Aboriginal Australia. Yet it uses Aboriginal cultural forms to make a different kind of sense of this new object. The coastline (which would have been focal for Cook) is lightly sketched, but outside it is a path, linking sites off the coast. Outside that is a jagged line indicating a wider boundary around Australia. Inside is a track that circles around Australia, linking many circles along the way. This is what Aboriginal iconography does so well, mapping space and territory with concentric circles, giving it solidity through a network of pathways. The concentric circles indicate a fuzzy boundary system composed of sets of boundaries around Australia. The pathways indicate the core principle and strategy by which Aborigines manage social relations. David Mowaljarlai (in Muecke 2004, p. 172) calls it 'the gift of pattern thinking'.

There are no state boundaries in this map, and no capital cities. At the centre, called 'the navel', is a prominent filled-in circle: Uluru, perhaps. Otherwise there is no hierarchy of places, only networks and links. Four bands cross the country like grids of latitude, linking places on the western and eastern seaboards, though the correspondence is not exact. There is also an asymmetry between east and west, if places are given their value in contemporary terms, since Geraldton, Carnarvon and Port Hedland are not normally seen as on a par with Sydney, Brisbane or even Townsville. But Mowaljarlai is from the west, and his map gives an image of the whole as seen from a particular region, in which Port Hedland, for instance, looks as large as a significant urban site.

More than a record of major urban centres, these lines are part of a strategy for interpreting the nation as a living body, with organs (lungs, sexual organs) and body parts (head, shoulders and arms, ribs, feet). Mowaljarlai does not state the gender of this body, but in Aboriginal traditions it is always feminine. This body has a pubic region, not a phallus, and the two northern capes look like breasts, so we can assume that this is the land as woman, as mother. This version of Australia does not have a huge, empty desert centre. Like Hau'ofa's 'sea of islands', it is full of life and multiple connections: an Australia that other Australians have been unable to see for two centuries.

Yet this Aboriginal tradition also resonates with other cultures in the European tradition. As we saw at the beginning of this chapter, 'Australia' is grammatically feminine in the original Latin. English has largely dropped its gendering of the inanimate world, but gender lingers as in the etymologies we have looked at. Might we not draw this analogy: just as European conventions triggered new developments that were latent in Aboriginal traditions, so this Aboriginal tradition triggers the latent European gendered world-view of this land and those who live in it? This is how non-reductive, creative multiculture can work: not absorbing all others into a single dominant form, nor levelling all differences to leave only what is common to all, but instead creating a space in which different traditions are enriched by mutual dialogue. Cosmogenesis. An Australian multiculture.

Appendix: Tools for analysing multiculture and borderwork

We hope that this book will help to lay a basis for further exploration of the issues it raises, in response to problems and events that may not yet have emerged. To assist in this task we bring together some of the key concepts, tools and strategies of analysis that we have used through the book.

1 The creative coexistence of unities and diversities is a core generative principle that underlies most human societies.
Multiculture exists within this dynamic play of unities and diversities as a pattern of relationships incorporating a diversity of peoples and cultures within but not subsumed by a larger unity. Contrary to the view that the same group will endlessly produce the same culture, we argue also for the theoretical possibility of **heterogenesis**—a process which we define by the claim that in any field (culture, class, profession, etc.) the new or the different can be generated by the 'same'. These unities are also inherently plural in that they involve the coming or being together of diversities around particular cultural locations or issues. This means that multicultures are themselves made up of multicultures, with multiplicity and unity all the way down.

Analytic point: in any situation, even one which seems hostile to multi-culture, look for traces of chains of multiculture.

2 Societies as dynamic systems are organised at every level through **borders**. These borders are the products of borderwork in a given society or state, present and past. Borderwork is an active process of meaning-making, designed to manage both separation and connection, in combinations that can often themselves become highly complex.

Analytic point: in any society, look for processes of meaning-making around borders—physical, social and categorial (i.e. traditional sociological categories, gender, class, ethnicity, profession, status, nation, etc.)—seeing how these three kinds of border interact in practice.

3 Arising out of the interplay of difference, all societies and cultures have **schismogenic tendencies**. These can focus around any and all of the primary social categories—language, culture, religion, ethnicity, class, gender, age, location—producing divisions along these potential fault lines within or between any given groups. Because a culture is a set of patterns and relations across all these categories, a multiculture consists of a relation between them all. Schismogenesis acts on this totality, producing both splits and alliances between the various elements of the culture. Because of this interrelationship, it is misleading to focus only on ethnicity in isolation. For this reason, the term **racism** is often unhelpful, since it often conflates issues of ethnicity with other categories, such as religion or culture, and is itself a poor descriptor of the complex interaction of all these categories in social identities.

Analytic point: in any society, look for the fissures (ethnicity, class, etc.) and see where they are growing; look for the patterns and connections between these various fissures.

4 In all societies and cultures (in different ways, to different degrees) there is a tendency to make connections, to aggregate into new forms. We call this tendency **cosmogenesis**. In keeping with the principle of contradiction above, cosmogenesis *coexists* with schismogenesis in all societies, producing all the various forms of culture, including multicultures. We tend to associate schismogenic patterns with destruction and cosmogenic patterns with creativity. This is often true, since the limit case of the former is warfare, while

the limit case of the latter is peace. But wars can be creative (these are often periods of great inventiveness), separations can be essential, and cosmogenesis can be stifling. The principle of contradiction is crucial to understanding that cultures can be creative and destructive at the same time, irrespective of whether they exhibit predominantly schismogenic or cosmogenic patterns.

Analytic point: since cosmogenesis coexists with schismogenesis, it is always worthwhile to look for it even if it is not to be expected.

5 After Bateson, we group schismogenic and cosmogenic tendencies into two types: **symmetrical** and **complementary**. Symmetrical behaviours concern groups that are alike in salient respects, which can be the basis for either cosmogenesis (like seeking like) or schismogenesis (like rejecting like). Complementary behaviours concern groups whose difference is crucial to the relationship: either cosmogenic (unlike attracted to what it lacks) or schismogenic (unlike rejecting or dominating unlike for reasons of difference).

Analytic point: be alert to the surprising role of similarity or difference, which can have opposite effects depending on the basic character of the relationship, symmetrical or complementary. Look for both elements present to some degree in most relationships, where there is always a range of qualities at issue.

6 A crucial factor in understanding the dynamics of a culture or society is the degree to which it is **close to** or **far from equilibrium**. When a society is close to equilibrium, it is relatively stable and predictable. The further it is from equilibrium, the more likely it is to be subject to explosions of schismogenesis, or the equally rapid and surprising emergence of cosmogenesis: complex new orders.

Analytic point: if there are some of the markers of far from equilibrium conditions present, such as unpredictability, non-linear causality, contradiction, paradox, action at a distance, then it is probably a far from equilibrium situation, so analysts should look specifically at borderwork processes in the society (both historically and symptomatically), and more generally, expect and look for the unexpected.

7 Also arising out of the play of difference, all cultures exhibit **contradictory tendencies**. Contradiction is both a social fact and an analytic device. Contradictory tendencies do not sit easily in formal social analysis, yet we live them all the time.

Analytic point: in any society, once you have identified fissures of ethnicity, class and so on (points 2 and 3 above), trace them in order to pick up the reasons for people being on the different sides at the same time, or for simultaneously holding two apparently inconsistent positions or beliefs.

8 In any complex situation, there will nearly always be very many forces and factors at play. But analysts and key players are tempted—often by language used by players themselves—to reduce this multiplicity to one or to two terms. **Two-term analysis** is a **binary structure**, typified by a pattern in which analysis is reduced to a choice of one side or the other. There are three useful strategies to resist such reductive tendencies. One is Derridean **deconstruction**, which identifies and resists weighted binaries. The second is **three-body analysis**, which pushes analysis away from binary structures towards the dynamic multiplicity inherent in the situation. The third is **fuzzy logic**, which effectively replaces crisp binary analyses with analyses that take account of the presence of indeterminacy, contradiction and coexistence of different factors.

Analytic point: in looking for relations in a multiculture, don't stop with one or two cultures: in analysing a complex situation or event, look for more than two factors and turn the analysis back on the various players to detect the signs and effects of crisp—usually binary—loaded logics.

9 A multiculture has a structure that can be described, but what is crucial is how it works in practice, as a complex, dynamic system in a complex, dynamic context. For this reason it is essential to study **structures in action**, in the form of stories, episodes, events or trends, each as a highly complex site where structures act and change. Multiculture exists at many levels, each level distinguishable yet interconnected, from the most local to the global, with the precise relationship always to be discovered, not assumed.

Analytic point: a highly fruitful way of studying and understanding the complexity of multiculture is through stories, set against the background of structures and events, seen as a nested set of frames and contexts, including the global.

10 Multiculture in its widest contexts in space and time is so complex a phenomenon that it needs to be studied in an **interdisciplinary** way, understanding interdisciplinarity not simply as a set of different facts or ideas or methods, but as also itself a form of multiculture, requiring the respect for difference that is a key quality in multiculture. We organise the necessary branches of knowledge as a three-body system. **Empirical social science research** provides essential data, as collected and interpreted by generations of researchers, government agencies and others. **Interpretive disciplines** draw on the study of language in its widest semiotic sense (verbal codes and texts), plus images and behaviours in various contexts. Like everything else in the human world, multiculture passes through and is created in language in this sense. **Theories** and **metatheories** come to us from many sources. In our case, we have found value in the traditions of analysis of class and gender, as well as in post-structural and postcolonial cultural analysis (the ideas of 'discourse', 'imagined communities', 'Orientalism'), and in postmodern science/ 'chaos theory' (including the ideas of 'three-body analysis' (Poincaré), 'far from equilibrium theory' (Prigogine), and 'fuzzy logic' (Zadeh).

Analytic point: interdisciplinarity, as a dynamic, open approach, respecting the difference of different traditions and their complementarity, is a highly creative approach to multiculture.

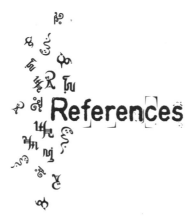

References

Academic sources

Ahmad, A. 1994, *In Theory: Classes, Nations, Literatures*, Verso, London

Anderson, B. 1991, *Imagined Communities: Reflections on the Origin and Spread of Nationalism*, Verso, London

——1992, 'The new world disorder', *New Left Review*, no. 193, pp. 3–13

Andren, P. 2003, *The Andren Report: An Independent Way in Australian Politics*, Scribe, Melbourne

Ang, I. et al. 2002, *Living Diversity*, SBS, Sydney

APIC and the Australian Ethnic Affairs Council (AEAC), 1979, *Multiculturalism and its Implications for Immigration Policy*, AGPS, Canberra

Appiah, A.K. 1990, 'Racisms', in *Anatomy of Racism*, ed. D.T. Goldberg, University of Minnesota Press, Minneapolis

Attorney General's Department 1996, *Migration Act 1958*, rpt no. 6, AGPS, Canberra

Attwood, B. & S.G. Foster 2003, *Frontier Conflict: The Australian Experience*, NMA, Canberra

Augustine, St 1958, *City of God*, trans. G. Walsh et al., Doubleday, New York

Balcarek, D. & G. Dean 1999, *Ned and the Others*, 3rd ed., Glenrowan Cobb & Company, Glenrowan

Barth, F. 1969, *Ethnic Groups and Boundaries: The Social Organisation of Culture Difference*, Little Brown, Boston

Bateson, G. 1972, *Steps to an Ecology of Mind*, Palladin, London

Bennett, T., Michael Emmison & John Frow 1999, *Accounting for Tastes: Australian Everyday Cultures*, Cambridge University Press, Melbourne

Bhabha, H. 1994 *The Location of Culture*, Routledge, London

Birrell, R. & T. Birrell 1981, *An Issue of People: Population and Australian Society*, Longman, Melbourne

Boogaart, E. van den 1988, 'The mythical symmetry in God's creation: the Dutch and the southern continent, 1569–1756', in *Terra Australis: The Furthest Shore*, International Cultural Corporation of Australia, Sydney, pp. 43–50

Brook, J. & J.L. Kohen 1991, *The Parramatta Native Institution and the Blacktown: A History*, New South Wales University Press, Sydney

Burchell, D. 2000, Multiculturalism and its Discontents: Majorities, Minorities, and Toleration, in possession of the author, University of Western Sydney

Carey, P. 2001, *True History of the Kelly Gang*, University of Queensland Press, St Lucia

Castles, S. et al. 1992, *Mistaken Identity: Multiculturalism and the Demise of Nationalism in Australia*, 3rd ed., Pluto Press, Sydney

Castles, S. & A. Davidson 2000, *Citizenship and Migration: Globalization and the Politics of Belonging*, Macmillan, Houndsmills

Clifford, J. 1994, 'Diasporas', *Cultural Anthropology*, vol. 9, no. 3, pp. 302–38; [rpt. Vertovec, S. & R. Cohen 1999, *Migration, Diasporas, and Transnationalism*, Elgar, Cheltenham and Northampton pp. 215–51]

Cohen, S. 1980, *Folk Devils and Moral Panics: The Creation of Mods and Rockers*, St Martin's Press, New York

Commonwealth Jubilee Citizenship Convention 1951, *Report of Proceedings*, 22–26 January, convened by the Minister for Immigration, Canberra

Cox, D. 1996, *Understanding Settlement Services*, AGPS, Canberra

Cunneen, C. and J. Stubbs 1997, *Gender, 'Race' and International Relations*, Institute of Criminology monographs, Sydney

Denoon, D. 1983, *Settler Capitalism: The Dynamics of Dependent Development in the Southern Hemisphere*, Clarendon Press, Oxford

Derrida, J. 1981, *Positions*, trans. A. Bass, Chicago University Press, Chicago

Dibb, P. 2003, 'The Arc of Instability and the North of Australia: Are they Still Relevant to Australia's New Defence Posture?', Charles Darwin Symposium Series, Conference paper, 29–30 September

DIMA 2000, *Population Flows Immigration Aspects*, DIMA, Canberra

Do, T. 2002, 'Statistics: Refugees and Australia's contribution', in *Refugees and the Myth of the Borderless World*, ed. M.-L. Hickey, Department of International Relations RSPAS, Canberra, pp. 41–48

Dodson, M. 1994, 'The Wentworth Lecture. The end in the beginning', *Australian Aboriginal Studies*, no. 1, pp. 2–13

Duarte, F. ed. 2001, *Voices From UWS Diasporas: Texts and Resources on Multicultural Themes*, Social Justice Unit, University of Western Sydney, Sydney

Duruz, J. 2000, 'A nice baked dinner . . .', *Continuum*, vol. 14, no. 3, 2000, pp. 289–302

Elias, N. 1982, *The Civilizing Process: State Formation and Civilization*, Basil Blackwell, Oxford

Evans, R. et al. 1997, *1901 Our Future's Past Documenting Australia's Federation*, Macmillan, Sydney

Fagan, R.H. & M. Webber 1994, *Global Restructuring: The Australian Experience*, Oxford University Press, Melbourne

Fiske, J. et al. 1987, *Myths of Oz*, Allen & Unwin, Sydney

Fleming, C. 2004, *René Girard: Violence and Mimesis*, Polity, Cambridge

Foster, L. & D. Stockley 1988, *Australian Multiculturalism: A Documentary History and Critique*, Multilingual Matters, Cleveland

Foucault, M. 1972, *The Archaeology of Knowledge*, trans. A.M. Sheridan-Smith, Pantheon Books, New York

Gans, E. 1993, *Originary Thinking: Elements of Generative Anthropology*, Stanford University Press, Stanford

Girard, R. 1986, *The Scapegoat*, trans. Y. Freccero, Johns Hopkins, Baltimore

——1990, 'Innovation and repetition', *SubStance*, no. 62/63, pp. 7–20

——2002, 'What is occurring today is a mimetic rivalry on a planetary scale', Interview with H. Tincq (orig. published *Le Monde*, 2001), trans. J. Williams, Colloquium on Violence and Religion, http://theol.uibk.ac.at/cover/girard_le_monde_interview.html

Goldberg, D.T. 1993, *Racist Culture: Philosophy and the Politics of Meaning*, Blackwell, 1993

Gordon, H. 1994, *Voyage from Shame: The Cowra Breakout and Afterwards*, University of Queensland Press, St Lucia

Gray, J. 2003, 'Enlightenment humanism as a relic of Christian monotheism', in *2000 Years and Beyond: Faith, Identity and the 'Common Era'*, eds P. Gifford et al., Routledge, London, pp. 35–50

Grynberg, R. 1993, *A New Oceania: Rediscovering Our Sea of Islands*, ed. E. Waddell et al., University of the South Pacific/Beake House, Suva, pp. 68–71

Guillaumin, C. 1988, 'Race and nature: The system of marks: the idea of a natural group and social relationships', *Feminist Issues*, vol. 8, no. 2, pp. 25–43

Hage, G. 1998, *White Nation: Fantasies of White Supremacy in a Multicultural Society*, Pluto, Sydney

——2003, *Against Paranoid Nationalism: Searching for Hope in a Shrinking Society*, Pluto, Sydney

Hall, S. 2000, 'The question of multiculturalism', in *Un/settled Multiculturalisms*, ed. B. Hesse, Zed Books, London

Hartz, L. 1964, *The Founding of New Societies: Studies in the History of the United States, Latin America, South Africa, Canada, and Australia*, Harcourt, Brace & World, New York

Harvey D. 1989, *The Condition of Postmodernity*, Blackwell, Oxford

Hau'ofa, E. 1993, 'Our sea of islands', in *A New Oceania: Rediscovering Our Sea of Islands*, ed. E. Waddell et al., University of the South Pacific/Beake House, Suva

——1997, 'The ocean in us', in *Dreadlocks in Oceania*, eds S. Mishra & E. Guy, University of the South Pacific Beake House, Suva, pp. 124–48

——2000, 'Epilogue: pasts to remember', *Remembrance of Pacific Pasts: An Invitation to Remake History*, University of Hawai'i Press, Honolulu, pp. 453–71

Hodge, B. 2005, 'Ute culture and what's left of theory: An Australian academic visits Mexico', *Continuum*, vol. 19, no.1, pp. 121–29

Hodge, B. & V. Mishra 1990, *Dark Side of the Dream*, Allen & Unwin, Sydney

Hoffman, J.E. 1984, 'Historical and geopolitical considerations of an immigrant nation in Asia', in *Australian Multicultural Society: Identity, Communication, Decision Making*, eds D.J. Phillips & J. Houston, Drummond, Blackburn, pp. 58–66

Holland, A. & C. Williamson, 2003, 'Kelly culture', in *Kelly Culture: Reconstructing Ned Kelly*, State Library of Victoria, Melbourne, pp. 8–32

Holland, W. 1996, 'Mis/taken identity', in *The Teeth are Smiling: The Persistence of Racism in Multicultural Australia*, eds S. Castles & E. Vasta, Allen & Unwin, Sydney, pp. 97–111

HREOC 1991, *Report of National Inquiry into Racist Violence in Australia*, AGPS, Canberra

Hughes, R. 1988, *The Fatal Shore: A History of the Transportation of Convicts, 1788–1868*, Pan Books, London

Immigration Reform Group 1960, *Control or Colour Bar? A Proposal for Change in Australia's Immigration Policy*, Pamphlet printed at Melbourne University Press, Melbourne

——1962, *Immigration: Control or Colour Bar? The Background to 'White Australia' and a Proposal for Change*, ed. K. Rivett, Melbourne University Press, Melbourne [substantial rewrite of the 1960 pamphlet, with an augmented historical background by D. Johanson added to the beginning of the book]

Jelloun, T. Ben 1998, *Le Racisme expliquée à ma fille*, Editions du Seuil, Paris

Joint Standing Committee on Migration (JSCM) 1993, 'Rationales for detention', in M. Crock, *Protection or Punishment? The Detention of Asylum-Seekers in Australia*, Federation Press, Sydney, pp. 21–24

——1994, *Asylum, Border Control and Detention*, AGPS, Canberra

Jonas, B. 1997, *Face the Facts: Some Questions and Answers about Immigration, Refugees, and Indigenous Affairs*, Pamphlet, Federal Race Discrimination Commission, Canberra

Jupp, J. 2002, *From White Australia to Woomera: The Story of Australian Immigration*, Cambridge University Press, Cambridge

Kabutaulaka, T. 1993, 'The bigness of our smallness', in *A New Oceania: Rediscovering Our Sea of Islands*, ed. E. Waddell et al., University of the South Pacific/Beake House, Suva, pp. 91–93

Kettle, S. & G. Smith 1992, *Threats Without Enemies: Rethinking Australia's Security*, Pluto, Sydney

Kingston, Margo 2004, *Not Happy, John! Defending Our Democracy*, Penguin, Camberwell

Kohen, J. 1993, *The Darug and their Neighbours: The Traditional Owners of the Sydney Region*, Darug Link & Blacktown & District Historical Association, Sydney

Kosko, B. 1994, *Fuzzy Thinking: The New Science of Fuzzy Logic*, Freemans, New York

Langton, M. 1993, *Well, I Heard it on the Radio and I Saw it on the Television*, Australian Film Commission, Sydney

Latham, J. 1968 [orig. 1961], 'Australian immigration policy', *Attitudes to Non-European Immigration*, Cassell, Melbourne, pp. 132–36

Layton, R. 1989, *Uluru*, Aboriginal Studies Press, Canberra

Lazarus, N. 1999, *Nationalism and Cultural Practice in the Postcolonial World*, Cambridge University Press, Cambridge

Levinas, E. 1994, *In the Time of the Nations*, trans. M.B. Smith, Athlone, London

Lewis, M.W. & K. Wigen 1997, *The Myth of Continents: A Critique of Metageography*, University of California, Berkeley

Locke, John 1966, *The Second Treatise of Government and a Letter Concerning Toleration*, ed. J.W. Gough, Blackwell, Oxford

Lyotard, J. 1977, *The Postmodern Condition: A Report on Knowledge*, trans. G. Bennington and B. Massumi, Manchester University Press, Manchester

Maley, W. 2002, 'A global refugee crisis?', in *Refugees and the Myth of the Borderless World*, ed. M.-L. Hickey, Department of International Relations RSPAS, Canberra, pp. 1–8

Mann, M. 1999, 'The dark side of democracy: The modern tradition of ethnic and political cleansing', *New Left Review*, no. 235, pp. 18–45

Martin, Jeannie 1996, 'Signs of the time: Race, sex and media representation', *The Teeth are Smiling: The Persistence of Racism in Multicultural Australia*, eds S. Castles & E. Vasta, Allen & Unwin, Sydney, pp. 145–59

Masood, M. & K. Sultana c.2002, 'The Ahmadiyah Community in Western Sydney', typescript, courtesy of the authors

May, S. 1999, 'Critical multiculturalism and cultural difference: Avoiding essentialism', in *Critical Multiculturalism: Rethinking Multicultural and Antiracist Education*, Falmer, London, pp. 11–41

McConnochie, K. et al. 1988, *Race and Racism in Australia*, Social Science Press, Wentworth Falls

McGregor, C. 1997, *Class in Australia*, Penguin, Ringwood

McIntyre, S. with Clark, A. 2003, *History Wars*, Melbourne University Press, Melbourne

McKiernan, J. 1995, 'Asylum, border control and detention', *People and Place*, 3.2, pp. 39–42

Milbank, J. 1990, 'The end of dialogue', in *Christian Uniqueness Reconsidered: The Myth of a Pluralistic Theology of Religions*, ed. G. O'Costa, Orbis, New York, pp. 174–91

Miles, R. 1989, *Racism*, Routledge, London

Mishra, S. 2002, *Diaspora and the Difficult Art of Dying*, University of Otago Press, Dunedin

Mishra, V. 1996, 'The diasporic imaginary: Theorising the Indian diaspora', *Textual Practice*, vol. 10, no. 3, pp. 421–47

Moallem, M. 1999, 'Transnationalism, feminism and fundamentalism', in *Between Woman and Nation: Nationalisms, Transnational Feminisms, and the State*, eds A. Kaplan & M. Moallem, Duke University Press, Durham

Moghissi, H. 2001, *Feminism and Islamic Fundamentalism*, Oxford University Press, Karachi

Muecke, S. 2004, *Ancient and Modern: Time, Culture and Indigenous Philosophy*, UNSW Press, Sydney

New Elizabethan World Atlas Illustrated, n.d., Colorgravure, Melbourne

Nicole, R. 2001, *The Word, the Pen, and the Pistol*, State University Press of New York, Albany

NSW Commission for Children and Young People n.d., *Ask the Children*, Sydney

Oodgeroo 1989, 'Towards a Global Southern Hemisphere', Occasional Address, ICPS, Griffith University, Brisbane

Oxenham, D. et al. 1999, *A Dialogue on Aboriginal Identity*, Gunada, Perth

Palfreeman, A.C. 1958, 'The end of the dictation test', *Australian Quarterly*, vol. 30, no. 1, March 1958, pp. 43–50

——1967, *The Administration of the White Australia Policy*, Melbourne University Press, London

Parker, D. 2000, 'Chinese takeaways', in *Un/settled Multiculturalisms*, ed. B. Hesse, Zed Books, London

Passey, K. & G. Dean 1991, *The Bushranger Harry Power: Tutor of Ned Kelly*, Bushranger Enterprises, Wodonga

Pearce, J. 1993, *Gold Nuggets Galore at Sofala from 1851*, pamphlet

People and Place 1993, 'An interview with Mr Gerry Hand, former Minister for Immigration, Local Government and Ethnic Affairs', *People and Place*, 1.4, pp. 1–9

Prigogine, I. & I. Stengers 1984, *Order Out of Chaos*, Fontana, London

Pryor, J. 2002, 'Our homes are girt by sea', *eremos*, no. 78, pp. 11–15

Ram, K. 1996, 'Liberal multicultualism's "NESB women": A South Asian post-colonial perspective on the liberal impoverishment of difference', in *The Teeth are Smiling: The Persistence of Racism in Multicultural Australia*, eds S. Castles & E. Vasta, Allen & Unwin, Sydney, pp. 130–44

Ratuva, S. 1993, 'David vs Goliath', in *A New Oceania: Rediscovering Our Sea of Islands*, ed. E. Waddell et al., University of the South Pacific/Beake House, Suva, pp. 94–97

Richmond, A.H. 1955, *The Colour Problem*, Harmondsworth, Pelican

Rizvi, F. 1996, 'Racism, reorientation and the cultural politics of Asia-Australia relations', in *The Teeth are Smiling: The Persistence of Racism in Multicultural Australia*, eds S. Castles & E. Vasta, Allen & Unwin, Sydney, pp. 173–88

Romm, J.S. 1992, *The Edges of the Earth in Ancient Thought: Geography, Exploration, and Fiction*, Princeton, New Jersey

Sadleir, J. 1973 [orig. 1913], *Recollections of a Victorian Police Officer*, Penguin, Harmondsworth [orig. G. Robertson & Co., Melbourne]

Said, E. 1995, *Orientalism*, Penguin, London

Schaffer, K. 1987, 'Landscape representation and Australian national identity', *Australian Journal of Cultural Studies*, 4.2, pp. 47–60

Sherwood, J. 1984, 'Multiculturalism: Including or excluding Aborigines?', in *Australian Multicultural Society: Identity, Communication, Decision-Making*, eds D. Phillips & J. Houston, Drummond, Blackburn, pp. 95–102

Silver, L.R. 2002, *Australia's Irish Rebellion: The Battle of Vinegar Hill*, Watermark Press, Sydney

Sloterdijk, P. 1987, *Critique of Cynical Reason*, trans. Eldred, University of Minnesota Press, London

Snyder, L.L. 1962, *The Idea of Racialism*, Van Nostrand Reinhold, New York

Stackhouse, M. 1999, 'Human rights and public theology: The basic validation of human rights', in *Religion and Human Rights: Competing Claims*, eds C. Gustafson & P. Jupiter, M.E. Sharpe, New York, pp. 12–30

Stevens, C. 2002, *Tin Mosques & Ghantowns: A History of Afghan Cameldrivers in Australia*, Paul Fitzsimmons, Alice Springs

Subramani 1995, 'The political logic of multiculturalism', in *Altering Imagination*, Fiji Writers' Association, Suva, pp. 247–57

——1997, 'Exiles in a park', in *Dreadlocks in Oceania*, eds S. Mishra & E. Guy, vol. 1, pp. 55–67

——2001, *Dauka Puraan*, Star, New Delhi

Summers, A. 1975, *Damned Whores or God's Police*, Penguin, Harmondsworth

Taylor, C. 1992, *Sources of the Self: The Making of Modern Identity*, Cambridge University Press, Cambridge

Thorne B. 1993, *Gender Play: Girls and Boys in School*, Open University Press, Buckingham

Van den Boogaart, E. 1988, 'The mythical symmetry in God's creation: The dutch and the southern continent, 1569–1756', in *Terra Australis: The Furthest Shore*, eds W. Eisler & B. Smith, International Cultural Corporation of Australia, Sydney, pp. 43–49

Vasta, E. & S. Castles, eds 1996, *The Teeth Are Smiling: The Persistence of Racism in Multicultural Australia*, Allen & Unwin, Sydney

Vertovec, S. & R. Cohen 1999, *Migration, Diasporas, and Transnationalism*, Elgar, Cheltenham and Northampton

Wallerstein, I. 1974, *The Modern World System: Capitalist Agriculture and the Origins of the European World Economy in the Sixteenth Century*, Academic Press, New York

Ward, A. 2000, 'Treaty-related research and versions of New Zealand history', in *Remembrance of Pacific Pasts: An Invitation to Remake History*, University of Hawai'i Press, Honolulu, pp. 401–19

Willard, M. 1967, [orig. 1923], *History of the White Australia Policy to 1920*, Melbourne University Press, Melbourne

Williams, R. 1976, *Keywords*, Fontana, London

Wilson, R. 1997, *Bringing Them Home*, HREOC, Canberra

Windschuttle, K. 2002, *The Fabrication of Aboriginal History: Van Diemen's Land 1803–1847*, vol. 1, Macleay Press, Sydney

——2004, *The White Australia Policy*, ed. G. Thomas, Macleay Press, Sydney

Yarwood, A.T. 1958, 'The Dictation test: Historical survey', *Australian Quarterly*, vol. 30, no. 2, June 1958, pp. 19–29

Media Sources

'8.45 am September 11, 2001: The Moment the World Changed', 2001, *SMH*, 15–16 Sept., p. 1

ABC News 2004, AM549, 7.45 am, 12 Dec.

Akerman, P. 2002b, 'Buoyed by a Less Rowdy Majority', *Telegraph*, 5 Feb., p. 14

Allard, T. 2004, 'ASEAN gives Howard a Prod over Peace Pact', *SMH*, 29 Nov., p. 2

Anon. 2003, An Appeal from the Asylum Seekers of Australia, public petition, Villawood

Australian, 2004, 'A Sorry Tale of Failed Politics', Editorial, 27 May, p. 10

Banham, C. 2003a, 'Life After Tampa: Australia's Castaways Are Happier to Call New Zealand Home', *SMH*, 2 June, p. 1

——2003b, 'Children of the Revolution', *SMH*, 26–27 Dec., pp. 19, 22

——2004, 'Compassion Back in Fashion as Australia Throws Refugees a Lifeline at Last', *SMH*, 13 July, p. 1

Barrett, C. 1992, 'Candlelight Vigil Held at Centre to Acknowledge Detainees' Plight', *North West Telegraph*, 15 April, p. 3

Berry, S. & F. Walker 2004, 'Lingering Pain of Tampa', *Sun-Herald*, 29 Aug., p. 37

Brown, M. 2004, 'Downer Pays Respects as Fiji Unites in Grief', *SMH*, 1–2 May, p. 20

Callinan, R. 2004, 'Raskols on the Rampage', *The Australian*, 8 Sept., p. 15

Cameron, D. 2003, 'Feel Like an Outsider, Habiib?', *SMH*, 31 May–1 June, p. 5

Chesterton, Ray 2001, 'Community United in Fury Over Sentence', *Telegraph*, 24 Aug., pp. 6–7

Chulov, M. 2004, 'A Simple Fence that Protects a Power Grid', *SMH*, 28 April, pp. 1, 6

Connolly, E. 2005, 'Rack off Hoges, We Just Don't Like the Way You Speak', *SMH*, 25 Jan., pp. 1, 5

Connolly, E. & L. Kennedy 2004, 'I'm Off to Jihad, Son Wrote', *SMH*, 30 April, pp. 1, 4

Dodson, L. 2005, 'Howard Explodes at MPs' Revolt', *SMH*, 25 May, p. 1

Dodson, L. & J. Kerr 2005, 'We've Failed Detainees—PM Caves In', 18–19 June, p. 1

Dodson, P. 2004a, 'No Threat in Giving Indigenous Ways a Place in the Life of Australia', *SMH*, 26 Jan., p. 15

——2004b, 'Goodbye ATSIC. Another Door Opens', *SMH*, 28 May, p. 15

Doherty, L. 2004, 'Globalism Circles Student World—Languages are Back', *SMH*, 19 Oct., p. 8

Double Trouble (short film) 1951, dir. L. Robinson, Australian National Film Board, (DVD re-release by Film Australia, 2004, *Immigration*)

Downer, A. & M. Vaile 2002, Press Release, Australian Government Office, Canberra

Eccleston, R. 2005, 'Price of Freedom', *Australian*, 20 July, p. 13

Farmer, D. 2003, 'Now Begin the Journey', *What's On in Benalla*, Tourist Magazine, pp. 24–29

Film Australia 2004, *Immigration*, DVD including *Double Trouble* (1951, dir. L. Robinson, Australian National Film Board)

Fraser, M. 2001, 'Stumbling Along a Path of Inhumanity', *SMH*, 18 Sept., p. 12

Georgio, P. 2005, 'We Have Abandoned Our Dearest Values on Asylum', *SMH*, 18 Feb., p. 15

Gittins, Ross 2004, 'We're Champion Workers—Don't Laugh, It's True', *SMH*, 1–2 May, p. 10

Grattan, M. et al. 2001, 'Howard's Tampa-led Recovery', *SMH*, 4 Sept., p. 1

Gray, D. 2004a, 'Fiji Farewells its First Chief', Photograph with unattributed caption, *SMH*, 29 April, p. 8.

——2004b, 'Earning their Place in Paradise', Photograph with unattributed caption, *SMH*, 1–2 May, p. 24

Heggen, M. et al. 2001, 'Traitor's Poem', *Telegraph*, 14 Dec., pp. 1–2

Horin, A. 2004, 'Being Choosy Works When it Comes to Immigration', *SMH*, 9 Sept., pp. 1, 2

'In Chief, A Skilled Fijian Statesman', *SMH*, 23 Apr. 2004, p. 28

Jones, I. 2003, 'Discover History', *What's On in Benalla*, Tourist Magazine, p. 24

Jopson, D. 2003, 'Funds Plea to Fight for Reconciliation', *SMH*, 9 June, p. 5

Karvan, C. 2002, 'Treat Asylum Seekers With Compassion—Not Cynicism', *SMH*, 4 Sept., p. 15

Kennedy, L. 2001, 'Bashed and Drowned in Bath at Fortress Home', *SMH*, 15 Mar., p. 2

Keskin, Z. 2004, 'No Pity Please, It's All My Choice', *Sun-Herald*, 4 April, p. 74

King, J. 2005, 'A Tale of Two Cities', *SMH*, Insight, 17 Jan., p. 12

Kotkin, J. 'Urban Collapse, the Next Terrorism Threat', *SMH*, 25 July, p. 9

Lacey, J. 2004, 'Morning Show', ABC Radio, 5 August, AM 549

Lake, M. 2004, 'In Defence of a Nation's Honour,' review of K. Windschuttle's *White Australia Policy*, *SMH Spectrum*, 23–25 Dec., p. 7

Lamont, L. 2004, 'Neutral School for Culture Clash Boy', *SMH*, 12 June, p. 1

Lawrence, J. 2003, 'Truth Is, We're Sick of Political Correctness', *Sunday Mail*, 6 July, p. 36

Lobley, K. 'Pacific Solution', Metro, *SMH*, 12 Nov., p. 28

Lowe, M. 2003, 'Residents Living in Fear of Youths: Rocherlea Hooliganism Claims', *Examiner*, 22 Dec., p. 1

Mackay, H. 2003, 'With Children Locked Up, Can We Still Call Australia Home?', *SMH*, 12–13 July, p. 30

Macken, D. 2003, 'The Asianisation of Australia Stalls', The Weekend Australian Financial Review, *Australian*, 12–13 July, p. 24

Manne, R. 2002, 'A Return to the Shame of White Australia', *SMH*, 4 Feb., p. 8

McDonald, H. 2003, 'Made in China', News Review, *SMH*, 18–19 Oct., pp. 29, 40

McGrath, A. 2004, 'Let's Look at the World Upside Down', *SMH*, 26 Jan., p. 15

McKell, R. 2004, 'Attacked: "They Told Me I'm Not Welcome in the Country", Gatamah Says', Photograph, *Australian*, Higher Education Supplement, 25 Aug., p. 41

Metherell, M. et al. 2004, 'Abbott Stirs Education Debate', *SMH*, 22 Jan., p. 4

Mike and Stefani (short film) 1952, dir. R. Maslyn Williams, Australian National Film Board (DVD re-release by Film Australia, 2004, *Immigration*)

Morris, R. 2003 'Sydney Loves Sultry Voice of Lebanon', *Telegraph*, 28 May, p. 25

——2004, 'Resorting to Rights', *The Australian*, 20 May, p. 9

Mukhtar, E. 2004, 'Switching Channels', *SMH Spectrum*, 26–27 June, p. 6

O'Brien, N. et al. 2001, 'Attacks Stir Racist Venom', *Australian*, 14 Sept., p. 9

Pearlman, J. 2003, 'The Healing Hand of Justice', *SMH*, 1 Sept., p. 17

Peatling, S. 2005, 'Shameful Case Forces Change', *SMH*, 8 Feb., pp. 1, 6

Pryor, L. 2004, 'Modern Traditionalists Get Wed on the Web', News Review, *SMH*, Weekend Edition, p. 11

'Racism Rise is Ignored', 2004, *Telegraph*, 4 June, p. 15

Redmond, N. 2004, 'Village Wish List', *Central Western Daily*, 28 Aug., p. 1

Rintoul, S. 2005, 'Long Walk to Freedom', *Weekend Australian Magazine*, 11–12 June, pp. 20–28

Robinson, N. 2004, 'Racist Taunts Draw Blood', *Australian*, Higher Education Supplement, 25 Aug., p. 41

Safe, G. 2003, 'Museum Told it's Lost the Plot', *Australian*, 16 July, p. 5

Shanahan, D. & M. Saunders 2001, 'Poll Backs PM's Stand', *Australian*, 4 Sept., p. 1

Smith, D. 2004, 'Families Share Roots in 1415 BC', *SMH*, 2–3 Oct., p. 3

Stevenson, A. 2003a, 'Fraser Advocates a Return to the Trenches on Multicultural Policies', *SMH*, 24 July, p. 6

——A. 2003b, 'All Together Now', *SMH*, 24 July, p. 13

Summers, A. 2001, 'The Day the World Changed', *The Australian*, Weekend Inquirer, 15–16 Sept., pp. 23, 26

——2002, 'Turning Away the Whitlamite Generation', *SMH*, 28 Jan., p. 12

Taylor, P. & P. Shadbolt 2004, 'Neo-Nazis Launch New Attacks', *The Australian*, 20 July, p. 6

Tomas, J.C. 2004, 'Dense Bush Thwarts Police Hunt for Body of Missing Drug Suspect', *SMH*, 9 Feb., p. 8

Totaro, P. 2002, 'Tunnel Vision', *SMH*, 23 Sept., p. 11

Toy, N. & L. Knowles 2001, 'Victim Tells How Racists Taunted Her "You Deserve It Because You're an Australian"', *Telegraph*, 24 Aug., pp. 1, 6

Wakim, J. 2004, 'Any Tom, Dick, or Harry Can Beat Prejudice', *SMH*, 27 Sept., p. 17

West, Andrew & Frank Walker 2002, 'Paranoia in the Lucky Country', *Sun-Herald*, 29 Dec., p. 4

Williams, L. 2004, 'Fading Expertise in Close Neighbour', *SMH*, 10 Sept., p. 4

Borderwork and multicultural Australia

Wise, A. 2004, "'I Wouldn't Know What's In There, Would You?": The Quotidian Experience of Chinese Language Signs Among Anglo Working Class Elderly', paper presented to the *Everyday Transformations Conference*, Murdoch University, Perth

Zion, L. 2004, 'Road Movie for Our Times', *Australian*, 1 Sept., p. 17

Websites

ABS 1995, 'Australian Social Trends 1995', <http://www.abs.gov.au/Ausstats/abs@.nsf/94713ad445ffl425ca25682000192af2/126fb> [1 Jan. 2005]

——1996, 'Australian Social Trends 1996', <http://www.abs.gov.au/Ausstats/abs@.nsf/94713ad445ffl425ca25682000192af2/ee212> [1 Jan. 2005]

——2000, 'Australian Social Trends 2000', <http://www.abs.gov.au/Ausstats/abs@.nsf/94713ad445ffl425ca25682000192af2/0820d> [1 Jan. 2005]

——2001, 'Australian Social Trends 2001', <http://www.abs.gov.au/Ausstats/abs@.nsf/94713ad445ffl425ca25682000192af2/6ba77> [1 Jan. 2005]

——2002a, '2001 Census Basic Community Profile and Snapshot', <http://www.abs.gov.au/Ausstats/abs@.census.sf/4079a1bbd2a04b80ca256b9d0028f92> [1 Jan. 2005]

——2002b, 'Australian Social Trends 2002', <http://www.abs.gov.au/Ausstats/abs@.nsf/94713ad445ffl425ca25682000192af2/6abbe> [1 Jan. 2005]

——2002c, 'Australia Now: Year Book Australia 2002 Population Clock', <http://www.abs.gov.au/Ausstats/abs@.nsf/94713ad445ffl425ca25682000192af2/1647> [28 Nov. 2004]

——2003, 'Year Book Australia 2003: Population Size and Growth', <http://www.abs.gov.au/Ausstats/abs@.nsf/Lookup/BDDA207CF3D7349ACA256CA> [1 Jan. 2005]

——2004, 'Australia Now: Year Book Australia 2003 Population Size and Growth', <http://www.abs.gov.au/Ausstats/abs@.nsf/Lookup/BDDA207CF3D7349AC256CA> [28 Nov. 2004]

'Australia's Defence Challenges in the 21st Century', *Defence Systems Daily*, <http://defence-data.com/features/fpage39.htm>

Dibb, P. 2001, 'Tinker with Defence Policy and Risk Attack', <http://www.online opinion.com.au/view.asp?article=1941> [22 Dec. 2004]

DIMA 1999, [National Multicultural Advisory Council] 'A New Agenda for Multicultural Australia' <http://www.immi.gov.au/multicultural/-inc/pdf-doc/agenda/agenda.pdf> [18 Jan. 2004]

———2003, [National Multicultural Advisory Council] 'Multicultural Australia: United in Diversity: Updating the 1999 New Agenda for Multicultural Australia: Strategic Directions for 2003–2006', <http://www.immi.gov.au/multicultural/-inc/pdf-doc/united-diversity.pdf> [18 Jan. 2004]

———n.d. 'What is Australian Multiculturalism?', educational kit, <www.immi.gov.au/multicultural/australain/multikit/multi culturalism.pdf> [17 Jan. 2004]

Fonte, J. 2002, 'The Fracturing of the West?', Spring, *Policy*, <file://D:\Data\Policy%20SPring%(Sept-Nov)%202002.htm>

'Fraser Says Howard Will Never Say Sorry' 2005, AAP, 27 Apr. <http://news.ninemsn.com.au/article.aspx?id=49122> [28 June 2005]

'Fred Chaney' 2001, Life Matters with Julie McCrossin, <http://www.abc.net.au/rn/talks/lm/stories/s399339.htm> [30 June 2005]

Gunew, S. n.d., <http://faculty.arts.ubc.ca/sgunew/RACE.HTM> [20 June 2005]

HREOC 2004a, 'Isma—Listen', <http://www.humanrights.gov.au/racial_discrimination/isma/report/exec.htm> [23 June 2004]

———2004b, 'A Last Resort? A Summary of the Important Issues, Findings, and recommendations of the National Inquiry into Children in Immigration Detention', <http://www.hreoc.gov.au/human_rights/children_detention_report/summaryguide/4f> [24 May 2004]

Kastoryano, R. 2004, 'The Reach of Transnationalism', Social Science Research Council, <http://www.ssrc.org/sept11/essays/kastoryano.htm> [16 Dec. 2004]

Monk, P. [c.2003], 'Rethinking the Defence of Australia', <http://www.austhink.org/monk/dibb/htm>

National Archives 2002, 'Fact Sheet', <http://www.naa.gov.au/fsheets/fs150.html> [20 June 2005]

Parliament of Australia 2003, 'Referendum Results', <http://www.aph.gov.au/library/handbook/referendums/r1967.htm> [20 June 2005]

Racism. No way <http://www.racismnoway.com.au>

Salteri, P. 2000, 'Australia's Defence Challenges in the 21st Century', Defence Systems Daily, http://defence-data.com/features/fpage39. htm, [29 Dec. 2004]

Williams, D. 2004, 'Myths, National Origins, Common Law and the Waitangi Tribunal', <http://www.murdoch.edu.au/elaw/issues/v11n4/williams114.html> [20 June 2005]

Index